In Trouble Again

Also by Redmond O'Hanlon

JOSEPH CONRAD AND CHARLES DARWIN

INTO THE HEART OF BORNEO

In Trouble Again

A Journey Between the
Orinoco and the Amazon

BY

REDMOND O'HANLON

HAMISH HAMILTON · LONDON

HAMISH HAMILTON LTD

Published by the Penguin Group
27 Wrights Lane, London W8 5TZ, England
Viking Penguin Inc, 40 West 23rd Street, New York, New York 10010, U.S.A.
Penguin Books Australia Ltd, Ringwood, Victoria, Australia
Penguin Books Canada Ltd, 2801 John Street, Markham, Ontario, Canada L3R 1B4
Penguin Books (N.Z.) Ltd, 182–190 Wairau Road, Auckland 10, New Zealand
Penguin Books Ltd, Registered Offices: Harmondsworth, Middlesex, England

First published in Great Britain 1988 by
Hamish Hamilton Ltd

British Library Cataloguing in Publication Data

O'Hanlon, Redmond
Amazon journey.
1. Amazon River Watershed – Description and travel
I. Title
918.1'10463   F2546

ISBN 0-241-12375-5

Typeset by Butler & Tanner Ltd
Printed and bound in Great Britain by Butler & Tanner Ltd, Frome and London.

CONTENTS

LIST OF ILLUSTRATIONS

Map
by Chartwell Illustrators   page xi

Photographs
Between pages 84 and 85

Indian rock drawing.
A gap in the trees above the Baria.
The bongos.
Simon. A pause on the climb to the waterfall.
The huts of the Siapa Yanomami.
Pablo with piranha.
Jarivanau in his hammock.
Jarivanau with his bow and arrow.
Off to hunt peccary.
Juan.

Between pages 180 and 181

The walk to the Yanomami. (*Juan Saldarriaga*)
Our first sight of the shabono.
The photograph before we entered the shabono. From the left:
Culimacaré, Reymono, Chimo, Pablo, Jarivanau. (*Juan Saldarriaga*)
A Yanomami mother. (*Juan Saldarriaga*)
Yanomami girls sitting round my pack.
Yanomami men. (*Juan Saldarriaga*)
Yavateiba in his spider-monkey tail headband. (*Juan Saldarriaga*)
Jarivanau gets his blast of yoppo. (*Juan Saldarriaga*)
Up the right nostril: I get my blast from Jarivanau. (*Juan Saldarriaga*)
The palm-frond dance. (*Juan Saldarriaga*)
The sneaked picture: Maquichemi, Yavateiba and their son.

Drawings
by Jane Cope

ACKNOWLEDGEMENTS

The author wishes to thank 22 SAS; Stephen Boyd and the *Sunday Times*; Bill Buford and *Granta*; Jeremy Treglown and the *Times Literary Supplement*; Galen Strawson; Craig Raine; Pat Kavanagh; Julian Evans; Gary Fisketjon; Elizabeth Grossman; Linda Hopkins; Alan Hollinghurst; Ernst Mayr; J. K. L. Walker; Lindsay Duguid; Penelope Hoare; Lucretia Stewart; Max Peterson; Douglas Matthews; Brian Morris; Rodney Needham; John Hemming; Robin Hanbury-Tenison; Raymond Woodhead; Tanky Smith; David Wileman; Jack Shaverien; John Perry; Julio Rivas Pita; Charles Brewer-Carias; Fernando Barrientos; Wladimir Torres Vega; Gustavo Orlando Lopez; Louis Gonzalez; Alberto Muller Rojas; Margaret Jull Costa; Stephen Rutland and Elizabeth Stockton.

R. O'H. Oxfordshire, 1988

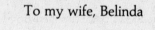
To my wife, Belinda

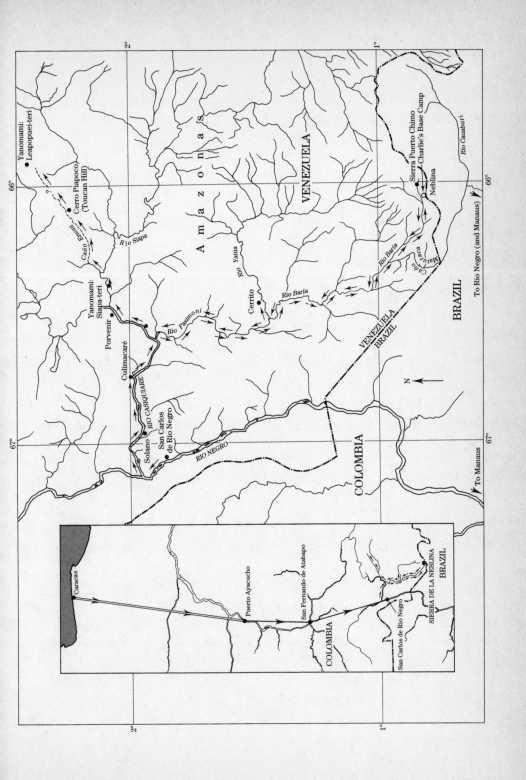

Mistle Thrush

1

Having spent two months travelling in the primary rain forests of Borneo, a four-month journey in the country between the Orinoco and the Amazon would pose, I thought, no particular problem.

I re-read my nineteenth-century heroes: the seven volumes of Alexander von Humboldt's *Personal narrative of travels to the equinoctial regions of the New Continent during the years 1799–1804* (trans. Helen Maria Williams, 1814–29); William H. Edwards' *A Voyage up the River Amazon* (1847); Alfred Russel Wallace's *A Narrative of Travels on the Amazon and Rio Negro* (1853); Henry Walter Bates's *The Naturalist on the River Amazons* (2 vols, 1863); and Richard Spruce's *Notes of a Botanist on the Amazon and Andes* (edited by Wallace, 2 vols, 1908).

There are no leeches that go for you in the Amazon jungles, an absence which would represent, I felt, a great improvement on life in Borneo. But then there *are* much the same amoebic and bacillary dysenteries, yellow and blackwater and dengue fevers, malaria, cholera, typhoid, rabies, hepatitis and tuberculosis – plus one or two very special extras.

There is Chagas' disease, for instance, produced by a protozoon, Tripanozoma crusii, and carried by various species of Assassin bugs which bite you on the face or neck and then, gorged, defecate next to the puncture. When you scratch the resulting itch you rub the droppings and their cargo of protozoa into your bloodstream;

between one and twenty years later you begin to die from incurable damage to the heart and brain. Then there is onchocerciasis, river-blindness, transmitted by blackfly and caused by worms which migrate to the eyeball; leishmaniasis, which is a bit like leprosy and is produced by a parasite carried by sandflies (it infects eighty per cent of Brazilian troops on exercise in the jungle in the rainy season): unless treated quickly, it eats away the warm extremities. And then there is the odd exotic, like the fever which erupted in the state of Pará in the 1960s, killing seventy-one people, including the research unit sent in to identify it.

The big animals are supposed to be much friendlier than you might imagine. The jaguar kills you with a bite to the head, but only in exceptional circumstances. Two vipers, the fer-de-lance (up to seven and a half feet long) and the bushmaster (up to twelve feet, the largest in the world), only kill you if you step on them. The anaconda is known to tighten its grip only when you breathe out; the electric eel can only deliver its 640 volts before its breakfast; the piranha only rips you to bits if you are already bleeding, and the Giant catfish merely has a penchant for taking your feet off at the ankle as you do the crawl.

The smaller animals are, on the whole, much more annoying — the mosquitoes, blackfly, tapir-fly, chiggers, ticks, scabies-producing Tunga penetrans and Dermatobia hominis, the human botfly, whose larvae bore into the skin, eat modest amounts of you for forty days, and emerge as inch-long maggots.

But it was the candiru, the toothpick-fish, a tiny catfish adapted for a parasitic life in the gills and cloaca of bigger fish, which swam most persistently into my dreams on troubled nights.

In Borneo, when staying in the longhouses, I learned that going down to the river in the early morning is the polite thing to do — you know you are swimming in the socially correct patch of muddy river when fish nuzzle your pants, wanting you to take them down and produce their breakfast. In the Amazons, on the other hand, should you have too much to drink, say, and inadvertently urinate as you swim, any homeless candiru, attracted by the smell, will take you for a big fish and swim excitedly up your stream of uric acid, enter your urethra like a worm into its burrow and, raising its gill-covers, stick out a set of retrorse spines. Nothing can be done. The pain, apparently, is spectacular. You must get to a hospital before your bladder bursts; you must ask a surgeon to cut off your penis.

2

In consultation with my friend at the Radcliffe Hospital in Oxford, Donald Hopkins, the inventor of the haemorrhoid gun, I designed an anti-candiru device: we took a cricket-box, cut out the front panel, and replaced it with a tea-strainer.

Released so brilliantly from this particular fear, I began, in earnest, to panic. Alfred Russel Wallace's resolution seemed the only one possible. Attacked by fever in his dugout on the Rio Negro in 1851, 'I began taking doses of quinine,' he tells us,

> and drinking plentifully cream of tartar water, though I was so weak and apathetic that at times I could hardly muster resolution to move myself to prepare them. It is at such times that one feels the want of a friend ... for of course it is impossible to get the Indians to do those little things without so much explanation and showing as would require more exertion than doing them oneself ... during two days and nights I hardly cared if we sank or swam. While in that apathetic state I was constantly half-thinking, half-dreaming, of all my past life and future hopes, and that they were perhaps all doomed to end here on the Rio Negro.... But with returning health those gloomy thoughts passed away, and I again went on, rejoicing in this my last voyage, and looking forward with firm hope to home, sweet home! I however made an inward vow never to travel again in such wild, unpeopled districts without some civilized companion or attendant.

That was the answer: I would persuade the civilised companion of my Borneo journey, the poet James Fenton, to visit the Venezuelan Amazons with me. He would be flattered to be asked. He would be delighted to come.

After supper at the long table in James's kitchen (a map of Borneo still hung on the wall), halfway through a bottle of Glenmorangie, I judged the time was ripe.

'James,' I said, 'you are looking ill. You are working far too hard writing all these reviews. You need a break. Why don't you come to the Amazon with me?'

'Are you listening seriously?'

'Yes.'

'Are you sitting comfortably?'

'Yes.'

'Then I want you to know,' said James, shutting his eyes and pressing his palms up over his face and the top of his bald head, *'that I would not come with you to High Wycombe.'*

I asked everyone I knew. I went to see the poet Craig Raine. 'It will increase your stock of metaphors,' I said.

'It will increase my stock of parasites,' said Craig.

I rang the photographer Don McCullin.

'To be frank with you', said Don, 'I thought you might get round to me sooner or later. You've come to the right man. It makes sense. Look, I don't want to be rude or anything, Redmond, but I've looked at a lot of pictures in my time, and well, frankly, *yours are the worst I've ever seen.* But I'm not interested. I've done it all. I cleaned up on the Xingu for Norman Lewis, and that was enough for me. Just at the moment, just for now, I want to get drunk a lot. And I also want to make love to Lorraine a lot – and where you're going you can't do either.'

And then I thought of Simon Stockton, a friend of my early twenties. Born in Cambridge, the high point of his education had been sharing a school classroom with the future novelist Martin Amis, an experience so demoralising it had decided him against any further study whatever, and sent him off to run his own discotheques. He had set up a nightclub in Hamburg and there, some time later, his partner had been found by the police one day, through no fault of Simon's, lying on a park bench with a bullet through his head. Simon's passport was stamped 'UNDESIRABLE ALIEN' and he was deported.

He started again as a croupier, worked his way up from club to club, and now helped to run the Kensington Sovereign. He would be a push-over. His secret ambition, I knew, was to abandon his wild, professional night-life and become something really peaceful, like a war photographer. I gave him a ring. It would be my first visit to a casino.

Simon, in his mid-thirties, suave in a dark suit, met me by the guard at the reception desk.

'Come on through and try to keep calm,' he said. 'We've got big punters tonight. Everyone's tense.'

We sat at the bar. Simon clicked his fingers and a Malay brought a bottle of claret. The dim red table and wall lights cast reflections along the rows of bottles, threw up warm, shiny patches on the oak panelling, reproduced themselves whole in the corner mirrors and hung transparent in the large, zig-zag glass partition. Through it we could watch the players hunched round the roulette and blackjack tables, and one or two wives or mistresses, sitting on stools behind their husbands or lovers, anxious, chain-smoking.

'So you're coming?'

'Of course I'm coming. It's the biggest opportunity of my life. I've bought a 500-millimetre mirror lens for the birds. I wouldn't miss it for the world. And besides, after fifteen years in this joint, it's the Amazon or the bin for me.'

'And there again,' he added à propos of nothing in particular, 'I'm good on the violence. See that?' He lifted the hair off his forehead to reveal a long, recently healed scar. 'Eight stitches. Some maniac lost all he'd got and thought I'd put the hex on him. Smashed me over the head with an ashtray. The doorman butted him in the stomach and we did him for assault.' Simon nodded at a waiter and a tray of oriental dishes arrived.

'What do they generally do,' I asked, 'when they lose everything?'

'They go home and top themselves,' said Simon, his mouth full of monkfish. 'We get a lot of that – but it's not our fault – it's just that we happen to be at the end of the line.'

'You'll be bored in the jungle.'

'I can handle it,' said Simon, turning round briefly to scan the tables. 'There's nothing much I can't handle. Why, we had three Iraqis in here only last week. Some Arab gangster thought we were cheating and these boys were his minders. So I promised them everything – my Aunt Sally, the cat, the piggy-bank, *everything* – while the car-jockey called the police. When the Old Bill rolled them we found their pockets were just wide slits: they'd got the hardware strapped down their thighs, eighteen inches long and curved at the ends. *It was the dimensions*. Right out of order, in my opinion.'

I was staring through the glass partition, admiring the half-naked girl croupiers by the dull lights above the green baize, when an elderly Japanese scowled, beckoned to a flunkey, muttered something and despatched him to Simon.

'Fatso,' said Simon, 'you just got yourself thrown out.'

'Thrown out?'

'For smiling.'

'Smiling?'

'Yeah. You were smiling at the girls. You upset Mr Yamamoto there. He thinks you put the jinx on him. You are interfering with his astral powers. You'll have to go. They're *gamblers*, you see. They come here to *gamble*. It's called a *casino*. If you want girls you go to something called a *brothel*.'

Outside on the pavement, with the lorries and cars and taxis soughing past in the drizzle, we stood and looked at Waterhouse's masterpiece, the great Victorian Romanesque façade of the Natural History Museum, its cleaned blue and cream brick, its window arches and mullions, its pinnacles and towers shining in the beams of floodlights: a secular cathedral sheltering the very collections (then housed at the British Museum at Bloomsbury) which Bates and Wallace and Spruce had visited before setting out for the Amazons.

'Isn't it beautiful?' I said. 'Don't you think it's the most tempting building on earth? Do you often slip over there when you're on a day shift?'

'Frankly,' said Simon, turning to go back down the steps past the uniformed doorman, 'I've never set foot in the place.'

I stood in the rain, unable to move, and continued staring at the celestial building across the road, a palace of disturbed yearnings.

And I imagined myself back on the late spring lawn of my Vicarage childhood. When I was about four and three-quarter years old, a mistlethrush which had been clearing out its nest flew high over my head and dropped one half of an empty eggshell in front of me, close by the sundial. Being unaware, at the time, of the empty cosmos, of the unfeelingness of causal connections, I concluded that this message of brown and purple blotches on a background of browny-white had been intended just for me.

I began an egg collection and kept it in a box on top of the chest of drawers in my little bedroom, whose window looked out over the kitchen-garden, across the small fields and thick hedges and woods of the cheese country, to the distant scarp of the Wiltshire downs. I took one blackbird's egg from a clutch of five in their rough cup lined with dried grass hidden in a thicket by the laburnum tree. I found a thrush's egg in its mud-rounded nest in a bush by the pond. I raided the nest of a fly-catcher that returned each year to rear its young on a ledge against the mellow ochre Bath-stone front of the house, where it was shielded from the sun by ivy leaves. With a teaspoon I scooped out the white, brown-speckled egg of a wren from its dome of dead leaves built into the leaf-litter behind an old wall-pinioned greengage tree. One day, sitting in the front of my father's two-seater canvas canoe on Bowood lake (which was part of his parish) I lifted the covering from a floating mound of weed moored in a lily-bed and removed the chalky egg of a Great crested grebe. It was the pride of my collection.

When I was seven, on the day I was sent away to board at a prep school in Dorset, my father gave me the two volumes of T. A. Coward's *The Birds of the British Isles and their Eggs*, my first proper books, which he had been given by *his* father, who used to watch birds and geologise with Coward all over Cheshire in the early 1900s. To go with them he gave me T. A. Coward's own custom-built binoculars which Coward had left to my grandfather: in fact a pair of matching telescopes, slim, black, brass tubes through which, one day, I hoped to see all the birds that Coward had seen, as mysterious in their marsh and coastland, on their moors and mountains and forests, as Thorburn had depicted them in his tempera plates.

On the first week of the school holiday I persuaded my father to take me to the Natural History Museum. It was all different then: you could actually go to the mahogany egg cabinets and pull out the drawers. And there were all the eggs of all the birds in the British Isles, thousands of them, lying in whole clutches, on their beds of cotton wool in the wood partitions under the glass. It was the guillemots' eggs that really astonished me – they had a whole cabinet to themselves: they were white or yellow or blue or green or purple or red or brown; and they were smeared or lined or blotched or spotted with all kinds of different colours. If these were the eggs of just one species, how could you ever hope to know enough? It was all variety and surprise and difference; and each egg looked so fine in itself. Perhaps it was *that* feeling, I now thought, standing in the rain on the Cromwell Road, which I had really been searching for – and which I had found – in the primary rainforest in the heart of Borneo, that sudden, passing, incandescent moment when you are not even sure if the something that is flying across the river in front of you is a bat or a bird or a butterfly. And it was that feeling which I vowed to experience again, if I could, in the vaster forests of the northern Amazons.

There was a hand on my shoulder.

'Are you all right, sir?' It was the doorman. He had a compassionate look on his craggy face. He had seen it all before.

'Not want to go home? Is that it? Listen to me, sir — it's always best to go straight home when you've had a spot of bad luck. You'll feel better in the morning. If you haven't the money for a cab, sir — if you don't mind my saying — the Kensington Sovereign will lend it to you. It's the policy.'

Over the next two months I made an unerring selection from different camping shops of seriously defective equipment. Having searched without success, I eventually found two pairs of heavy-duty-plastic 'campaign-tested' water bottles which fastened to belts; I took them home and filled one with water: it was so designed that when you screwed the lid home the bottle split down the sides.

Exasperated, I once again invoked the talismanic name of my uncle, Colonel Egerton-Mott, who had run Special Operations Executive in Borneo against the Japanese during the war, and I went to see the sponsors of our Borneo journey, 22 SAS.

At their Headquarters near Hereford I was absurdly pleased to see that I had been promoted, from Training Wing to Regular Stores.

'Well done, lad,' said the Quartermaster as we walked from his office to the equipment shed. 'I liked your book on Borneo. You made us sound almost human.'

Then I got that wrong, too, I thought, as we passed a platoon of young soldiers on the apron making a last check on their bergen packs before jumping into two parked lorries. They were fit and lean and possessed by a ferocious energy. They didn't even *look* human.

In the stores I had a reunion with Ernie and Eddie and signed for two complete sets of the jungle equipment I had taken to Borneo, plus an outfit of special lightweight jungle fatigues (large) and a floppy camouflage hat (it had two pairs of large airholes set above the brim, covered with wire mesh fine enough to keep out blackfly). Over-excited, I put on the clothes. I felt tough at once. I was ready for anything.

'We can't let him go like that,' said Ernie, sounding genuinely distressed.

'Why not?' I said. 'Am I missing something?'

'No,' said Ernie, in an agonised voice, 'it's just that you're a disgrace to the Regiment. You look like Benny Hill.'

*

A week later, I took Simon's share of the equipment down to his house in a suburb of West Drayton. It was easy enough to find. The villa was dramatically distinguished from the row of look-alikes because Simon had painted it purple all over, and an enormous blown-up photograph of his head entirely blocked off the left upstairs window.

It was three in the afternoon and Simon came to the door in his flannel dressing gown.

'Hi, Fatso. Brought the kit? Lob it in here,' he said, helping me carry the bergen into the room on the right. Against one wall, there was a stack of tuners, amplifiers, record and tape decks topped with shelves of records. An outsize television and several video machines stood by the window. In the corner, a wooden girl, her big wooden breasts painted cream, held out an ashtray. We spread the olive-drab basha-top, the canvas hammock, the mosquito net and the pole-bed across the carpet on top of one pair of small, red dancing shoes, one pair of black fishnet stockings, one black suspender belt, and one black G-string with a tiny, scarlet silk heart sewn onto the front.

'It's okay,' said Simon. 'She's asleep upstairs. She wears anything I ask her to, comes on a Thursday night, and goes away again on Friday. She *never* gives me any aggravation. Want a tour of the house? Stocky's maximum-pleasure dream-machine?'

We walked across the corridor.

'This is the front room', said Simon. 'We take tea in here when very special guests, like Mother, come to pay their respects. We eat cucumber sandwiches and little cakes.'

The floor was fully occupied with a large work-bench. The walls were covered with a comprehensive collection of tools in hanging rows which stretched right round the room, their categories marked in an index of fluorescent red paint beside the light switch, 'CHISELS, HAMMERS, DRILLS, SAWS, PLANES AND MISCELLANEOUS'.

On our way upstairs we climbed past an even larger inscription: 'REMEMBER REMEMBER THE FIFTH OF NOVEMBER'.

'What's this? Did you forget the fireworks?'

'No,' said Simon, 'it's the day my wife left me.'

'I'm not surprised she went,' I said.

'I'll never forgive her,' said Simon.

I looked out of the landing window, to take the air.

An old plum tree was growing in the middle of the lawn. From its lowest branch there hung a bedraggled outsize Snoopy, a riding-hat on its head, a much-holed target pinned to its chest. It swayed, slightly, in the breeze.

'What's that?'

'That,' said Simon, 'is an *image*. It's my ex-wife. That's her crash helmet. She had a *horse*. Whenever I get depressed I take my crossbow, lean out, and bolt her one.'

'And this,' he said, flinging open a door marked 'DANGER, HIGH VOLTAGE OVERHEAD CABLES', 'is the master bedroom. This is where the maid brings me my croissant and I read the *Financial Times* every morning.'

He switched on a red light. It was a darkroom, the window obscured by black shutters and a light proof ventilator. Tables ran round the edge of the room, with filing cabinets beneath them. There were two big Durst enlargers, a set of developing and fixing trays and three plumbed-in washing sinks. The cameras and lenses were neatly arranged on a shelf. A set of Bowens flashlights stood half-rigged in a corner, their heads on tripods, their folded umbrellas and barn-door, cone and bowl reflectors piled beside them. But the chief glory of the room was the girls. They pouted from Simon's sofa in soft-focus black and white. They sat naked in full Cibachrome on Simon's flower-bed. They perched in sepia on the knob of his banisters and giggled; they sprawled long and languorous on his carpet; they were caught by remote-control on the bed, with the master himself undressing them.

'Good, eh?' said Simon.

'They look surprisingly happy about it,' I said. 'They must actually like you.'

'Of course they do,' said Simon, 'it's only natural. They love me to death. But it's wham, bam and thank you mam with me, I'm afraid. Not like you. How long you been married? Fifty years?'

'Eighteen,' I said.

'Eighteen!' said Simon, walking across the passage and easing open another door. 'Eighteen! Well, if we ever come out of the jungle you *might* make it to your silver wedding — if Belinda's fool enough to wait for you — and I could give you a round fat teapot with a quarter-inch spout.'

10

We peered round the door.

'This is the romper-room,' said Simon.

A very young girl lay asleep on the double bed; she was half-covered by a duvet, curled in the foetal position. Three Siamese cats snuggled together, pressed into the hollow between her buttocks and the back of her thighs. Her yellow hair fell forward across the pillow.

'She's lovely,' I said, as we went downstairs.

'Lovely cats,' said Simon.

'Aren't you *very* fond of her?'

'Look here,' said Simon, 'don't you get heavy with me. She works in the casino. I'm in charge of personnel. I'm not kidding, Redmond, I'm *exhausted* with pretty girls. I'm *manhandled* by them. There are days when I can hardly call my dick my own.'

We sat down at the table in the appliance-choked spaceship of a kitchen.

'You're a lucky man,' I said.

'It's just a problem I have,' said Simon, reaching over to a wine-rack and pulling out a bottle of Châteauneuf du Pape, 'I wanted someone to come here properly and look after me, so I put a notice up in the local newsagent. "*Unbelievably* ugly charlady wanted," it said. "Top rates for real old bag. No one under sixty need apply." I interviewed for *two weeks*; and chose a right old horror. Mrs T. She does for me. My Mrs Treasure. She's the best. I think I'm falling in love. In fact, one of these days, I'll have to give her one.'

'What's in the other rooms?' I said, as Simon filled up two half-pint-sized wine glasses.

'Nah. They were my wife's; I hardly go in them; I haven't colonised them yet. There's a full set of Encyclopaedia Britannica's *Great Books of the World* in the garden room. I bought them for her. They're still in their shrink-wrap. Bloody dire. Which reminds me — when we're on this trip, when we're stuck in the old jungle — you've got to educate me.'

'Educate you?'

'Yeah. I want to change my life. I really do. You tell me what books to read — and, come to that, why are we going on this trip, anyway? Why aren't you still teaching in Oxford, you fat berk? *That's* the life. Free port, as much as you want, laid down *hundreds* of years ago. Old codgers handing you expensive lardy-dahs all day. Young students all over you.'

'I was only on trial,' I said. 'And I taught my undergraduates the wrong century, just before their exams. It was terrible.'

'Shit a brick,' said Simon, looking seriously alarmed. 'I thought you were safe to go with; I thought I could trust you.'

'They made the same mistake. It wasn't their fault.'

'Jesus,' said Simon, uncorking another bottle.

'It's all right,' I said. 'We're going to take a nineteenth-century route. And that *is* my period. I thought we'd follow Humboldt up the Orinoco and through the Casiquiare; pick up Spruce and Wallace on the Rio Negro; go down to Manaus and join Bates, and then maybe go up the Purus. I've been wobbling round our local wood every morning. I'm fitter than I used to be.'

'Are you hell,' said Simon, pouring himself another glass. 'You drink too much.'

'And as for changing your life,' I said, 'with your through-put, sooner or later you're bound to find the right woman. That's the way to change your life.'

Simon relaxed and leant back in his chair.

'Well, as it happens, I *may* have found the right woman, scumbag. And it might just have something to do with you. I think she likes it – Stockton the explorer and photographer. Yeah. She doesn't know I've hardly seen daylight in my working life, let alone a jungle. She's a genuine schoolteacher-lady. Her husband died. She's got three lovely kids. I like kids. I might just go for her in a big way. In fact, as far as I'm concerned, she's angel-drawers.'

'But you've only got two weeks.'

'Easy-peezy. Lemon squeezy,' said Simon, 'she's coming to see me off. And if it comes to that – you're a monster.'

'What do you mean?'

'How can you do it?' said Simon, looking suddenly wild about the eyes. 'How can you leave your wife and daughter? Belinda just out of hospital. Puffin two weeks old. You ought to be shot. Just for thinking of it.'

'It was planned a year ago,' I said, looking away, focusing on a photograph in a stand-up frame on the table. 'I didn't know it would be like this. It's now or next year. We have to catch the rainy season. We may want to go up some very small rivers.'

'Spoken like a psychopath,' said Simon.

'Who *is* this girl?' I said, picking up the photograph. Simon stared out of the picture, carrying a silver cane and wearing a blazer, a boater, a high collar, a silk shirt with ruffles and a silk cravat. On his arm was a dark-haired girl in a 1920s dress and a wide-brimmed hat with ostrich feathers, carrying a furled umbrella.

'The Mr Cool in the boater is me,' said Simon, 'and the sexy bit in the dress is me. It's my last year's Christmas card. Good, eh? Don't you ever slip into a pair of knicks?'

That evening, as I was driving back to Oxford, it gradually dawned on me that it was too late to change anything: I was not just going to the jungle, I was going to the jungle with Simon.

Yoppo

2

I left Simon reading *Pride and Prejudice* in the flat I had rented in the centre of Caracas and took a taxi to the Country Club to meet Charlie Brewer-Carias.

Charlie, the great explorer and photographer of Venezuela, is a man whose hobby is dropping by helicopter onto jungle mountains like the Autana or Sarisarinama, and then abseiling into their caves and sink-holes; an ex-dentist who has now written six illustrated books about the mountains and plants of his country, he has led so many scientific expeditions into the interior that thirteen new species and one genus of plant, one new species and one new sub-species of bird and one aquatic insect (Tepuidessus breweri, Spangler, 1981) now bear his name. A popular hero, every taxi driver in Caracas likes to tell you about his term of office as Minister of Youth. To draw attention to the lands that Venezuela claims from the former British Guiana, now Guyana, Charlie gathered a band of young admirers and invaded the territory. Guyana mobilised her army and airforce. Charlie unscrewed a brass nameplate proclaiming 'British Guiana' on a frontier post, and withdrew. The Communist government of Guyana was not amused. The democratic government of Venzuela was not amused. Charlie lost his job.

I found him sitting at a table in the cloister of the central, flower-filled quadrangle, sipping a glass of water.

'Care for a session in the gym?' said Charlie, stroking his enormous drooping moustache.

'Certainly not,' I said, panicking. 'Couldn't we talk over a bottle or two?'

'That would be very bad for you. A very bad idea. You must stay away from drink altogether. The Indians have not adapted to it. You must not take it with you. The Amazonas, Redmond, is not a kind place.'

'Look here – I haven't been to a gym since school.'

'Now's the time,' said Charlie, getting up. 'You must fight that belly. Everyone should go to a gym.'

He picked up an athlete's bag from the paving stones, swung it on to his muscled shoulders, and pointed to a leather pouch on the table.

'Bring that,' said Charlie, 'and give it to me if there's trouble. Come on. We can get in a full hour before lunch.'

The pouch was extraordinarily heavy. I half-undid the zip and looked inside. It was a large, black Browning automatic.

'Jesus,' I said.

'Everyone out there,' said Charlie, 'wants to kill me. From the government of Guyana to the lowliest nut. Only last month some drug-crazed lunatic in a suburb came up to my car at some traffic lights and said he'd wanted to shoot me every day for years, but that his doctor had just talked him out of it. "Yeah. Thanks. Wild news," I said. "Just let me know if you change your mind."'

In the locker room Charlie changed into shorts, socks and gym shoes. I took off my shirt and shoes but held my trousers firmly in place by taking in another notch of my belt. We collected two towels and entered the gym.

A huge man was lying flat on his back on a small bench and lifting above his chest a bar whose weights seemed about equivalent to that of three buses on one side and half a small house on the other. It was just possible to make out his head amongst the muscles. Every time he drew in a breath it sounded like a jet taking off.

'Nobody else here can do this,' said Charlie, hoisting himself up and down between the parallel bars and kissing his knees. He nodded at the young men upside-down on wall bars and flying through the air on a succession of trapezes. 'I'm forty-six. But they just don't have the strength *and* the flexibility.'

'So what do you think of my route?' I said, my feet numb under a pair of leg irons I found impossible to move.

'Not now,' said Charlie, 'don't talk to me when I'm doing my exercises. I concentrate on a different set of muscles every day. If I throw a rope to a man who is drowning in a rapid, Redmond, I *must* be strong enough to pull him to the bank.'

'I shouldn't talk to *him*, anyway,' said a glistening hulk next to me with a super-signal wink (you probably train your eyelids, too, I thought). He was undulating his biceps with weights like bogeys from a railway truck. 'You need to get, ah, *strong*. I'm a surgeon myself, but I see plenty of jungle diseases at the hospital. If you take my advice, you'll stay in Caracas.'

'It's a *ridiculous* plan,' called Charlie from the cold shower next to mine.

'Next stage,' he said, ushering me into the dry-heat room. We joined a line of men sitting sweating and joking in front of directional heaters. It's just that I am not yet used to this climate, I told myself; there is no need to feel so outclassed by the mere bulk of dicks flopped along this bench.

'Those rivers,' said Charlie, 'I've been thinking about it. They're as big as the sea. What could be more boring? People have done it *in a hovercraft*. But I like you. You're bizarre. You're helpless here. You give me your old volumes of Spruce and Wallace — I've never even seen those books bound up — and I'll make you photocopies and I'll give you a little project all of my own, something that has not been attempted since the seventeenth century.'

'It's a deal,' I said, sweating.

'Then let's go next door,' said Charlie, 'it's the Club rainforest.'

In the steamroom my glasses misted up. Charlie, pacing up and down, went in and out of focus in the swirling murk.

'There's no point following Humboldt and Bonpland down the Casiquiare,' said his disembodied voice. 'You won't find your birds and animals. But there's another river that connects the Orinoco and the Rio Negro, the Maturaca — it's marked on the maps but it rises in a dendritic delta, an inland swamp to the south-west of Neblina. We don't know exactly where. You must go and find out; but it's wild country — the trees meet overhead all the way, the streams are criss-crossed with fallen trunks, you must cut your own way through; the last people to try — the Border Commission officers — were lost in there for two months in 1972 and gave up; the country is so remote that Neblina itself, the highest mountain in South America outside the Andes, was not discovered until 1953.'

We took another cold shower.

'You will come to my apartment,' shouted Charlie from his stall. 'I have low-level radar and high-level NASA infra-red satellite maps of the area. It is a small obsession of mine.'

In his eight-cylinder Chevrolet, Charlie told his driver to take us to the flat. One wall was hung with assorted blow-pipes, another obscured by a map-drawer cabinet and files of photographs. Books and papers lay everywhere. An adjoining room, furnished with metal shelves, contained a Sten gun, a Hasselblad, a combined .22 rifle and .410 shot-gun, a 7×8 Pentax with a wooden carrying handle, a 12-bore shotgun, a Linhof panoramic, a 16-bore shotgun, a pair of Olympuses and a case of lenses. On the floor stood a large radio transmitter. On a spare piece of table various bits of a knife and its accompanying plans were spread.

'This is the Brewer Explorer Survival Knife,' said Charlie, taking a complete model out of a drawer, '$6\frac{1}{4}$-inch stainless steel blade, Rockwell Hardness 56–58; $2\frac{3}{4}$-inch saw extending from the handle towards the point; on the left here a 180-degree clinometer for calculating the height of mountains; on the right instructions for five ground-to-air signals and a six-centimetre ruler. This small hole in the blade is of course for sighting when you use it as a signalling reflector; this large rectangular hole converts it into wire cutters when engaged with this T-type fitting on the tip of the sheath. It can also be made into a harpoon with another special device of mine. This end-cap screws off like this and, inside the hollow handle, here's a compass and a waterproof container with the morse code printed on its sides: holding six fish hooks, a monofilament nylon fishing line, two lead sinkers, one float, an exacto blade, two sewing needles, three matches, a flint stick and a suture needle with suture material attached. It's made by Marto of Toledo and imported into the US by Gutman at $150. But you and Simon can have one. It's good for skinning alligators. And when the Yanomami have had a go at you you can sew each other up round the arrow holes.'

'The Yanomami?'

'Yeah. The most violent people on earth. Some anthropologists think they were the first peoples to reach South America from the North. They have very fair skins, occasionally green eyes. They are the largest untouched group of Indians left in the rainforest. The other Indians are terrified of them. My friend Napoleon Chagnon called his book on them *The Fierce People* — I'll give you a copy, and Jacques Lizot's too, *Tales of the Yanomami*. It's all perfectly understandable — they grow a few plantains, but basically they're hunter-gatherers and there's not much food in these forests. So when times are hard they kill the new-born girls; so there are never enough women to go round; so they fight over them. Within the tribe, in formalised duels, they hit each other over the head with ten-foot long clubs. Outside the tribe they raid each other's settlements for women and kill the enemy men with six-foot-long arrows tipped with curare. And on top of all that they've no concept of natural death, so if anyone dies from a fever it's the result of malign magic worked by an enemy shaman. Each death must be avenged.'

I stood there stupidly, holding the enormous Brewer Explorer knife.

'And this still goes on?' I said, shaken.

'They are killing each other,' said Charlie, *'right now.'*

He pulled open a map-drawer, took out a 20 × 16 photograph and spead it on the carpet. On a deep red background were patches of white and long black squiggles.

'This is the infra-red picture on a good day with minimal cloud. You will charter a light aircraft in Puerto Ayacucho on the Orinoco and fly south onto the map — to here' — a tiny white cross and blob, the only sign of settlement in the whole area, beside the biggest of the squiggles — 'San Carlos on the Rio Negro.'

Charlie's callused, muscly forefinger tapped emphatically at the spot. He was getting excited.

'There you will employ my men. It will be their only job this year. You will pay the Indians eight dollars a day and Galvis, the radio-operator and cook, ten. Half in advance. You start when they sober up. Allow a week. Chimo is an old motorman of vast experience, and he claims to know this route. Valentine is an old prow-man. Pablo is very strong and good with an axe. I am giving you the best crew in Venezuela. You will hire my two outboard motors and two of Chimo's dugouts. I will call San Carlos on the radio tonight, atmospheric conditions permitting.'

'Two dugouts?'

'Redmond, you are going to one of the most isolated places on earth. If you break a boat, running it over tree trunks, you could *never* walk out of that swamp.'

'Do you think we're up to it?'

'That's your affair,' said Charlie, with an annoyed shake of the head. 'You will travel north up the Rio Negro, turn east into the Casiquiare; and then swing south down the Pasimoni which narrows into the Baria' (the squiggle grew faint) 'just after the Yatua joins it from the east. Almost at once you will begin to see all kinds of monkeys, two species of otter, sloth, anacondas, tapir, peccaries, jaguar, deer, ocelot, everything. And here' (Charlie spead out his fingers and set them travelling south-east) 'the river divides into a thousand tributaries. It disappears entirely beneath the red, the forest. You can say goodbye to the sunlight. Believe me – I've flown over bits of it in a helicopter and you can't see the streams from the air. But you'll be going in the wet season. There'll be plenty of water. You should be able to get through to Brazil.'

'So why don't you want to do it?' I said, suspicious.

'I'm fully occupied with this,' said Charlie, tapping a mass of cliffs and ridges ringed with cloud in the south-east corner of the picture. 'I lead expeditions to Neblina for the American Museum of Natural History and the Venezuelan Foundation for the Development of Science. We go in by helicopter to my base camp and then by helicopter to the summit. There's a 250-square-kilometre lost world up there – 98% of the plants are new species: Neblinaria, for instance, like an artichoke; new orchids; bromeliads; mosses. The tepuis are islands of life, cut off from each other by the jungle and from the jungle by 3000-metre-high cliffs. They're remnants of the Guyana shield, 100-million-year-old blocks of sandstone that pre-date the drifting apart of Africa and South America. We have so many results, so many new species to describe, that I'm setting up a new Journal with the Smithsonian. I'm a very busy man.'

Charlie put the photograph away. We heated up a cheese and tomato pizza in the kitchen. Charlie's wife-to-be, Fanny, came home just long enough to collect some books, a passionate kiss and piece of pizza. Small, dark and beautiful, still at university, she was in training for a place in the rhythmic gymnastics team that Venezuela would be sending to the Olympics.

'She is also studying for her exams,' said Charlie, 'and so, at the moment, she only adorns me with her presence by night.'

He made a guava juice.

'Come to that – you could try and reach Neblina by the Baria. Just follow the strongest current and you'll get there eventually. You could rest in my base camp and then go up the canyon. You'd be the first people to reach it by the Baria route. Bassett Maguire and William and Kathy Phelps went by the Siapa in 1953.'

'And where are the Yanomami?'

'Oh, *them*,' said Charlie, grinning. 'You won't meet them around Neblina. It's entirely uninhabited and probably always has been – *they* won't kill you until you're halfway down the Maturaca.'

'So what do we do now?' I said, trying to look calm.

'You stop panicking,' said Charlie, flexing his huge shoulders and massaging the back of his neck with his right hand. 'In Brazil on the south of their range they do knock off the odd fur-trapper or gold-panner, but it's not systematic. I actually did some work down there with my friend Julian Steyermark in 1975. We wanted to find out which plants go into yoppo.'

'What the hell's that?'

'It's a drug they blast up each others' noses through a metre-long tube. It produces peripheral vision colour disturbances and enables the shamans to summon their *hekura*, their tutelary spirits. It also produces severe shock in the ear, nose and throat system and the pain blows your head off: Julian and I never tried it. The other Indians swear it causes brain damage. But it's probably harmless. You must have a go if you get the chance.'

Charlie strode over to a different filing cabinet.

'Here, you can have an offprint of our joint paper from *Economic Botany*. Our particular Yanomami used Justicia pectoralis, Virola elongata, and the bark from the tree Elizabetha princeps.'

I picked up the knives and took my second Venezuelan gift, a small green pamphlet entitled '*Hallucinogenic Snuff Drugs of the Yanomamo Caburiwe-Teri in the Cauaburi River, Brazil*'.

'Now I must kick you out,' said Charlie, seeing me to the door, 'I have work to do. Tomorrow morning I will collect you at your flat at ten o'clock sharp. We must visit three different Ministers. You will need a whole sheaf of official letters to the Regional Military Governor. With me, it will take a week, maybe two. Without me, you would never get in there. Not a chance. The entire area is restricted. The Guardia will think you're a spy or a gold prospector. However, it so happens that I am a Special Adviser to the Venezuelan

Army on all its jungle training. I will pull rank on any soldier who bothers you. But remember, Redmond, the frontier posts are there for a reason. It doesn't matter a damn about you. But it's bad for the Indians if they kill you. It's bad for public opinion. You can't have just anybody going in there and getting themselves stuck full of arrows like a porcupine.'

Back in the flat, Simon was curled up on the sofa, watching a football match on the television, *Men Only* spread open on his knees. A glass and a half-empty bottle of Chilean wine were on the table beside him and a further empty bottle lay discarded on the floor, together with three empty packets of Marlboro cigarettes, *Playboy*, *Penthouse*, *Fiesta* and *Pride and Prejudice.*

'GooooAAAAl!' yelled Simon. 'When there's a goal, they say GooooAAAAl!'

'I thought you were meant to be educating yourself,' I said.

'I am,' said Simon, not taking his eyes off the match. 'I've been reading a lot of new stuff here about the G-spot. Find the G-spot. Drive them *wild*.'

'What about Jane Austen?'

'She's great. I love it. I'm saving her up. Just when you think you've sussed it all out you find it's really someone else's second cousin who wants to get the leg over.'

'There's been a small change of plan,' I said.

'Yeah,' said Simon, still watching, 'I've been thinking about all this. When your old friend asks you to the country by the Caribbean, don't pack your bikini, that's what I say.'

I took one of Charlie's knives out of its black metal sheath and laid it on the sofa beside him. Its thick, highly polished blade with the jagged saw-top and engraved reminders for helicopter signals (v assistance + medical) glinted in the table-light.

'Oh god,' said Simon, looking down, 'that's *horrible*. That would give *Hitler* the screaming ab-dabs.'

'It's a present from Charlie,' I said, sitting on a chair. 'This change of plan – we're going to try to be the first people to reach Neblina, the highest mountain in South America outside the Andes, via the vast Baria swamp. Then we'll be going down a river that nobody's been down since the seventeenth century, to try and find a fierce people called the Yanomami. Apparently they hit each other over the head in duels with ten-foot-long clubs and they hunt each other with six-foot-long arrows.'

'Oh, thanks,' said Simon, concentrating at last, kicking out with his legs on the floor and pushing himself hard back into the angle of the sofa. 'Out of sight. Thanks a bundle for telling me in London. I've *always* wanted to be slammed up the arse with an arrow and then whacked on the nut with a pole.'

Black Curassow

3

Three weeks later, very early on the first morning of our stay in the little frontier town of San Carlos, I woke up in my room in the shack which served as the research station for the *Instituto Venezolano de Investigaciones Cientificas Centro de Ecologia Proyecto Amazonas* and identified the source of the high-pitched, metallic chattering that came from a corner of the roof. I lay in my hammock, switched on my small torch, focused the beam and mesmerised three very black, very glossy, very furry bats a quarter-way down the rough wall. They stopped talking, recovered their composure, moved crabwise up to the runnels beneath the corrugated iron ceiling and disappeared. I lifted the mosquito net, swung out of bed and stepped on one of a pair of neatly formed, dryish and surprisingly large Cane toad turds.

Fred, the toad, imagining himself camouflaged, was sheltering beneath the metal frame of my bergen. He looked apologetic in a warty kind of way. I rubbed my sock and cleaned up with a piece of discarded graph paper. Every thirty seconds Fred would blink, once.

I made my way across the concrete-floored hall and into the large, high space of the kitchen-cum-storeroom. At once pots banged; plates jumped into each other; suspended wire-cage caches of bread and rice packets swung on their chain hangings; and the metal mosquito grille, which comprised the top half of the two back walls, pinged like a tennis raquet. I shone the torch up along the beams and admired the scurry of white stomachs and brown backs, the fluffy urgency of retreating rats, making for their nests somewhere in amongst the boxes and abandoned pieces of soil-sampling equipment on the topmost shelf by the door, their tails flipping along behind them.

Outside in the garden it was almost light. The odd lizard rustled away over the leaves beneath the two orange trees. At this time of day they were sluggish: by noon they would be much more impressive, picking themselves up like dinosaurs and rushing to cover on their back legs. The main water tank was empty, so instead I gave the cockroaches a fresh meal in the lavatory hut with the hole in the ground. Then the town generator and the river-pumping motor puttered into life (two hours in the morning, two in the evening); an officer shouted orders for the soldiers' warm-up exercises in their compound up the street; the girls in the bungalow opposite, wasting no time, put on the first Venezuelan pop song of the day. I went back inside to make coffee.

Juan Saldarriaga emerged from his room. Juan, dark, small, bearded, wiry and worried, was a Colombian ecologist I'd met on the airstrip of the capital of Amazonas, Puerto Ayacucho. After five minutes' conversation I'd asked him to come with us; and he'd invited us to stay at the research station. Simon had disliked him from the start.

Juan unbolted the front door onto the grassy street with his quick, awkward movements that gave him an air of suppressed rage. A turkey walked past.

'Brekfax?' said Juan. 'Porridge? Peanut butter and hot bread?'

He opened rat-proof tins of oats and sugar and powdered milk.

He was perhaps the only man in South America with a real reason of his own for joining us. Personally and professionally obsessed with his theory that the rainforest was not the stable environment it was generally imagined to be, he wanted to prove that almost all of it had burned down in patches at one time or another during irregular dry periods; and to suggest that such repeated small-scale devastations might provide the answer to the ecological problem of its extraordinary diversity of species. To do that he needed to journey to the remotest possible areas, to dig for samples of carbon in soils that had probably not been disturbed by the shifting agriculture of the Indians, the burning and clearing of small pieces of jungle in which to grow plantains or manioc. And to do that he needed me. In return he would, I felt sure, translate any Spanish I found difficult and, in general, tell me all he knew.

Simon emerged, looking a little strained.

'Those friends of yours in the SAS,' he said, 'they pygmies?'

'What do you mean?'

'It's their hammocks. You can only sleep in one if you're four feet long.'

Agitated, he banged his toothbrush on the table.

'Their hammocks have to be small,' I said. 'Everything they carry has to be as light as possible.'

'Well, it's not natural. I can't say I go around slinging sodding hammocks in the normal course of things, not as a general rule, but it can't be right. You *can't* be meant to sleep with your legs in the air and your knees locked and your hooter practically stuffed down your strides. It's the pits. It really is.'

'You're meant to sleep across it,' said Juan, laughing.

'I've tried that,' said Simon, rounding on him, 'I've tried *that*. You wind up with your head on the floor and your nuts in the air. You might as well bung up a meat hook and string yourself to that and be done with it.'

'Don't make a fret,' said Juan, 'we'll find you a proper hammock. The best hammocks come from Colombia.'

'I am *not* fretting,' said Simon. 'In England only girls fret. I am throwing a wobbly. In English it's called *throwing a wobbly*. And another thing — you can't breathe in that mosquito net. You can't breathe. And then there's lizards or something throwing bricks about in the roof all night.'

'It's not lizards,' said Juan, pouring the coffee into mugs, 'it's rats. It's okay.'

'Rats!' said Simon.

'I've seen them,' I said. 'They're well turned out. They use the best shampoo.'

'Very funny,' said Simon.

'I had a cat,' said Juan, 'but one day he made a shit in my dried and weighed soil samples. I was annoyed. So I threw him out into the street. I threw him by the tail. Since a year already we have had no cat.'

'Charming,' said Simon.

Just as the porridge was ready, Galvis walked in from the street. Tall, gangly and ingratiating, he had a small moustache and a squeaky voice. We shook hands and he joined us for breakfast.

'I've talked to Charlie on the radio,' he said in Spanish, 'he's sending

25

a replacement outboard motor and two big tarpaulins. It'll take a week to get here. But I've gathered the crew – Valentine and Pablo are here and Chimo has brought his nephew down from Solano. He's called Culimacaré because that's his village. He's a Curipaco. Chimo says we need an extra man. Chimo says it will be very difficult. No one has been there before. There will be fallen trees across the rivers. We must cut a way through with axes. It will be the biggest adventure of my life. The Expedición Maturaca.'

'It'll be the biggest adventure of my life,' I said.

We shook hands again, all round.

The door slammed right back on its hinges against the wall and the toughest-looking old man I'd ever seen swayed into the room. The skin on his face was as thick and leathery as that of one of Professor Glob's dug-up bog people, tanned by several hundred years under the peat. The furrows, where his face met his neck, were folded like the sides of a bull's dewlap. He wore gum boots; khaki trousers restrained his bulging thighs; a khaki shirt stretched across his mass of stomach; he held a smoking pipe in his gums; and on his head he wore a dark blue, heavy-duty-plastic construction worker's helmet. He stopped close in front of me. He smelt of shag, rank male and sweated beer. He looked me up and down with his hooded, deep, brown, ancient eyes. He was not reassured.

'Chimo,' he said, putting out a hand. It felt as rough as a pineapple.

Anxious to please, I bent down nervously and drew a presentation machete out of the bundle I had put ready under the table.

Chimo took it with one hand, looked at it carefully, drew his pipe out of his mouth and gobbed a small pond of gunge some six feet away to the right. It spattered, star-shaped, on the side of a petrol drum.

'Thank you, chief,' said Chimo in Spanish. 'This is Brazilian. This is the worst machete you can buy.'

Simon, uncharacteristically, whispered in my ear, 'This is the real McCoy', he said, in his advisory mode. '*This is one big heavy.*'

'I want my wages in advance,' said Chimo, standing four-square, 'I need beer.'

I went to my room, disturbed Fred, dug about in the bottom of my bergen and found Chimo's envelope, half his pay, 300 dollars' worth of small-denomination bolivar notes (fifteen to the pound) which I had prepared the night before. When I returned, Chimo was shaking his head at the huge pile of stores stacked along the left hand wall. A young man, obviously very shy, hung about in the doorway.

'There's not enough petrol,' said Chimo.

'It's too bad,' I said, knowing we could only get more by flying back to Puerto Ayacucho. 'When we get to the Maturaca it'll be down stream. We'll paddle.'

Chimo grunted. 'Culimacaré,' he said, nodding towards the doorway. 'We need an extra man.'

'He's just trying it on,' said Simon, 'he probably wants you to hire his whole family.'

Culimacaré, small and strong, looked at the floor. As I tried to shake his hand, he snatched it away. An extra thumb stuck up, I noticed, inactive and hooked over at the top, just above the base of his true thumb.

'You're coming with us,' I said grandly, 'welcome to the Expedición Maturaca.'

Chimo gave me an enormous grin, walked over to Culimacaré and put an arm round his shoulders.

'Now you can buy a gun,' he said.

An old pock-marked Indian, wearing a helmet like Chimo's, and a well-built, very dark Indian of about forty entered the room.

'Valentine and Pablo,' said Chimo. 'Now we're all here. Now you must pay up.'

I handed out the money, gave every one a machete and Culimacaré and Pablo an axe, and we agreed to meet again in the morning. The journey proper had almost begun.

Juan locked up and, carrying our towels and three small piles of washing, the three of us walked down to the river for a swim. The wide, grassy streets, arranged on a grid plan, led past whitewashed bungalows and wattle-and-daub huts, some thatched and some roofed with corrugated iron. The Government, Juan said, flapping along in his sandals, had provided the money for the new roofs, and for a trainee doctor, a clinic, a primary school, a carpentry shop and an agricultural co-operative. But there was nothing much to carpent, no agriculture and no jobs. So the young men married, played football, swam and got drunk every Friday and Saturday at the regular party (held in a different house each week). There was a Justice of the Peace. He was paid full-time by the Government, but there were no cases to try. So he sat all day outside his house under a palm-thatch roof enclosed by a small wooden stockade, reading thrillers to keep in training. The Chief Road Mender was one of the three people in town who owned a Toyota truck, flown in by Hercules transport, and he drove it about his roads all day, which was why they needed mending. There was a detachment of conscript marines from the Venezuelan Navy, but they owned no boat. The barracks housed sixty soldiers, who were waiting for the Colombians on the opposite bank to invade San Carlos and capture the Justice of the Peace. Things were ordered better, said Juan, in Colombia.

Still, as we crossed the main square, deserted but for a few women sitting and talking in doorways, it all seemed as well arranged as Wallace had thought it in February, 1851: 'The village of São Carlos is laid out with a large square, and parallel streets. The principal house, called the Convento, where the priests used to reside, is now occupied by the Commissario. The square is kept clean, the houses white-washed, and altogether the village is much neater than those of Brazil.'

At the waterfront a soldier sat in a small hut above the bathing place, his feet up on the parapet, his Sten gun across his knees, watching the empty river. It was the end of the dry season and the water was exceptionally low. It indeed ran, as Humboldt describes it, 'in a straight line from north to south, as if its bed had been dug by the hand of man.' In the great heat of the morning and the fierceness of the reflected light I could well believe that our latitude was the 1° 54′ 11″ which Humboldt calculated it to be; but nothing I had read had prepared me for the actual colour of the Rio Negro. Its blackness made the vegetation on its islands look richer, its far bank seemed much more than 600 yards away, the clear sky a whiter blue. Smooth granite rocks shelved steeply down into the water. We stripped to our underpants and went for a swim; our legs looked lustrous and marble-like wading in the black coffee shallows. We scrubbed our clothes on the rocks.

'I know all the crew,' said Juan. 'Chimo is famous for travelling the rivers; he is Headman of the Baré in Solano; but he is also an old rogue with lots of mistresses and a big family. He will steal the petrol. Culimacaré is a Curipaco; he is strong and also reliable. Valentine is Geral and too old to come at all. He is an unhappy man. He beats his wife when he is drunk, so she threw him out of the house and now he lives with his son. But he speaks Geral, so perhaps he can help us when we reach Brazil. Pablo is strong but he, too, is unhappy.

28

He has a son and a daughter, but his wife was fishing in her little canoe just up the river here, eight years ago, and a storm came up and she drowned in the waves. As for Galvis – it is Galvis who will give you real trouble.'

'What sort of trouble?' I said, feeling important.

'It is hard for him,' said Juan. 'As we say here, everything he makes with his hands he destroys with his elbow. His father is a double-murderer: he was a security guard in a factory in a small town in northern Venezuela and he killed an unarmed thief. That was all right. But then he made himself a little shop; and one day he shot a customer who tried to bargain with him. So then he went to prison. Galvis joined the Guardia but was thrown out for drinking. He took a hotel catering course in Caracas but failed to finish. And then he came to San Carlos, with no money, and did a little trading – and now he has a house, an Indian wife and two children, and he even tried to be Mayor. But the people would not allow it.'

'Why not?'

'They say he cheats them whenever he can. The Baré may be ignorant, Redmond, but they are not stupid. He is in big trouble. Charlie Brewer is the only friend he has. Chimo says if he makes one more bad move the Baré will petition the regional Governor in Puerto Ayacucho and have Galvis thrown out of San Carlos.'

'Fuck a priest,' said Simon, gathering his wet clothes off the hot rocks and stuffing them back in his plastic bag. 'He sounds just like me.'

We went back to the house, hung our clothes out to dry on the line in the garden, and then made our way, past the low buildings of the school and the well-kept clinic, to visit Mariano, the most influential Baré in town. A good word from Mariano, said Juan, was the first essential step in winning the last great prize, a *zarpe*, a written permission from the Guardia to leave San Carlos by boat.

Mariano had quick, intelligent eyes, and the air of a man who is used to controlling his appetites, as befitted a retired First Sergeant of the National Guard. We sat in his ordered front room and his wife, Jacqueline Eliana, brought us coffee in little cups. One wall was hung with plastic dolls, a portrait of the Pope and picture of the Virgin Mary; a wardrobe surmounted with family pictures occupied another; but the entire far end of the room, shrine-like, was devoted to his collection of Baré artefacts: wooden manioc graters with pebbles set into the surface in intricate patterns; baskets covered in simple dyed-black geometrical designs; blow pipes and dart-holders of different sizes; curare pouches; bows and arrows; small, worn, stylised ceremonial paddles with thin blades and tops like spear-points; ten stone axeheads and necklaces of jaguar teeth.

Yes, he was a Baré like most people in San Carlos, but he was a pure Baré and proud of it, that was the difference. We knew Charlie Brewer? We had seen him in Caracas? We were using his men? Good. San Carlos was the oldest town on the Rio Negro. The Baré were the first Indians to be civilised in Amazonas province, in the 1760s. If the Government gave the young men jobs of some kind, his people might survive another three generations or so. If not, they would gradually leave for the shanty towns around Caracas, and that would be the end of them. We were going to Neblina? We were looking for carbon? Not gold? Good. He himself had been thirty years in the army, in Apure, in Caracas, in the North; but he had come back. Would we like to see his animals?

At the rear of his house he had catfish (all fins and whiskers) in one tank and Red-headed turtles (of which Wallace never managed to find a specimen) in another. Two Black curassows, turkey-sized birds, walked painstakingly back and forth at the bottom of their cage beneath the fruit trees; and, beyond his small orchard, three tapirs lay asleep in an enclosure. They woke up as we approached, wiffled their extendable, flexible snouts shortsightedly in our direction and came to the fence, low-slung donkeys on hoofed toes with their oval ears erect, to have their backs scratched. The parents were grey with short bristly coats but the calf was still young enough to have its yellow and white stripes, its camouflage in the broken light of the deep jungle. Mariano's son had brought back the parents as babies from his hunting expeditions to the Casiquiare. We congratulated Mariano on the success of his captive breeding programme, shook hands and walked back to the research station.

The heat under the corrugated iron roof was only just endurable. Expanding variably in the midday sun, it cracked and banged above our heads as if someone was hurling rocks at an empty oil drum. We had a tin of sardines each and retired for a siesta.

It was too hot to sleep, so I flicked through the photocopies of my books that Charlie had made, under the 'San Carlos' sections. It was easy to sympathise with Spruce, who had arrived in the town, in 1853, just at the right moment to take part on the wrong side of a planned massacre: 'I had been here a very short time and had had no quarrel with any one ... but I was accused of the crime of having a white skin and of being a foreigner, and as with my little stock of merchandise I found myself the richest merchant in San Carlos, pretty pickings were calculated on in the sacking of my house.' He joined forces with the two resident Portuguese and

at the hour of Ave Maria, when all were praying in the church, I betook myself to the place of rendezvous, where I found my companions already assembled with their families. Our dispositions were speedily completed, and we set ourselves to await the event, our arms being so placed as to be seized at a moment's warning. But though throughout the night parties of drunken Indians paraded the streets with tambourines and carizos, it passed over without our being attacked. You may imagine our state of anxiety, which must have been greater on the part of my comrades than on mine, surrounded as they were by their trembling families. Whenever a drunken party was heard approaching the house with shouts, beating of drums, and occasional firing of muskets, our conversation was suspended, and with our hands on our weapons we awaited what for aught we knew might be the commencement of the attack.

Towards 4 o'clock in the afternoon of the following day, though there still remained a considerable quantity of bureche, and indeed fresh supplies had come in, every one had left off drinking. At sunset, not a person was to be seen in the streets and all was still as death. The Portuguese, who had lived in San Carlos many years, and had never seen the night of St. John's Day passed otherwise than in drinking, dancing, and quarrelling, were filled with apprehension that this unwonted silence was the prelude to an attack, and that the Indians were merely keeping themselves sober for the sake of making it with more effect. We have reasons to conclude that such was really their intention, one of the principal being that in the morning the drinking, etc., were resumed and kept up for several days afterwards. When night closed in we remarked that two men were walking up and down the street in front of the house; these were a sort of scouts or sentinels, and were changed at short intervals throughout the night. The Indians, however, never screwed up their courage so far as to venture to attack us.

They knew of our warlike preparations, and, as it would seem, calculated that a good many of the foremost in the assault must necessarily forfeit their lives. Of their ultimate success against us there can be little doubt, for they were 150 against three. My firm resolve, in case of being attacked, was not to allow myself to be taken alive, and so suffer a hundred deaths in one.

Whilst awaiting this attack Spruce in fact calmly wrote a long letter to William Hooker detailing his plans, which he never carried out, for finding the source of the Orinoco. All his routes would have brought him out from eighty to 200 miles too far to the south-west, but he was remarkably well-informed by Indian report and rumour. It was not until 1950 that a joint Venezuelan–French expedition actually followed the last 120 miles of the Orinoco's course to a stream trickling 3400 feet down a mountain in the Sierra Parima, more or less where Spruce places the source of the Siapa on his rough map. Spruce could not follow this logical route, because it would have meant entering the territory of 'the hostile Guaharibos' (an earlier name for the Yanomami). Both the Spanish and Portuguese habitually took slaves from remote Indian tribes; and Spruce rightly believed that the Guaharibos had every reason to be hostile:

> Shortly after the separation of Venezuela from the mother country, and whilst there was still an armed police in the Canton del Rio Negro – there is none of any kind now – the Commandant of San Fernando was sent with a considerable body of armed men to endeavour to open amicable relations with the Guaharibos. He reached the Raudal de los Guaharibos with his little fleet of fifteen piragoas, and as the river was full, the whole of them might have passed the raudal, but it was not considered necessary, and his own piragoa alone was dragged up, the rest being left below to await their return. A very little way above they encountered a large encampment of Guaharibos, by whom they were received amicably, in return for which they rose on the Indians by night, killed as many of the men as they could, and carried off the children. Treatment such as this of course, is calculated to confirm, and perhaps it was the original cause, of the hostility of these Indians to the whites.

One of the routes which Spruce considered but never attempted was the very one which we proposed to take: 'The Rio Cauaboris is easily reached from San Carlos by proceeding up the Pasimoni, a tributary of the Casiquiare, and up its southern branch the Bariá, from which there is a short portage to the Cauaboris; but nothing of bulk could be taken this way....'

Intrigued, I turned to the photocopy of volume V of Humboldt which I had made in Oxford. Sure enough Humboldt had known about it too: the Cauaburi (a note even informed me that the 'upper part of the Cababuri [sic] was called Maturaca') is

> divided near its source into two branches, the western most of which is known by the name of Bariá. The Indians of the mission of San Francisco Solano gave us the most minute descriptions of its course. It affords the very rare example of a branch, by which an inferior tributary stream, instead of receiving the waters of the superior stream, sends on the contrary a part of its own waters to that stream, in a direction opposite to that of the principal recipient. I have collected on one plate of my atlas several examples of these ramifications with counter-currents, those apparent movements against the general slope, these bifurcations of rivers, the know-ledge of which is interesting to hydrographic engineers. This plate will remind them, that they must not consider as chimerical all that deviates from the type, which we have formed for ourselves from observations collected in too limited a part of the Globe.

It was all very disappointing. Humboldt knew about it. Spruce knew about it. Everybody knew about it. I fell asleep.

Simon, disgruntled, was the first to emerge.

'I've been strung up *and* fried alive,' he shouted. 'Where *is* the beer in this one-horse hell-hole?'

'It's in the Colombian shop,' replied Juan from his room.

'Bring your equipment,' I said. 'Let's pay homage to Humboldt and measure his tree. In 1801 "We found in the village a few juvia trees," he says here, "that majestic plant, which furnishes the triangular nuts called in Europe the almonds of the Amazon. We have made it known by the name of the *bertholletia excelsa*. The trees acquire a height of thirty feet."'

'You can measure your own nuts, for all I care,' said Simon, 'but be quick about it.'

There was a knock on the door and Juan drew back the bolt. A distraught old man in shorts and tee shirt muttered something; Juan disappeared into his drying room and came out again carrying a jar and a big syringe. The visitor took them and left.

'*That's* a needle and a half,' said Simon. 'What's *he* shooting up?'

'It's not for him,' said Juan. 'It's formalin. His aunt died yesterday. He wants to preserve the body for the party tonight and the funeral tomorrow. You rot fast here.'

'Oh god,' said Simon, taking a step backwards.

Humboldt's tree, huge, spreading, oak-like, with gnarled bark and small leaves, filled most of the space in the garden at the back of the church. In the mission building beside it very small children clustered round two very large nuns. The priest, a missionary from Madrid, was simultaneously refereeing and playing in a furious game of football with the young men of the town on the mission pitch. We extended Juan's lightweight set of telescopic measuring poles: the tree was now twenty-five metres high. We pulled out the tape: its crown spread over an area of 22 by 16.3 metres and its trunk was 1.72 metres in diameter at 1.3 metres above the ground.

'So how do you know it's the same one?' said Simon.

'You prove it isn't,' I said, huffy.

The Colombian, in his tiny General Store on the slipway side of the square was very sorry – he had almost sold out of beer and he intended to keep the rest for himself. The river was too low for boats to come up from Brazil. Beer had to be flown in by Hercules transport. But there was always Carlos. He knew where Carlos lived. He would shut his shop and go and wake Carlos.

'Wake him up?' I said. 'It's not important. We'll come back in the morning.'

'He'll be just as drunk in the morning,' said the Colombian. 'You go and wait by the bar.'

The bar, beyond the far side of the square, was easy to find. It stood on a grass bank above the river, a hut proclaiming itself to be Las Delicias, marked at the entrance not by twin pillars, but by twin oil drums full of empty Polar beer cans, on an imaginary street signposted as the calle Simon Bolivar. A mangy dog joined us.

'There were many dogs in San Carlos,' said Juan, 'but the medical orderly, either because he was drunk or because he feared an epidemic, put out poisoned meat for them one night. He dumped the bodies in the jungle. He was still doing it in the morning. He had a wheelbarrow.'

The Colombian arrived with Carlos (fat, smiling deliriously, too drunk to speak but just able to walk with assistance) and, using Carlos' key, let us all in. The dog curled up on the bare floor. Carlos collapsed onto a chair behind the bar, his head level with the counter.

'That old Carlos,' announced Simon, 'has OD'd on the Polar.'

Carlos grinned up at us as the Colombian took the beer from the fridge and gave us two cans each. I leant over and pushed the money into Carlos's shirt pocket and we went down to the river for an evening swim.

The football team were there, swimming in their shorts and tee shirts. The young girls of San Carlos were there, large, voluptuous, standing in the shallows in their thin, wet, clinging cotton dresses. They soaped themselves with a quiet suggestiveness, putting one hand and then the other down their plunging necklines, lathering their breasts beneath their bodices, and watching the football team.

Five little boys beside us, having commandeered a one-man fishing canoe, a curiara, would jump in all at once, paddle frantically until it sank beneath their weight, shriek with laughter, empty it of water and start again.

Nighthawks, in the short dusk, flickered back and forth about thirty feet above the surface of the river.

'Sometimes,' said Juan, 'the tonina, the fresh-water dolphin, comes in here at this time of day. They come close in shore and blow bubbles as they breathe.'

People were gathering by a whitewashed hut on the left-hand edge of the little bay. We wandered up to investigate.

'It's the party for the dead woman's family,' said Juan. 'Shall we join them?'

'What do you want to see corpses for?' said Simon. 'I'm going back to read my book.'

Outside the hut, under a group of lemon trees, tables and benches had been arranged. Groups of men were drinking aguardiente and playing dominoes. Friends and relatives arrived bearing presents, a tin of coffee, a basket of manioc. A few girls were sitting in a circle playing pass-the-ring. Children kicked a ball about half-heartedly, a bit overawed by the cadaver which was spread out on a table just inside the door. Candles stood at the four corners, and a water-filled bowl of herbs and cut lemons had been placed on the floor beneath to mask the smell.

'She was an old lady of seventy-five. She fell over and fractured her skull,' said Juan. 'But it is not just an ordinary death. She was the last speaker in San Carlos of the Baré language. Professor Manuel Francisco Asabache can speak a little Baré, but that is not the same thing. The language is now dead.'

We walked back in the dark, by a different route. Halfway home we came across a body lying on the path. It was Pablo, our axe-man, sleeping soundly, his legs splayed out, one arm over his head and the other straight out along the ground with a wad of notes in his clenched fist. They had been torn off where they stuck out between his thumb and forefinger. Juan felt in his pockets. Nothing.

'His friends wait until he is drunk,' said Juan, 'and then take all the wages you gave him.'

'What do we do? Drag him back with us?'

'No, Redmond, he would not like us to know, to see him like this. It is better to leave him. It will not rain tonight. He will wake up before the morning.'

In the research station we were all preparing to go to our hammocks when the outside door swung violently open. Chimo stood on the path. He swayed from side to side and then lurched backwards against the fence.

'I just came to tell you,' he said, 'that I will be a responsible man in the morning.'

Silky Anteater

4

Early the next day Simon began his self-appointed task of checking the stores. He opened Charlie's big waterproof tins which we had filled in Caracas market, listed their contents on a piece of graph paper clamped to the research station clipboard – coffee, salt, flour, manioc, cooking oil, brown sugar, spaghetti, dried onions, lentils, rice, black beans – and marked them with one of his fluorescent pens. Concentrating hard, sweating in the mounting heat, he emblazoned their tops and sides: STALE SPAG, FARTING DAGO BEANS, BORING LENTILS, FUCKING HORRIBLE MANIOC.

He tabulated his pile of cigarette cartons, his box of lighters and crate of tomato ketchup, the spare sparking plugs, the bag of cartridges. Pigeon-toed in scarlet-and-white basketball boots, ready for the jungle in brown, army-surplus cotton trousers that were slightly too short for him and a green lumberjack shirt that was too large (two packets of Marlboro safe in its chest pockets), he began to look absorbed and happy for the first time since our landing in South America.

Maybe everything really will be all right, I thought, as Charlie's ominous prediction in Caracas market came back to me yet again.

In one of the covered alleys Charlie bought a bag of guavas for himself and offered one to each of us.

'Get away,' said Simon, looking at the yellow, egg-sized, pear-shaped fruit in Charlie's hand, 'I'll try that kind of weirdo when I have to and not before.'

As we took a couple of sacks of manioc to the car Charlie drew me aside.

'Either you are a complete amateur at choosing your men,' he said, thrusting his face close to mine, 'or you are a sadist. I like Simon. He amuses me. But you should have left him in London. Biologically speaking, Redmond, he is a specialised animal: he is adapted for life in the city and nowhere else. You are playing a very dangerous game. You are playing with the lives of my Indians.'

'Christ!' said Simon, spinning round and breaking into my thoughts. 'We're *twenty* one-litre cans of motor oil out. We're twenty cans short. Some wide boy's nicked our oil!'

'It's normal,' said Juan, counting the stack himself. 'It could be the Cessna pilot. It could be the Guardia. It could be anybody. You have to allow for it in the cost, Redmon. For a year already the Government have been trying to build a receiving station for television here: they want to bring the people television, so that the Government can speak to them. But every time the airforce fly in cement in the Hercules the Guardia borrow the fishermen's canoes in the night and take the cement to the other side of the river, to Colombia. In Colombia they pay twice as much.'

'So what do we do, smartarse?' said Simon.

'Redmon must pay for Galvis to fly to Puerto Ayacucho when the Cessna comes tomorrow. He will buy motor oil and two hammocks and two big tarpaulins; Galvis will like to go. He has a girlfriend in Ayacucho.'

'Bloody marvellous,' said Simon, sitting down at the table and holding his head in his hands. 'It's Minister this and Minister that and Generals and Regional Governors and Restricted Areas and evil-looking bastards with Sten guns and then it's maniacs with arrows at the end of it all, and now we've got no fuel. This is one big fuck-up, Fatso. This is one long aggravation.'

'It is okay,' said Juan. 'We can still leave in one week. Tomorrow, Simon, I will help you to pack your kit bags. You must divide up everything you really need, like the medicines for fever. You must place some in each bag. Then if we turn over and lose some in the rapids we do not worry.'

'Rapids?' said Simon, looking up sharply. 'What rapids?'

'We have to pass one set on the Casiquiare,' said Juan. 'But don't throw the wobbly. Just a few people have died there already. It is not like the Raudales de Atures at Puerto Ayacucho. The only man in Venezuela who is not afraid of *them* is Charlie Brewer-Carias. In 1972, on one of his training courses, he took twenty young people down that piece of the Orinoco. The bowman had a panic. They hit a rock. The boat broke up. Eighteen young men drowned.'

'That Charlie,' said Simon, 'is well out of his tree. He is seriously bonkers. He ought to be put away. And here you are, Fatso, *doing everything he says.*'

'He is the only man to go up those rapids as well as down,' said Juan. 'It took him one month to find all the bodies. They were trapped under the rocks. They were held downstream under the banks. Every night he returned to the Hotel Amazonas and rang up the parents of the boys still missing. That is why he no longer likes to stay in Puerto Ayacucho.'

'Dear God,' said Simon, getting up. "I'm going to get lost in *War and Peace* and then I'm going out. When Carlos opens up he can get legless with me. He's the only sane geezer in the whole stinking shithouse.'

'It is late already,' said Juan to me. 'I must now inspect my experimental plots. I must go and see Pedro.'

'Come on Simon,' I said, 'come and see the forest.'

'Stuff that,' said Simon.

We collected Pedro, Old Valentine's son, from his two-room, wattle-and-daub house beyond the red dirt airstrip and walked out of town. Pedro, wearing a white tee shirt, cotton trousers and gum boots, with a baseball cap on his head and a machete in his hand, walked fast and said little. Eventually he turned off the track and entered the jungle.

'Here it is not like Borneo,' said Juan. 'You will be disappointed. This is tierra firme forest — it is never flooded — but the soils around San Carlos are some of the poorest in the Amazon basin. They derive from the Guiana shield, the oldest rocks in the world, and almost all their nutrients were leached out of them long ago: natural selection has favoured those species which grow slowly and make minimum demands for food. We have up to ninety-six different kinds of tree in each 900-square-metre plot, but big individuals are very rare.'

Nevertheless, even in the relatively impoverished San Carlos jungle, I at once felt a flicker of that delight which Darwin recorded in his diary on first entering a Brazilian forest in 1832:

> amongst the multitude it is hard to say what set of objects is most striking; the general luxuriance of the vegetation bears the victory, the elegance of the grasses, the novelty of the parasitical plants, the beauty of the flowers, the glossy green of the foliage, all tend to this end. A most paradoxical mixture of sound and silence pervades the shady parts of the wood: the noise from the insects is so loud that in the evening it can be heard even in a vessel anchored several hundred yards from the shore: yet within the forest a universal stillness appears to reign. To a person fond of natural history such a day as this brings with it pleasure more acute than he ever may again experience.

If there were any rain-forest flowers, they were blooming way above our heads in the canopy; dull-green, broad-leaved jungle grasses grew only at the edge of Pedro's paths in the leaf litter; small fan-leaved palms and etiolated shrubs clustered only in the gaps between the thin-stemmed, lichen-covered trees; there were few lianas, and in twenty minutes' walking we passed only five plank-buttressed forest giants. But, high up, on the edge of the first clearing we reached, a huge butterfly, a morpho, was sailing along, and when it flapped its wings intermittently, like a bird in a thermal, their upper surface flashed an iridescent blue brighter than the backs of kingfishers.

The clearing was Pedro's conuco, his plantation, an elliptical space covered with tree stumps and felled, charred trunks, between which he was growing manioc and pineapples.

'I have ninety-six different study sites like this but of varying ages,' said Juan, in his official, lecturing voice, as Pedro hacked open a pineapple and gave us a piece each. 'Recovery rates from this type of small-scale slash-and-burn farming are five to seven times longer in the upper Rio Negro than in other parts of South America, but in approximately 140 to 200 years the basal area and biomass values here will be comparable to those of a mature forest.'

On the way to the next plot Pedro pointed to a large, worn hole in a trunk, which he said was the home of an animal that carried its young in a pouch (probably a Southern opossum); Juan paused to admire a tree – it looked much like all the others – Visma apurensis, which is fertilized by bats; and Pedro stopped by a tree which he said was a tabari, cut out a section of the light brown bark with his machete, bashed it at one end with the back of the blade, peeled off a series of strips, tore one to size, took his tobacco out of his trouser pocket and rolled a bark-paper cigarette.

At site two, a recently abandoned conuco, Juan measured various red-tape-marked shrubs, counted growth tips on sample branches and compared them against diagrams in his rucksack. On the next stretch of path Pedro, warming to his unaccustomed role of guide, showed us a large tree whose bark, when boiled and the water drunk, relieved stomach and muscle pain. My shirt and trousers were soaked with sweat in the clammy heat. I felt as if I had been for a swim in the Rio Negro fully clothed, and I was beginning to wish that I had taken a piece of bark myself (worth 50 bolivares per two hands' breadth, said Pedro, in Ayacucho market) when we stopped by a clump of very odd-looking palms.

'This is the cumare,' said Juan. 'Some local people live by collecting the fibres. They make brooms, brushes, hammocks and ropes.'

It was clearly the palm which Wallace calls the piassába, peculiar to the area and abundant:

> In the whole of the district about the Upper Rio Negro above San Carlos ... It grows in moist places, and is about twenty or thirty feet high, with the leaves large, pinnate, shining and very smooth and regular. The whole stem is covered with a thick coating of the fibres, hanging down like coarse hair, and growing from the bases of the leaves, which remain attached to the stem. Large parties of men, women, and children go into the forests to cut this fibre ... Humboldt alludes to this plant by the native Venezuelan name of chiquichiqui, but does not appear to have seen it....

Pedro cut a pole with his machete from a sapling and thwacked the bushy side of the nearest palm.

'Get back!' said Juan, tugging at my arm. 'It is dangerous, Redmon. Many snakes make their home in the cumare.'

To my disappointment nothing stirred. No twelve-foot bushmaster came curling through the air.

'Chimo says that Culimacaré began to cut the fibre full-time when he was twelve,' said Juan. 'It is not right. Of all your crew only Galvis has been to school.'

41

A little further on, Pedro suddenly broke into a run in front of us, dropped to the ground and covered his head with his arms.

'Wasps!' shouted Juan. And then, turning to me with a triumphant grin: 'Where we are going,' he said, 'you will be stung ten times a day.'

Pedro rolled another cigarette and we sat down beside him on an exposed root.

'Five stings,' said Juan, with interest, counting the punctures on Pedro's swelling hands. 'He must have touched a branch where a new small colony had hung its nest. Normally there are more individuals.'

'How did you become a scientist?' I asked.

'I work very hard,' he said, looking at his feet. 'I never stop. I won a scholarship to university and then I left Colombia. I won another scholarship, to the University of Tennessee. I am studying for my doctorate at Oak Ridge National Laboratory. My wife, Mercedes, she is a Colombian student of art at Tennessee. People think well of her work. We write to each other only in English, to improve ourselves. I love her very much, but I have not seen her for six months. And now, because I must take the chance to journey with you, it will be nine months, maybe ten. It is hard for us.'

'What about the rest of your family?'

'I have an elder brother. But it was different for him. He worked hard, too. He came second in the competition for a scholarship to the university. My father has a business in telephones, but it was worse then. His cheque was no good, so my brother had to leave the university. He joined a mining company. He is left-wing and he became the secretary of the union. So then he had to leave the company. He went prospecting on his own account, and he found gold.'

'So he's rich.'

'He is very rich. But it is difficult for him. His gold mine is in an area where there are many guerillas. He helped to build the local school, so he is okay so far. But one day they will kill him.'

'Why? Because he's the boss?'

'Yes. And because we are a violent people. The whole of South America is violent. Look at it! I don't know the exact figures, Redmon, but what can you do? Peru has only had four years of democratic government, Ecuador eight, Brazil one, Uruguay four months. Bolivia has had 180 presidents in 160 years. Even Venezuela suffered from dictators from the 1940s to the 1960s and here in Amazonas, from

1921 to 1927, there was a mad cruel military governor, Thomas Funes, who wanted the Amazonas to be an independent state. He persecuted the Indians and conscripted them into his army, so they abandoned their settlements and took to the forest and many died. But we Colombians, we are the worst. Between 1946 and 1966 300,000 people died in my country. The Conservatives, the Church party, fought the Liberals – the church said that all Liberals were sons of the devil and must be killed. Now it is the communists against the Government. The army branch of the Communist party is called FARC, *Fuergas armadas revolucionarias de Colombia*. It protects the narco-traffickers, and they are more violent than the Mafia. We still live with *la Violencia*. We are used to it. In my country we are tough and wary. We have to be. Perhaps it is something in our character, a mix of the Spaniard and the Indian – I, too, have a terrible temper. I feel it inside, all the time. Your Simon – I think he can be violent. But you, you are very English, dishonest. You never show your feelings.'

Juan had worked himself into a rage against all this violence. Pedro finished his cigarette, stood up, cut through a liana at head height with his machete and, holding the upper severed end to his mouth, drank at the flow of water. When he had had enough, Juan and I followed suit.

On the way back, near his own conuco, Pedro drank again, kneeling down beside a little stream and putting his lips directly to its surface. Standing up, he caught sight of something in the undergrowth and jumped across the stream to investigate.

When we caught up with him Pedro grinned at us and then at a tall bush. In a fork at chest-height was a squirrel-sized animal, furry, golden, curled up and asleep. About the least violent roundel of life you could imagine, his bushy tail looped muff-like round his back feet, which gripped one of the thin branches. His front legs were wrapped over his head. Knowing that he was as inoffensive as he looked, the yellow or white form of the Silky anteater, which feeds by night on ants, and which Wallace heard about but never saw, I stroked his back. The fur was thicker, finer and softer than a kitten's. He woke up, gently unfurled his tail, and re-wound it tightly round the other branch of the fork. He slowly stretched himself, straightening his back, and, on either side of his face, held up his front feet: armed with one large and one small black, hooked claw apiece, they framed his tiny eyes and, on their bare insides, they matched the bright pink of

43

his downward-curving snout. I tickled his golden stomach until he tired of such uninvited affection, lazily drew back his head, hissed, and nodded sharply forward as if trying to spit. We left him in peace.

'Simon!' I said, as we burst through the door of the research station. 'We saw a Silky anteater!'

'Did you?' said Simon, looking up from his book, a crate of beer at his elbow. 'Then why the hell didn't you grab it by the back legs and drag it back here? There's ants *everywhere*. They're all over the kitchen. It's bloody disgusting. They've been at my spam.'

'You must put it in water,' said Juan.

'Take a running jump,' said Simon.

'And we almost saw a Southern opossum,' I said. 'And that would interest you. They've got a bifurcated penis, and people used to think they mated through the nose and then blew the young into their pouches.'

'Probably do,' said Simon. 'There's no telling. There's things out there, I shouldn't wonder, with dicks like pitchforks.'

Over the next few days we made short trips down the Rio Negro with Old Valentine in his bongo, to test Charlie's outboard motors and to visit the few sites around San Carlos where Indian petroglyphs are found. On flat granite slabs at the head of half-hidden creeks, and on rocks at the edge of the river itself that were exposed by the exceptionally low waters, we photographed the engraved picture drawings of uncertain age and origin which Humboldt and Wallace and Spruce describe: matchstick men with multiple arms or box bodies, abstract designs of whorls and circles and lines, crude representations of iguanas or fish. Spruce thought such art had been 'involved in unnecessary mystery', and tells us that having 'carefully examined a good deal of the so-called picture writing, I am bound to come to the conclusion that it was executed by the ancestors of Indians who at this day inhabit the region where it is found; that their utensils, mode of life, etc., were similar to those still in use; and that their degree of civilisation was certainly not greater – probably less – than that of their existing descendants.' But to me, then, standing beside Juan, whom I had only just met, and Simon, whom I momentarily felt I no longer knew, they seemed as enigmatic as the vast trees on the high bank above us, as impenetrable as Old Valentine's pock-marked face.

The next night, as we were returning upriver from a visit to a similar set of rocks, I was imagining Galvis drunk, happy, and almost penniless in bed with his Puerto Ayacucho girl in the Hotel Amazonas; worrying about a fault in the small Yamaha outboard motor; and wondering anxiously why, even with our sheaf of official letters, it was proving so difficult to persuade the Teniente, the military commander of San Carlos, to grant us our final permission to leave, when we passed two huts on the left bank backed by an old clearing. I recognized the farm at once. Four hours paddling downstream from San Carlos, it was surely that place where, in all his travels, Spruce had been most bitterly lonely. It was the conuco of his pilot Pedro Deno, not much changed in 130 years. Spruce was suffering from diarrhoea and slung his hammock early while his Baré Indians got drunk on bureche. Hearing endless discussion about 'heinali', the man, he began to pay attention:

> I heard them begin to lash themselves into a fury by recapitulating all the injuries they had received from the white men, all of which they considered themselves justified in retaliating on my devoted head – though in my short intercourse with them I had shown them only kindness, and particularly to Pedro Yurébe, whose little daughter I had a short time before cured of a distressing colic, which for many consecutive days and nights had allowed her no rest. . . . I heard them all whispering one to the other, 'Iduali! Iduali!' ('Now it is good – now it is good'), and as Yurébe hesitated a moment, I got up and walked leisurely towards the forests as if my necessities had driven me thither again; but instead I turned when I got a few paces and walked straight down to the canoe, unlocked the door of the cabin, which I entered, and having fortified the open doorway by putting a bundle of paper before it, I laid my double-barrelled loaded gun, along with a cutlass and knife, by my side, and thus awaited the attack which I still expected would be made. At intervals I could hear angry exclamations from the Indians, wondering that I did not return to my hammock; and it may be imagined in what a state of mind I passed the rest of the night, never allowing my eye and ear to relax their watchfulness

for a moment.... I took care throughout the rest of the voyage that the Indians should never approach me unarmed, and I never spent a gloomier time.

But the very next morning Juan returned from his regular visit to the barracks bearing that document of documents, the zarpe, our licence to go, plus a Venezuelan flag on a three-foot pole which we were to fly at all times on the lead bongo. Plumb in the middle there were a couple of bullet holes.

To celebrate, we crossed the river to the Colombian bank, and walked over the earth-and-stonework ditch and bastions of the ruined Portuguese fort of San Felipe which, in Humboldt's time, contained a garrison of two soldiers and fifteen cannons ('the greater part dismounted').

An enormously fat man with a long white beard emerged from a hut beside the northern wall. He was wearing swimming trunks and sandals and a muscovy duck waddled at his heels. Hearing that Juan was a scientist, he told us to wait on a rock by his door, disappeared inside again, and came out carrying a tin, a book and a plastic bag. As his stomach was twice as big as mine and Simon's slopped together, I warmed to him at once. He sat down and opened the book, a pocket history of Colombia. The duck sat down, too, breast-first onto its feet; it cocked its head and watched us with one eye. The fat man tapped his index finger on a conventional representation of a mountain surrounded by cliffs, a rough rectangle with short, straight lines fanning out round its edge. It was lavelled 'MESA MONTANA (URANIO?)' ('Table Mountain [Uranium?]). He pulled a bit of ironstone out of the plastic bag, laid it carefully on the rock, unscrewed the lid of the tin and shook out a shower of iron filings. The lodestone held the iron filings to itself like the prickles on a hedgehog.

'You see!' he said. 'I am going to be very rich. I have a large piece of uranium like the picture in the book.'

I looked at his expectant eyes, and I hoped that it was not his sustaining dream. Juan disabused him gently. The fat man turned his face away for a moment, and then smiled at us, as if it was now too late to do anything else.

The following afternoon Galvis arrived with the oil, the tarpaulins, two hammocks and a bright red dress for his wife. Chimo arrived with his bongo and Culimacaré and all Charlie's tools for repairing outboard motors. We could leave at last. Then the Government Hercules arrived with supplies for the Marines and the Guardia, and with enough free aguardiente for the remote outpost of San Carlos to celebrate Labour Day (and to remember to vote for the right party when the election came). Two days later, when everyone could stand up, we left.

Screaming Piha

5

Halfway through the morning the town council pick-up, an old Toyota with wood-slat sides at the back and 'CONCEJO MUNICIPAL' painted on its doors, juddered to a halt outside the research station. We loaded the stores and followed the truck down to the landing stage. Closely watched by the soldier with the Sten gun, who made random searches through some of our storage tins for acetone in case we were really bound for the Colombian jungle to set up a cocaine factory, we rolled the fuel drums down the sloping granite rocks, manhandled them into the two rough-hewn dugout canoes, and packed in everything else according to Chimo's instructions. There was just enough room for Simon and me to perch on the plank seat in the middle of Chimo's dugout, our backs against our bergens, and for Galvis and Juan to do likewise against a sack of rice in Old Valentine's boat. Valentine and Culimacaré squatted as lookouts in the two bows and Chimo and Pablo, the motormen, punted the boats out from the shore with ten-foot poles, swung the bows upstream, stowed the poles, sat down, and started the outboard motors with one pull of their strings apiece. The soldier, shedding his official manner, suddenly looked wistful, abandoned.

'Good luck!' he yelled above the putter of the motors. 'And stay clear of the Yanomami!'

*

We kept close in to the banks of long forested islands in the middle of the great river, under the vast expanse of sky. But Charlie was right: the Rio Negro was far too wide to show us much except the tall trees and thick lianas, the impenetrable-seeming, light-loving plants which crowd out over the water at the jungle's edge. We disturbed little but small flocks of White-winged swallows resting on overhanging branches, who simply resumed their zig-zagging flight low across the choppy surface of the river, hawking for insects; and an hour or so upstream we startled a different species, pairs of Black-collared swallows, neater, less approachable, perched on the rounded granite rocks. Simon pulled his pocket tape-recorder out of his bergen and began his devotional diary to Liz, his school-teacher-lady.

'Dateline May 3rd,' he intoned. 'We're on the move, Angel-drawers. Every boring mile brings me closer to you. I bite your bum. Simon.'

'That's not the right spirit,' I said. 'Just think of it: Humboldt and Bonpland set off from San Carlos exactly like this — except that their Indians had to paddle — on 10 May 1801, on their way to prove that the Casiquiare really did connect the Orinoco and the Amazon.'

'Update,' said Simon, clicking his machine on again, 'Redmond says that some crazy Kraut and his sidekick came this way 184 years ago. *Get that for a bundle of fun.* I grab your suspenders. Simon.'

Valentine and Culimacaré, lookouts with no snags to look for in the deep water, surrendered to their hangovers and fell asleep. Simon put his recorder away and pulled out *War and Peace*. A giant white-fronted and black-bellied bird, standing halfway up a tangle of branches and lianas, grew increasingly agitated as we approached, raising and dipping its black-crowned, black-plumed head, and then, on broad grey wings, it laboured up over the trees and out of sight. I took Schauensee and Phelp's *Guide to the Birds of Venezuela* from its waterproof bag in the front pocket of my bergen and identified it at once — a White-necked heron. Shortly afterwards the right bank gave way to a great expanse of water. We turned east into the Casiquiare.

Humboldt estimated the Casiquiare to be 'from two hundred and fifty to two hundred and eighty toises' wide, and Robert Schomburgk, passing on his way downstream in 1838 from the mission of Esmeralda, after becoming the first European to cross the mountains from British Guiana, put it at 550 yards. To me it just seemed as wide as the Rio Negro, but mud-coloured rather than black. It was a white-water river, most of its flow deriving from the mountain-stream-fed Orinoco rather than from the low-lying rivers, stained with tannins from rotting vegetation, which supply the Negro network.

Drowsing against my bergen as the great trees slid endlessly by, I thought of Schomburgk's travels and I envied him for one sight above all others. Crossing the ranges to the east he

> hit upon a flock of those glorious birds, the Cock-of-the-Rock ... I had the opportunity of being present at the birds' dance which indeed the Indians had often talked to me about, but which I had always considered to be a fable. We heard at some distance off, the chirping notes that are so peculiar to the Rupicola, and two of my guides nodded to me to sneak cautiously with them in to the spot that at some distance from the path formed the gathering-place of the dancers. It was from four to five feet in diameter, cleared of every blade of grass, and the ground at the same time was smooth as if human hands had levelled it. It was on this spot that we saw one of the birds dancing and hopping around while the others apparently constituted the wondering spectators. He now spread out his wings, threw his head in the air or spread his tail like a peacock: he then strutted around and scratched the ground up, all accompanied with a hopping gait, until exhausted he uttered a peculiar note, and another bird took his place. In this way three of them one after another stepped onto the stage, and withdrew one after the other with the proudest self-consciousness back again amongst the others who had settled on some low bushes that surrounded the dancing ground. We counted ten males and two females, until all of a sudden the crackling noise of a piece of wood, that my foot had inadvertently stepped on, scared them — and bang flew the whole ballet-troupe away.

In my half-waking dream I imagined the flame-orange males waiting for us to the south in the world's oldest mountains, or, perhaps, as Schomburgk had watched them display in February, we might even be greeted by a female in her mud nest, high in the vault of some secret cave.

About an hour later we arrived at Solano, pulled the canoes up the granite slab of the landing stage, and went to present our pass to the army. In front of the barracks, a concrete bungalow with a corrugated iron roof, a young soldier in fatigues and a tee shirt sat at a table under a sunshade, reading a novel.

'That's okay,' he said, glancing at the zarpe, 'they told us you were coming on the radio. We don't get many messages here.'

'What are you looking for?' I asked. 'Gold prospectors? Colombian Communists?'

'What? Here? At Solano?' He jumped to his feet, grabbed his Sten gun from the table, and roared with laughter.

'Nothing happens here,' he said, sitting down again. 'Nothing at all. We watch Chimo. And every night the boss and I pray to the Virgin for a posting to Caracas.'

He gestured at two long sheds beside the bungalow. 'That's what I do all day. Go and have a look. Feel free. Enjoy the only available girls of Solano.'

The first shed was a deep-litter house full of hens, Rhode Island reds panting in the heat, too hot to squawk; the second was spread with pigs, Large Whites, fast asleep.

'Last year in the rainy season,' said Juan, 'the Hercules couldn't get into San Carlos for months. There was nothing to feed to the animals. The Guardia had to kill them all.'

Juan took us on a tour of the village, past an abandoned, never-used school building in a crumbling wire compound; a large hut, part of an unfinished palm-fibre factory; and a row of empty Government houses.

'In the oil boom,' he said, turning back towards the river, 'the Government had great plans for Solano and San Carlos – a grand programme, *la conquista del Sur*, the conquest of the South. But the money ran out. Nothing came of it.'

As we headed back to the boats, clambering over the black granite rocks, two young men paddled into the shore in a bongo with a long, low, tube-like palm-thatch shelter set towards its stern. They wore tee shirts and green baseball caps, said they were Chimo's cousins, and had come from a hunting trip upriver.

The bows were piled with long lengths of a special wood, lighter than balsa, which is used for making fishing floats, and they had caught sixty turtles – the ordinary Amazon river turtles, with smooth brown shells, blackish skin, red-tipped snouts and a red band across the top of the head. We bought two for 20 bolivares. As Juan and I carried one each back to our boats they folded their necks sideways beneath their shells – unlike other turtles and terrapins which retract their heads directly backwards like a collapsing telescope. A primitive species, they are probably descended from sea-living ancestors which moved up the Amazon: when breeding they still behave like the turtles of the open sea, crowding onto sandbanks at night to dig pits and lay their eggs. Given the great harvest which the Indians then make (and which all the nineteenth-century traveller-naturalists record) I was surprised to find that there were still so many left to hunt.

We gave the turtles to Galvis, took our bergens up to the guest hut, an open-sided dome of thatch beside the army bungalow, and slung our hammocks. After a supper of spam and rice, as I lay swinging gently beneath my mosquito net and reading my photocopy of Bates, I was distracted by something whirring and buzzing from one red flower to another on a small bush growing just to the other side of the path. Big-bodied, grey-brown, its wings no more than faint worries in the air to either side of its back, it was plainly a hawkmoth. Then no, I thought, as it flew off like a bumblebee, it's not a moth: it's my first humming-bird. Perhaps, I decided, feeling not quite so stupid as night arrived, it was really a humming-bird hawkmoth of the kind which Bates kept shooting for his collection by mistake:

> This moth (Macroglossa Titan) is somewhat smaller than hum-ming-birds generally are; but its manner of flight, and the way it poises itself before a flower whilst probing it with its proboscis, are precisely like the same actions of humming-birds. It was only after many days' experience that I learnt to distinguish one from the other when on the wing. This resemblance has attracted the notice of the natives, all of whom, even educated whites, firmly believe that one is transmutable into the other. They have observed the metamorphosis of caterpillars into butterflies, and think it not at all more wonderful that a moth should change into a humming-bird.

The Guardia shut down their small generator, the stridulation of cicadas replaced and mimicked its humming. As I began to fall asleep, it seemed that almost anything in the Amazons might change into almost anything else.

At dawn the wisps of high cloud in the momentarily gold and purple sky were reflected in the smooth surface of the river, and we went down for a swim. Valentine and Pablo, having spent the night sleeping by the bongos to guard the stores, were boiling water over a fire.

'What's *that*?' said Simon, stopping suddenly.

Out of the corner of my eye I thought I saw a bat move on the stones. I looked closer: it was the top of a turtle flipper, beating to and fro; on a low fire the turtles were being roasted alive in their shells, on their backs; they held their beaked mouths open in one long soundless scream.

'For Christsake,' said Simon, turning away.

Juan shouted something to Pablo, who picked up his machete, ran forward, and cut off their heads.

'Why the hell don't they kill them first?' said Simon, frothing his words slightly and rounding on Juan.

'It is the custom,' said Juan, with a quick shrug of his narrow shoulders. 'The Indians always cook them like that.'

'Well, it's terrible,' said Simon, walking off on his own down the shoreline.

Juan and I stripped to our pants and washed, clinging to the side of the floating raft which held the Guardia's water pump. There was a loud *whoosh* behind us, a little further out in the river.

'Tonina!' said Juan.

'Dolphin!' I shouted stupidly, and turned too late to see anything but spreading circles of ripples.

Chimo and Culimacaré joined us from Chimo's house for breakfast and Simon returned, silent, from his walk. We ate turtle (rich, chewy) and manioc (like sawdust). Simon, declining both, opened a tin of spam and sat apart on a rock of his own. Galvis, intending to cheer up his new friend, went to sit beside him.

'Simon!' said Galvis. 'No problema!'

'No problem,' said Simon.

Galvis took a severed turtle head out of his mess tin, picked its brains out from the neck with a fork, ate them, and turned to Simon. He held the blackened head in his fingers in front of Simon's face and moved the jaws open and shut.

'Quack!' said Galvis. 'Quack! Quack! Quack!'

'Savages,' muttered Simon. '*Nothing but savages.*' He put down his tin of spam, got to his feet, and walked fast up to the guest hut.

Everyone laughed except me.

'Chief,' said Chimo as we re-packed the boats, 'I want to tow my son-in-law up to his conuco. And I want to give him two tankfuls of petrol.'

'If he is asking,' said Juan quickly, in English, 'he must like you.'

'That's fine,' I said, at once.

'Sod it,' said Simon, 'whatever it is. You say yes to everything. Sooner or later you must show these people who's boss.'

'It's not like that,' I said.

Chimo's son-in-law, daughter, four children, two dogs, and assorted cooking pots, baskets, fishing harpoons, axes and machetes, were waiting in their bongo (with idle outboard motor and empty petrol tins) by a creek (obviously Chimo's creek) upstream. Chimo, Culimacaré and the son-in-law secured the two boats together, like the twin hulls of a catamaran, by laying the two punt poles across and lashing them down to the plank seats bow and stern. Pablo took Chimo's curiara, a two-man fishing canoe, from its mooring by the rocks and roped it to the stern of his dugout.

As we made our way slowly eastwards against the current, flocks of ten to twenty Great egrets, hunched figures of dazzling white, would stand impassively on their long black legs in the tumbling foliage of the trees or on loops of liana, gangle into the air as we drew level, form into a long line, and fly off downriver behind us. Two parrots (perhaps the Red-lored) crossed the river high above our heads with fast, shallow beats of their very broad, very green wings. And later we disturbed an anhinga – which must have been fishing in our course – a bird like a cormorant but with a much longer and thinner neck, head and bill, and with a long, fan-shaped tail. It rose splashing and flailing from the surface, as if with a great effort, and then flapped and sailed in front of us, shiny and greenish-black in the sunlight, its wings streaked with white like droppings on a branch. Tired of our pursuit, it flipped into the river some thirty yards away to our left, submerged its body and watched us go by with just its head and a short length of neck visible, snake-like, above the water.

Two very odd-looking terns with black tips to their wings and enormous yellow bills sat together at the end of a sandbank.

'Guanaguanare!' called Chimo, seeing me staring through the binoculars.

Large-billed tern, said Schauensee, as I cross-checked from his Spanish to his English index. Chimo obviously knew his birds. The

Chief of Solano was an ornithologist. Life could not be better.

'Simon,' I said, 'I've seen my first parrots, my first anhinga, those are Large-billed terns, and we've only just begun!'

Simon put *War and Peace* away, unzipped the watertight camera-case at his feet and drew out a Minolta body and a long lens. He clicked on his tape recorder.

'Angel-drawers. I'm about to start my new career. I'm fixing my 500 onto the best camera. I'm going to zap some bird with an outsize hooter. I may even be about to enjoy myself. With my Stormtrooper Charlie knife I cut off your knicks. Simon.'

We swung into a straight stretch and a block of grey granite rose sheer on the right bank ahead of us, some three hundred feet above the forest canopy: the Rock of Culimacaré, from whose foot Humboldt fixed his position as 2° 0′ 42″ (slightly too far to the north) and which looked exactly as Spruce drew it in 1853. At its side was a smaller, chaotic assemblage of rocks, fractured towers, broken pinnacles, boulders perched one on top of the other. Further upstream, on the outer curve of a bend which swung the Casiquiare to the south-east, we passed the village of Culimacaré. From our low position, I could see nothing but the little landing-stage and two huts close by, their windows hung, as Humboldt described them, with palm-thatch and bamboo-frame defences against mosquitoes.

'*Now* I'll show you some rock-paintings!' shouted Chimo, pointing the boats towards one of the many small islands in the middle of the river.

A dead branch stuck out of the water near our landing-place and, as the hulls scraped onto the rocks, a cloud of tiny bats burst away from it like pieces of kicked puff-ball. They flickered over the water towards the upended roots of another place of flotsam – and disappeared. Focusing the binoculars I could just make them out, clustered down the sides of the bare wood like clumps of lichen.

Chimo led the way to a big granite boulder. On its one flat side (as if a piece of stone had split away in the heat) it was closely packed with engravings – a sitting monkey with a curlicue tail; an iguana with three pairs of limbs to show that it was running; and rows of square, oblong and penis-shaped manioc-oven trays (or so his Baré guides told Spruce of similar drawings), each one dotted with manioc cakes. Whoever had etched these designs in the rock knew what it was like to be hungry.

Pablo beached his bongo and Juan joined us. He took a piece of chalk out of his small rucksack, whitened the lines in the stone, and we took photographs.

'They were hungry,' I said.

'Soon we will all be hungry,' said Juan with excessive emphasis, as if giving voice to a private fear. 'In England, Redmon, there is always food. And in Borneo, too, where the rainforest is full of hills. But here the wet season is coming. And then the rivers flow over their banks and flood through the trees for hundreds of kilometres. The fish live in deep water and are difficult to catch. That is when the Baré and Curipaco have no protein and their young people lose their teeth. That is why Chimo and Pablo and Culimacaré have so few teeth – to eat meat in the wet season you must be a real hunter, a Yanomami.'

'If I lose my noshers,' said Simon gloomily, 'I'll flip my lid. I really will. You keep the manihock and I'll stick to spam.'

'The spam will run out,' said Juan, moving off to photograph another set of rock-paintings.

Simon and I wandered up over the smooth boulders. Scraggy bushes with small leaves grew in every crevice where soil was trapped, and from beneath one of them we flushed a family of nighthawks. They flew in front of us for twenty yards with stiff, stilted wing-beats, as if loath to fly at all in full sunlight, and then flopped down on the rocks. Probably Sand-coloured nighthawks, their backs were a light buff colour, speckled and squiggled with black, and, when at rest and folded, the tips of their long pointed wings crossed and scissored out behind them. Through the binoculars I could clearly see the forward-sprouting bristles round their bills. We put them to flight repeatedly, following them slowly round the island until they doubled back to their favoured resting-place, airy, insubstantial, noiseless as moths.

We reclined on a hot, almost flat slab of rock, waiting for Chimo to finish syphoning our precious petrol into his son-in-law's outboard motor and five-gallon reserve drum, and watching the river's mesmerising flow beneath the great chaos of foliage rearing up into the sky on the opposite bank.

'Raaaak! Raaaak! Raaaak!' called something, like a carrion crow with a megaphone.

'Guacamayo azul y amarillo', said Chimo very slowly, for my benefit, looking up from his bent position over the motor and pointing with his free hand.

High above us two big, orange-yellow birds entered our field of vision, their long tails streaming, the topsides of their wings flashing a bright cerulean blue on each deep and steady downbeat. I caught them briefly in the binoculars: their great hooked bills were jet-black as they looked down at us, their faces black-lined as though with the wrinkles of extreme old age. They passed easily across our gap of sky and out of sight.

'Our first Blue-and-yellow macaws!'

'Now get that,' said Simon, stretching out on the stone, putting his hands behind his head and shutting his eyes.

I became aware of a faint, high-pitched, low-volume bickering noise, like a fieldful of shrews all fighting in the grass at once. It was coming from the edge of the rock beside me and I knelt down to listen. There was a three or four-inch slit, a dark recess, between the underside of our slab and the next rock down. Putting my eye to it I could just see small black pieces of an intenser darkness scrabbling back from the entrance. It smelt oven-hot and musky.

'Simon, it's a bat roost.'

'Oh great,' said Simon, jumping to his feet. 'Here I am, just getting peaceful, kipping on the beach – and all the time *there's a bunch of vampires under my butt.*'

'They're not vampires,' said Juan, laughing, climbing into Valentine's bongo, 'it's just another species of small bat. We have hundreds of species of bat. Of all the mammals in the rainforest, bats have the highest biomass. The weight of bats is heavier than any other genus.'

'Well,' said Simon, aggrieved, 'they should piss off and roost somewhere else.'

We stopped again, to disconnect the boats before we reached the rapids, by a patch of open, scrubby land, perhaps an abandoned conuco. A flat-topped, acacia-like tree grew at its centre, beyond a waist-high clump of some kind of purple orchid, and from its branches there hung seven yard-long, thickly-woven nests, several of them set so close together that their sides touched. Yellow and black thrush-sized birds flew back and forth, whistling in the air and tut-tutting harshly at us from the branches by their nest entrances.

'Keep well back,' said Juan, joining us, 'Chimo says they nest with wasps.'

And at that moment there was a buzz like a straining moped past my ear; the air was full of hornets. Through the lenses I could see two unobtrusive, inverted cones, parchment-coloured, suspended beneath the leaves by the main clump of bird nests. We retreated back to the boats. 'Yellow-rumped caciques,' said Schauensee. 'Nests .... placed in high branches near wasps' nests.'

The rapids were no more than a series of gentle steps in the flat granite bed of the river, the water level far too low to make them dangerous. Valentine (too old), Galvis (the cook), Simon ('I'll take your photograph'), Juan ('I don't have that kind of strength') and the women and children watched from a rock as Chimo, Pablo, Culimacaré, Chimo's son-in-law and I dragged the bongos through the knee-high water, one at a time, for an hour.

We said goodbye to Chimo's relations, whose clearing was somewhere nearby, and Chimo and Pablo opened up the throttles on our motors. The river was wide, straight, canal-like; and in the narrow track of sky above it different species of parrots would suddenly appear, flying rapidly from above the trees on one bank and vanishing, all too soon, cut off from view by the massed trees on the other. Parties of up to twenty Orange-winged, always in pairs, would screech down at us: *quick quick quick*; flocks of up to fifty Yellow-crowned (equally green, rounded and fast but with scarlet wing-patches) would pass over us barking like excited spaniels: *bow-wow-wow, bow-wow-wow*; and the slightly bigger but otherwise identical Mealy parrot signed itself with a guttural *cho-oke, cho-oke*.

The air seemed remarkably free of mosquitoes. Humboldt, I decided, must have been exaggerating: his journey on the Casiquiare, he tells us, was the most miserable of all his time in the Americas — the vicious clouds of biting insects were such a torment that he and Bonpland slept in their nets by day and travelled only at night. We were bothered by nothing worse than a lustrous, dark-green, persistent fly, as big as a horsefly and with a bite like one.

Occasional Large-billed terns and the much smaller, freshwater tern, the Yellow-billed, flew low and very white against the trees; as they quartered the surface their reflections skittered over the water, abruptly closing to meet them, at splash-point, as they plunge-dived for small fish. And by a rocky stretch of shore we passed a black, eagle-like bird, which disregarded us entirely, promenading thoughtfully on long yellow legs and stopping, every now and then, to hunch its shoulders, lower its head, and inspect something of consuming interest near its feet.

'Chimo!' I yelled, turning round and pointing. 'What's that?'

'Aquila negra,' said Chimo, unimpressed, but then brightening, clearing his throat and gobbing over the side. 'That one eats well,' he added as an afterthought, as the beach and the Great black hawk receded in our wake, 'he eats like Chimo. He eats what you will eat with Chimo. Lizards, frogs and the babies of alligators.'

In the late afternoon a prow of trees appeared in the middle of our horizon ahead; the lines of vegetation to our left and right began to diverge: the Casiquiare moved gently apart into two equal halves.

We kept well in to the right, entering the fork of water flowing from the east. Our old left bank, behind us, picked up its new partner and curved away to the north.

'The Pasimoni,' announced Chimo solemnly. Facing forward and holding the helm with his right hand behind him, he got to his feet, put his right leg up on the gunwale (the flesh on his thigh hanging down like the underbelly of a sow), hooked his penis out of his shorts with his left hand and, directing the jet under the raised leg, pissed with impressive volume and velocity to starboard.

'I am honoured to have such an uncle,' said Culimacaré from the bow, 'because his pinga is so big.'

'That's because it's done so much work,' said Chimo, putting it away. 'I have sixteen children, Reymono. Nine from my own wife and seven from other women. I am sixty-seven years old, but everywhere I go there is always someone who will make me comfortable. I shoot as straight as a young man – with my gun and with my pinga.'

'Yeah, yeah,' chorused Culimacaré, taking off his baseball cap and waving it in the air. (He had heard it all before.)

His gesture started a Ringed kingfisher from a low bough on a tree in front of us: as big as a wood-pigeon, a feathery burst of blue-grey, white and chestnut with a bayonet bill, it flew upstream *krek krek krek*-ing its alarm call like a football rattle, and perched in a small bush growing out over the bank. As we approached Simon drew the camera with the mirror lens out of his case and took its portrait.

'Beautiful, Fats, there's no other word for it,' he said, taking a notebook and a couple of fluorescent, waterproof-ink-pumping, antigravity, state-of-the-art astronaut pens out of the leg pocket in his army trousers, 'I could almost get happy here.' In their respective neatly-marked columns he entered the date in orange ('May 5'), the subject ('Bird'), the film number ('400/1') and, in purple, the comment ('ACE SHOT'). He then put away his camera, lay back against his bergen, swatted a horsefly on his arm, smiled a genuine smile and treated himself to his twenty-eighth cigarette of the day.

The Pasimoni, wide, slow and black, began to narrow dramatically; trees no more than fifty feet high and ragged, thin-leaved shrubs replaced the great towering trunks; and small parties of Greater anis, magpie-like birds whose black plumage shone briefly purple or blue or bronze as they changed their position against the light, fussed from bush to bush in front of us, until their leader decided he had gone far enough, when they would all flap and glide back in the other direction, bubbling their collective annoyance as they went.

Just to look at such a group of swearing, quarrelling, thoroughly united anis would be enough to put you in mind of your friends, I thought, and those absurd birds alone should have saved Humboldt from his other, deeper unease in these regions – the loss which opened up inside him, the indifferent emptiness that threatened to draw out and engulf his – exceptionally rugged – sense of self. To begin with, he felt,

in proportion as we draw near to an object we have long had in view, its interest seems to augment. The uninhabited banks of the Casiquiare, covered with forests, without memorials of times past, then occupied my imagination.... In that interior part of the New Continent we almost accustomed ourselves to regard men as not being essential to the order of nature. The earth is loaded with plants, and nothing impedes their free development. An immense layer of mould manifests the uninterrupted action of organic powers. The crocodiles and the boas are masters of the river; the jaguar, the pecari, the dante, and the monkeys, traverse the forest without fear, and without danger; there they dwell as in an ancient inheritance. This aspect of animated nature, in which man is nothing, has something in it strange and sad. To this we reconcile ourselves with difficulty on the ocean, and amid the sands of Africa; though in these scenes, where nothing recalls to mind our fields, our woods, and our streams, we are less astonished at the vast solitude through which we pass. Here, in a fertile country adorned with eternal verdure, we seek in vain the traces of the power of man; we seem to be transported into a world different from that which gave us birth.

'These impressions,' he added ominously, 'are so much the more powerful, in proportion as they are of longer duration.'

At about four o'clock Chimo decided it was time to make camp. He signalled to Pablo in the boat behind and they brought the two canoes in to a long spit of rock at the edge of a lagoon.

A few yards into the forest we cut down the saplings and bushes between the taller trees and cleared a patch with our machetes that was large enough for the communal shelter. Chimo selected the right kind of liana for lashings, a mamure vine, tugged down a coil, cut it into lengths, and he and Pablo bound on four cross-poles from which to sling our hammocks and mosquito-nets. A sapling tied between two taller posts centrally placed at either end of the rectangle completed the basic structure, and Culimacaré, shinning up, spread Charlie Brewer's big, heavy tarpaulin to serve as a roof. We secured it by the eye-rings at the sides and corners and thrust sticks up underneath to maintain the pitch and to stop pools of water gathering in sagging craters over our heads.

Valentine and Galvis chopped wood for the fire, Chimo sat on a log smoking his pipe, and I persuaded Culimacaré and Pablo to take Simon, Juan and me for a paddle round the lagoon. Simon crouched behind Culimacaré in the bow, his long lens at the ready; Juan sat beside me in the middle; and Pablo dug the water gently with his big heart-shaped paddle at the stern.

Beyond its entrance the lagoon opened out into acres of calm water, its smoothness disturbed only by the wild activity of two tern-like birds near its centre. Black above, white below, they flew on long angular wings close to the water, their heads down – and their wide red bills ploughing its surface. Every now and then they swerved as if hit with an electric shock, and put a small squiggle in the straight line of their wakes. Watching through the binoculars I could see that the lower mandible of their quarter-opened bills was longer than the top: each twist marked the scooping-up of a small fish. As we paddled closer round the edge of the shoreline they suddenly broke from the surface of the water and rose steeply and sharply into the sky, jinking wildly away towards the main river with harsh, barking cries.

'Almost all these trees live only here – in habitats where the waters rise,' said Juan, looking at the low tangle of vegetation which bulged out over the water and which was spattered with the odd burst of red or purple or orange flowers. 'They bloom every year when the rains begin. They must drop their fruit, disperse their seeds, before the rains are ended. There is wide diversity. They are very elastic. They survive five months of the flooding, sometimes with only a few leaves showing. Inland, on *tierra firme*, they are all replaced by other species. There the trees may make flowers only once in four or five years. In 1982, it was a very dry year. All the trees of the *tierra firme* expected to die. So they all bloomed together and made their seeds. For once, Redmon, for a moment, the high-canopy forest was full of colours.'

A pair of big black Muscovy ducks flew past us flashing their white wing-patches, and, in the shallows at the head of the lagoon, six Green ibis were probing the mud with their long curved bills. They, too, took to the air, with stiff, flicking wing-beats and a rapid, gobbling call, *koola kooola koola*. We turned back.

Night came as we ate our fried spam and rice round the fire; the cicadas rasped and whirred with maniacal fervour; the tree frogs (I thought) *peep-peep-peep-*'d, and the river frogs quacked like a farmyard of Aylesbury ducks. I took my torch and Simon his camera and flashgun and we walked slowly along the sloping rock of the shore. Motionless, sleeping tadpoles hung in a six-inch-wide band where the water lapped gently against the granite; and where the first broad-leaved forest grasses grew, higher up the rock, we homed in on a particularly persistent peeping. We crept forward, agreed in whispers where the exact spot was, and I flicked on the torch.

'Freeze!' shouted Simon. 'Armed police!'

In the brightly-lit circle of dead leaves there was at first nothing to be seen – and then a tiny granite-backed, dead-leaf-bellied frog raised its head in dazzled bewilderment. Simon pressed the shutter and the flash went off.

'Ace shot,' I said.

'Macro-zoom,' said Simon. 'I'm the biz. And if that's a tree-frog, dickhead, I'm an alligator.'

We hunted the duck-frogs, but the quacking moved its source as we turned our heads — it reverberated over the rocks, out of the water, up in the trees.

'Flying frogs,' said Simon. 'Farting faggots.'

We gave up and returned to the firelight. I opened Schauensee and found the tern-like, water-ploughing birds: Black skimmers. Chimo leaned forward from his log and looked at the drawing, so I turned to the figure of one of the birds I most wanted to see, the hoatzin.

Blue-faced, red-eyed, about the size of a pheasant and looking as ancient as the dinosaurs, the wing structure of the hoatzin chick closely resembles that of the prehistoric archaeopteryx, the earliest known fossil bird. The first archaeopteryx skeleton, complete with impressions of its feathers in the rock, was found in 1861 in the Ottmann quarry in Bavaria, and coming to light just two years after *The Origin of Species* was published, it was imagined to be Darwin's missing link between the reptiles and the birds. And the young of the hoatzin, like archaeopteryx itself, have two large claws on each wing, moveable by special muscles, with which they hoist themselves about the branches like a climbing reptile. I was already beginning to feel, like Conrad's Marlow on the Congo in *Heart of Darkness*, that in this land where vegetation rioted on the earth and the big trees were kings, we might at any moment turn a corner and discover an ichthyosaurus taking a bath of glitter in the river, and the hoatzin seemed the emblematic bird of such a place.

'No, not here,' said Chimo, shaking his head, 'they live further up the Casiquiare. They hiss like snakes.'

Well, I thought, before I went to sleep — whenever Chimo turned over the shelter shook and we all bounced in our hammocks — even if we miss the hoatzin, maybe on the Baria we will see a pack of the rare, amphibious bushdogs; or perhaps a jaguar will pay us a visit after lights-out, or an ocelot (one size down) or a margay (one size down again) — or even (pushing it a bit) a kinkajou, a peaceful, golden-brown, foot-long, furry relative of the pandas, with an eighteen-inch prehensile tail, which sleeps all day in hollow tree-trunks and comes out at night, big-eyed, small-eared, snub-nosed, to move cautiously through the tree-tops, sniffing about for fruit.

*

The next day huge clouds began to stack themselves up to the south; and as we passed the long clumps of spindly, pale-stemmed trees standing on promontories or along the edges of lagoons the flood-mark, some forty feet up their trunks, just beneath the scraggy tops of their wiry branches and small leaves, seemed directly threatening. If the water really did reach such levels, where would we camp?

At noon we paused by a rare piece of rocky shore to make coffee and swig manioc-and-water, and I wandered up from the boats to take a pee by a cluster of grass tussocks. As my urine spattered into the stalks there was a dry, rustling noise – and out ran seven outraged baby caymans, scuttling for the river. Pablo jumped out of his bongo, cornered two behind a boulder, and picked them up by their tails. They protested with loud mechanical clicking sounds and scrabbled at the air with their long fingers and toes. Black all over apart from grey bands on their tails, they looked new and shiny and hyperactive and the insides of their little mouths were a delicate pink. When Pablo replaced them by the boulder one ran straight down to the water, but the other – all seven inches of it – turned round and went for Pablo's foot. 'You've got a temper like Juan,' he muttered, picking it up again and popping it in the river. It submerged in the dark water and disappeared.

We motored flat out all afternoon, accompanied by whole anxious institutes of anis in relays; solitary giant herons; the rattle of Ringed kingfishers; the *chat chat chat* of the big green Amazon kingfishers; and the flurries of anhingas, flapping away from us with their necks held slightly back towards their crops with an odd, downward kink.

In the early evening the reason for Chimo's hurrying became clear: the day's first piece of high, well-defined shore.

We made camp amongst the low, lichen-covered trees, which were almost free of lianas, and Chimo and Pablo unrolled two fishing lines, baited the large hooks with rotted chunks of turtle flesh and tossed them out, just beyond the immediate eddies by the bank. Almost at once the lines went taut: Pablo and Chimo hauled them back in fast, the water skirled, something flashed dark blue and silver, and then two deep-bodied fish, about fifteen inches long, with red-ringed eyes and mouths set very low on the steep curve of their hunched heads, were thrashing on the rock. They made a curious half-hissing, half-screaming noise.

'Get back!' said Chimo as I knelt down to look. 'Caribe take your fingers off.'

Pablo hit them hard on the head with the back of his machete, their tails flapped a tattoo on the stone, and then they lay still.

Simon wandered over, lighting a cigarette.

'Stocky,' I said. 'They're *piranhas*! They're twice as big as I'd imagined.'

'Great White Minnows,' said Simon, blowing smoke at the flies round his head. 'Jungle Jaws.'

'Apparently all that's exaggerated – they only go for you if you're bleeding.'

'Super-dooper,' said Simon. 'I'll take your word for it.'

Pablo picked one up, opened its mouth and extracted the hook. Large, flat, triangular teeth with very sharp points stuck up from the centre of the lower jaw and graded progressively down in size to either side.

'Fats,' said Simon, looking closer, 'you swim first. It's my time of the month.'

Pablo shut the piranha's mouth again, pulling back the lips to expose the teeth. The opposing triangles in the upper and lower jaws fitted together exactly.

'He has big muscles and many teeth,' said Pablo, grinning, so that his own bare gums made a sorry show in comparison. 'He cuts as clean as my razor.'

Chimo took a clasp knife out of his trouser pocket and slit the piranhas' silver bellies. He pulled out a handful of guts from each and lodged the soft mess carefully against a half-submerged root a few yards upstream. Pablo hacked off their heads, stuck them on the hooks, and he and Chimo began to catch piranha with every throw of the line.

Juan, having finished unloading his carbon-prospecting equipment, persuaded Pablo to let him have a go; lobbing in the hook and weight (at about half Pablo's length of cast) he pulled out a particularly fine fish, larger than the others and of a darker blue.

'Redmon!'' he shouted, sparkling like a child. 'I catch my first fish! I never catch a fish before!'

Pablo cleaned Juan's increasingly large pile of piranha and, with the Charlie knife, I gutted Chimo's, throwing each scoop of innards back into the swirling water. When we had twenty-five, Chimo called a halt; Galvis took five to make into a fish stew; and Valentine built a slatted table of saplings over a slow fire, a smoking rack for the rest.

After dark, we sat round the fire carefully sucking the white flesh off the sharp little bones, and I remembered my protective device against that other watery nightmare, the candiru. I went to the bongo with my torch and found it in the kit-bag which Simon had labelled, in fluorescent blue, 'MISCELLANEOUS'. My one reserve rum bottle, stashed away for emergencies, lay beside it, wrapped in a pair of Y-fronts. Simon, I knew, had transferred his to his bergen and had been taking secret nips with his coffee every morning, so on an impulse I decided to throw a one-bottle party.

I put the cricket-box in the pocket of my SAS trousers and bore the bottle to the fireside.

'Eeee-do-do,' said Chimo, brightening.

I poured a medium-sized tot into everyone's mug and handed them round.

'Eeee-do-do,' repeated Chimo, getting up casually as if stepping into the darkness for a piss but then walking smartly back into the firelight from behind me, enclosing the bottle in a giant fist, and whisking it back to his manioc-tin seat.

'Reymono,' he said, emptying the rest of the rum into his pint mug and shaking his leonine head as if to indicate that he, personally, did not like it one bit, but that there *were* certain duties attached to his position as the most experienced motorman on the Rio Negro. 'I need an empty bottle for the engine oil.' He took an enormous draught as if drinking beer, turned his mug upside-down to show that he had done the decent thing, and gave a regal belch.

'Fuck a pig,' said Simon, admiringly.

I pulled out my anti-candiru device and held it up. Everyone looked puzzled. I explained that in the middle of Borneo well-bred locals defecated only in the river but that here, on the contrary, I had noticed that everyone went behind a bush. Was it because of the toothpick-fish? Did they know anyone who had lost his penis? And, come to that (I was getting carried away in the excitement of pure scientific enquiry), did they know anyone with a fish up his arse?

There was a shocked silence. Even Culimacaré looked at me oddly. Chimo wrinkled up his eyebrows in amazement.

'At home,' he said at last, 'do you shit in your river? Do all the English shit in their river?'

'In England,' said Juan, coming to my rescue, 'it is too cold to go to the lavatory in the river.' Redmon was plainly a little crazy, he said, looking at me in kindly fashion, and although he, Juan, had never heard of it, the English believed that there was a very small catfish in these rivers which normally lived in the gills of bigger fish, but which sometimes, when a swimming man dropped his trousers, made a mistake.

Chimo leaned right forward, fell off his manioc tin, and howled with laughter.

'Galvis!' he spluttered, slapping the sides of his thighs, 'Galvis! That's why he has a voice like a woman! Galvis has a fish for a pinga! Everyone knows! That's why we didn't vote for him! You can't have a Mayor with a fish for a pinga!'

Hilarity erupted. 'Eee-do-do!' shouted Pablo and Valentine, beginning a rhythmic clapping.

Chimo jumped up with surprising speed, grabbed the cricket box, held it over his fly with one hand, and, with the other extended round an imaginary partner, did a waltz-like dance round the fire. On each turn, accompanied by a series of mincing steps and a leering leathery wink, he sang a little song in falsetto. Roughly translated, it went like this:

> Eeee-do-do
> Eeee-do-do
> I'm waiting for you
> Eeee-do-do
> I'm fit to bust
> Eeee-do-do
> I'm wet, I'm wet, I'm wet with lust
> Eeee-do-do
> I know, I know, I know it's true
> Eeee-do-do
> I'm by far the biggest girl in town
> Eeee-do-do
> But, just for you
> Eeee-do-do
> I'll take my knickers down.

Everyone, including Galvis, clapped and cheered, and Chimo, pleased with himself, set his manioc tin upright again and sat on it.

'Reymono,' he said, beaming at me toothlessly, 'it's my song. I invented it.'

'It's terrific,' I said.

'So now you can get another bottle. And then I'll tell you about the pinga fish.'

'That rum was all there is. I was keeping it for an emergency.'

'Chief,' said Chimo, suddenly solemn, 'every night without rum is an emergency.'

'What about the little fish?' said Juan.

'You find it in dead bodies,' said Chimo, losing interest and handing back the cricket-box. 'When you pick a dead person out of the river and he's been drowned a long time you find the little fish up his ear-holes and his nose-holes and his arse-hole, and in his pinga, too, I dare say, but I'm not a girl like Galvis, so I don't look.'

In the morning Juan and I left Simon reading on a rock, Galvis shampooing himself at the edge of the river, and Valentine and Chimo loading the boats, and, with Culimacaré carrying two small collapsible tables with sieve tops, Pablo a long-handled spade and Juan his rucksack, we set off to dig for carbon. About a hundred yards in amongst the low, thin trees, Juan found a clearish patch of forest floor to his liking, and measured out a small rectangle with his yardstick. Culimacaré set up the two tables and, under instruction, Pablo dug steadily across and down, ladling spadefuls onto alternate sieves. Juan entered the place and habitat ('low igapo forest, flooded often') in his notebook, and he and Culimacaré then sifted the light, sandy soil. It was full of hard little lumps of charcoal which Juan enclosed in a series of small plastic bags, labelling each one; between thirty and forty centimetres down, chips of brown pottery appeared.

'There were Indians camping here,' he said with satisfaction, 'prob-ably Baré, approximately three hundred years ago. We are still too close to the big rivers. But near Neblina, Redmon, I will prove my thesis. I will win my doctorate. No one, not even the Baré, could live in those swamps.'

Thirty carbon-free centimetres further down the trench began to fill with water; we packed up the equipment and returned to the boats.

Upriver the temperature dropped, the heavy grey clouds lowered themselves gently onto the trees and rolled over the waterway. Chimo put on his olive-drab, Venezuelan army oilskin and hood, and the rest of us took out Charlie's white capes with 'YAMAHA' painted in big red letters across the back. The drizzle gradually increased in volume and density. We huddled under our plastic capes, cold and soaked, hour after hour; the surround of water fell straight and heavy, shutting us into our own small worlds; the noise induced a trance-like state of washed-out emptiness. There was nothing to see but the occasional blur of the near bank and the little circle of lashed-white river surface which we seemed to pull forward with us. Simon and I baled in silence with our mess-tins.

In the late afternoon the onslaught eased and then stopped; the cloud lifted, the air cleared, and we pulled in to a large group of rounded, moss-covered boulders on the right bank.

'It's an old village,' said Chimo, unloading the tarpaulin. 'Our ancestors lived here. They fought Funes with bows and arrows and the blow-pipe. But the soldiers killed them all with guns.'

'Culimacaré is expert with the blow-pipe,' said Juan, as we cleared a space for the camp in the undergrowth behind the boulders. 'It is very interesting. All the Indians use the blow-pipe, except the Yanomami. They use only the bow-and-arrow and in many other ways they are different from all the others. They are perhaps more ancient. They have an odd blood-group. They are Diego-positive, Redmon, and no one else is Diego-positive.'

'I'll bet you're Dago-positive,' said Simon, with a yap of laughter.

Juan attacked a clump of saplings with quick, vicious swipes of his machete.

'Wee-weeeeeeeeee-peee-o,' whistled something, adding to the tension.

'The Minero,' said Chimo, pile-driving a corner-post stake into the wet ground. 'It sees everything. It drives a man mad.'

I put down my machete, sat on my bergen and drew Schauensee out of its front pocket. A shy, grey, thrush-like bird, sitting quietly on plate 26, it was well named: the Screaming piha. I imagined it perched equally inoffensively in the canopy above us, and then, suddenly deciding to liven things up a bit, sticking two grey claws in the sides of its beak and delivering the brain-shredding piha wolf-whistle.

'Wee-weeeeeeeeee-peee-o,' sang the real bird, and again, at irregular, short intervals 'Wee-weeeeeeeeee-pee-o, Wee-weeeeeeeeee-peee-o, wee-weeeeeeeeee-pee-o, wee-weeeeeeeeee-peee-o.'

'Jesus Christ,' spat Simon, as if it was my fault, 'that's all we need.'

*

Culimacaré took Chimo's shotgun, an old Brazilian sixteen-bore with its single barrel bound to the stock and the cracked forepiece with wire, and disappeared into the trees; Simon went down to the river to help Galvis sort out the evening's supplies of rice and corned beef and smoked piranha; Old Valentine, tired out by a day peering into a moving waterfall for hidden rocks, retired to his hammock for a snooze; Pablo fished for piranha; and Chimo, Juan and I went for a stroll.

'We Baré are a brave people,' announced Chimo, leading the way, his pipe in his mouth and puffs of Brazilian Alligator Brand, the strongest tobacco known to man, hanging in the air behind him.

We came to a steep-sided, fifteen-foot-deep cut curving away between the trees.

'They built a ditch to defend themselves and filled it with stakes,' he said, proudly. 'And they put a circle of stakes in the river, too. But it was no use. The soldiers killed the men and they took away the children and the wives.'

We crossed the ditch — a few decayed stumps still stood at its bottom — and followed it round on the overgrown perimeter ditch. At its end, on the downstream side of the camp, just where it ran into the river, the sides and base were churned up into mud with cow-like slotted tracks and slip-marks.

'The danta comes here to drink,' said Chimo.

'Tapir,' said Juan. 'The men say it tastes like the best young bull. For them, the tapir is the greatest prize of all.'

On a nearby boulder there was a neat pile of five, large, slightly curled droppings.

'What's that?' I said. 'It's too dense for a herbivore. Bush dog? Giant otter?'

'Yes, yes,' said Chimo, pausing to look, taking his pipe out of his mouth. His stomach began to wobble with suppressed laughter. 'Well done, Reymono. It is the first sighting by an Englishman.' He bent over and laughed till his thighs shook, too. 'You can take it from me, Reymono my Naturalista — this is a treasure, a great find. This is the shit-pile of the Giant Pablo bushdog!'

'Redmon,' said Juan in English, with only half a smile, delicately taking my arm as I wondered why Pablo did not use our huge supplies of lavatory paper, 'do not worry. The Indians are not subtle. Their sense of humour is always of the ground.'

70

'Naturalista!' said Chimo with a great gummy smile, clapping me on the back. For the first time, I felt warm inside, a part of things.

'Pablo!' shouted Chimo as we re-entered the camp. 'The naturalista Reymono says you shit turds like a bushdog!'

'What? What?' said Valentine, waking up and scrabbling out of his hammock.

Pablo grinned.

'There are no piranha here,' he said, ignoring Chimo like a gentleman, and pointing, by pouting his lips, at a line of fish at his feet. He had caught six pavón ('peacock-fish'), white-stomached, shaped like pike, with gold scales along their backs and three wide, black, transverse stripes on their sides; and seven bocachico ('little mouth'), purple with racing lines like a mackerel and regular, diamond-shaped scales.

'The bocachico are moving up the river to lay their eggs,' said Chimo. 'The wet season has arrived. Soon the termites will swarm. From now on, Reymono, we will have four days of rain for every one day of the sun.'

Pablo and Chimo gutted the fish and then Galvis simply cut them into sections, cascaded the pieces from his chopping-board into the huge bubbling pot of smoked-piranha soup, added two concentrated-chicken-flavour cubes and returned to his study of the *Reader's Digest*. Perhaps pavón was as good to eat as sea-bass. There would be no way of telling.

Culimacaré returned, pleased with himself, holding three large black birds by their necks in his right hand and Chimo's gun in his left.

'Pauji,' he said, laying the biggest of the three at my feet and giving the other two to Pablo. It was plainly a curassow of some sort, related to the Black curassow which we had seen in Mariano's garden, but with a red bill and legs, and with deep chestnut on its belly, flanks, under-tail coverts and in a band at the tip of the tail itself. Lesser razor-billed curassow, said Schauensee. Chimo stooped down, pulled out a tail feather, trimmed it carefully with his clasp knife, inserted it into his right ear, rotated it, and then repeated the process, his eyes shut the while, in his left.

The two other birds were smaller, chicken-sized, but obviously of the same family: they had long necks and tails, streaked-white wing-patches, shaggy white crests, and red legs; but their most striking feature was the matching, bright cobalt blue of the tips of their bills, their dewlaps and their throats. 'Pava,' said Pablo, pausing in his plucking to give five high whistles, ascending in pitch, in imitation, presumably, of their song, and then rolling himself a bark-paper cigarette. 'Blue-throated piping guan,' said Schauensee, long-winded as usual.

Pablo and I plucked and cleaned the birds and stowed them under the tarpaulin in the middle of Valentine's bongo beside Galvis's mysteriously locked medicine chest. What was in there that was so precious? Morphine? Cyanide pills? Plans for the revolution in San Carlos?

At supper the moon shone intermittently through gaps in the clouds and for the first time we heard the hollow, booming call of another member of the curassow family, the Nocturnal curassow, a simple set of six unvaried notes, *hum hum dee dee de dum*, a basso profundo imitation and two-note continuation of the Screaming piha whistle, a deep, resonant insistence designed to send his mate berserk with desire and you just plain berserk.

'What a *horrible* sound,' said Simon, putting down his mess-tin. 'And what god-awful food.'

Culimacaré, I noticed, sat slightly apart as always, withdrawn outside the lighted circle, eating with his back towards us and shielding his extra thumb in the shadows.

In my disturbed, quick-changing dream, I was sitting paddling in the front of my father's canvas canoe on the river Avon, above the weir at Kellaways, safely back in childhood. But when I turned round I saw that it was not my father who sat behind me, but Simon; his big brown eyes wide, his pupils were dilated in terror, fixed on something ahead. We were about to go over the weir, I thought, but no, the sluice was behind us. Simon, without altering the direction of his stare, reached down and pulled Chimo's shotgun off the duckboards. He put its barrel, very slowly, into his mouth; his right hand, I saw, closing round the trigger, was simultaneously growing an extra thumb. The shock-waves from the bang lifted me gently out of the boat and laid me on my back on the surface of the water; and when I woke up I was still wet and cold and the gun was firing like a howitzer. The claps of thunder above us and the bursts of white light in the clearing around us followed so closely on one another that they were almost continuous.

'Sod this for a laugh,' said a familiar voice, and Simon's face emerged from his mosquito net to my left.

'Thank god you're alive,' I shouted.

'Steady on,' said Simon. 'It wasn't *that* good a J. Arthur.'

The rain drummed on the canvas as if each drop were trying to get at us, personally. It rebounded off the leaves and the trunks and sliced into the shelter at a thousand different angles. Fragmented droplets snapped across the ground sheet.

Culimacaré, illuminated by lightning flashes, his tee shirt and trousers clinging to his body, his hair and face streaming with water, walked down the edge of the line of hammocks, poking off the pools of water on the roof tarpaulin with a pole.

'What a hero,' said Simon, lighting a cigarette.

'It won't last long, doctors,' said Culimacaré, adding more wood and a slurp of kerosene to the hissing fire.

'It's weird being called a doctor,' said Simon, as the storm moved gradually further off and the rain lost its edge of hysterical violence.

'Tell me,' he said suddenly, 'do you think I'd be able to control my emotions if I was better educated?'

'Of course not,' I said, startled. 'You should see some of the dons in Oxford. And, come to that, Tolstoy, say – he certainly couldn't control his emotions. He leapt on his serfs' wives and daughters all over the shop – in his barns and haystacks and woods. In fact his poor wife got so desperate she dressed up as a peasant herself and waited in a barn and he very nearly jumped on her, too, only he recognized her, just in time.'

'That's not it at all,' said Simon, agitated.

'Okay, then what about Dostoyevsky? He'd have been one of your punters. He used to force his wife to slip him the housekeeping roubles so he could go down the St Petersburg Kensington Sovereign – he'd come back at dawn, out of his nut with excitement, open up the end of the bed, suck all his wife's toes one by one, and then make his way up, as slowly as he could, kissing her everywhere as he went. He describes it in some of his later letters to her – she inked those bits over, but with infra-red photography we can read all about it.'

'That's not what I mean,' said Simon, lighting another cigarette.

'Well – Proust wrote his masterpiece on a gram of bull's adrenalin to speed himself up all night and a gram of veronal to knock himself out all day. And Painter reports a rumour that he could only get an erection by watching someone transfix rats with a hatpin through the bars of their cage. How's that? And he loved his mother so much that after a hard night's work he'd unroll a giant photograph of her head across the floor and shit on it.'

'Be serious with me for once,' said Simon, slowly. 'Stop hiding behind all these silly jokes. It's this *place* that gets me – I thought the jungle would *change* every day. You never told me it just went on and on the same for ever. You never said we'd be marooned out here with this Colombian bastard lecturing us like ten-year-olds. Something terrible is going to happen. I just know it is. *I can feel it already, all the time.'*

'Go back to sleep,' I said, lamely. 'You don't sleep enough. It'll all look different in the morning.'

'What kind of a reply is that?' said Simon, exasperated, flicking his cigarette-end out into the rain. 'Why can't you treat me like a human being?'

Dawn merely lightened the lines of falling water from grey-black to grey, and through the gap at the end of my hammock I could see out for no more than ten or twelve yards. I unwrapped myself from my SAS groundsheet, a defence against the big biting flies, whose proboscides, I had discovered, lance through cotton shirts and hammocks and trousers without a pause, but buckle against canvas; I sat up and drew a deep breath of wet, rancid air. Already covered in microscopic algae and fungus, the hammock and mosquito net and I and everyone else were beginning to smell of rotten butter.

I changed fast out of my dryish clothes, stuffed them back into their plastic bag inside my bergen, collected my wet clothes from the parachute-cord line strung above our heads under the tarpaulin, and shook them free of ants. When everything is wet, a wet shirt offers the least initial shock to the system, so I put that on first.

Simon, the night's conversation apparently forgotten, stuck his head out of his nest and turned on his recorder.

'Dateline May 9th. Pasimoni river. Angel-drawers, news despatch: Redso is playing toy soldiers again. He's just got into his wet (and baby I mean *wet*) shirt which now covers the top half – which is just as well because Redso's looking untasty like you wouldn't believe. Cos why? Cos for he's covered in big red lumperoonies from his friendly neighbourhood horseflies and mossies. Oh here we go – on with the wet blue y-fronts. No, correction: he's squeezing them out first. Eee-yuck. On they go. Over his bottle and glass. Oh yes, I'm right again – he's head down in the toy-soldier bergen. He's after his POWDER. There we go. One handful on the hampton. Give it a quick gander. TWO handfuls on the hampton. Next – on with the Jungle Formula all over the boat race and arms and ankles – and yes, he wants me to tell you what a GOOD CHAP he is. You see, angel, he likes to be loved by just *everybody*. Which is why he has everything under control here. Does he hell. On with the wet trousies. Pause for Canesten cream between the toesy-wosies. On with two pairs of wet socks. God, how *disgusting*. And all so way over the top, darling. Because your Stocky, as you know, has four sets of everything and fully intends to stay dry *all the time*.'

'Scumbag – why's it called a hampton?'

'Hampton Wick. Dick!' said Simon, switching off the machine.

Crouched under my cape behind a bush, hose-piped from above (but free of mosquitoes) I admired the way that the saplings around me shed the great volumes of water pouring over them. Although most of them must have been widely different species one from another their leaves were almost all the same shape – long ellipses with a little pointed gutter at their ends, a drip-tip which drew the water from their surfaces in one continuous runnel. Watching the tiny waterfall from a particularly large leaf and wondering if it was true, as I had read somewhere, that drip-tips helped to keep a leaf free of algae, fungi, lichens and briophytes, and thinking that I could do with a drip-tip or two myself, I noticed that the water was splashing onto a piece of wood that was of a different colour from all the rest of the debris. I leant forward and picked it up. It was a carved piece of the wood-lighter-than-balsa, a crude statuette, about six inches long, with a round head, vertical eyes-slits, square body and club foot (one leg was broken off), very much like some of the figures in the petroglyphs. An Indian on a fishing expedition had probably whittled and abandoned it. Unable to resist a proffered talisman or a passing fetish, I put it in my pocket.

It seemed hopeless to travel on such a day.

'Okay, chief,' said Chimo, grumpily, 'if that's your wish, that's okay, it's all the same to us.'

Pablo, Culimacaré and Valentine rigged up the spare tarpaulin from four trees beside Galvis's cooking fire. Chimo took the kerosene can and an armful of Valentine's axed-up pieces of rotten log and stoked up his personal night-time fire which he had built, for the past two nights, close to the head end of his hammock.

'Don't use too much of that kerosene,' shouted Juan. 'We're going to need all we've got.'

Chimo walked back, still holding the can, and joined everyone else in the sheltered semi-circle in front of the fish-stew pot. He drew up his manioc tin and sat down, keeping the can at his feet.

'There must be a flame,' he said slowly. 'Especially at night. But also when it is wet like this and no one can see far — because that is when the anaconda will come for you.'

Galvis, ladling chicken-flavoured fish-mess and manioc into our bowls, gave his high-pitched giggle. Juan, without looking up from his soup, laughed too,

Chimo got to his feet and rolled up his baggy trouser-leg.

'See that?'

There were four large scars, two on each side of his thigh, just above the knee.

'You scientists don't believe us,' said Chimo, sitting down again, 'but then you don't go fishing up little rivers in a curiara for hours on end, just to get something to eat. You should try that! You'd soon end up in the stomach of the Culebra de agua. He has his tail round a tree and he pulls you underwater and he eats you when you're drowned. That's what he does. *He* doesn't say excuse me, Doctor Juan, thank you, Doctor Juan, please would you be so kind, Doctor Juan Sir, but I'd like to swallow you, if you don't mind. He just goes right ahead and does it. He may be big — but he's quick as a rat. And you don't see his small brown head in the big brown water till he's got you in his jaws. Both times he was pulling me out of the curiara by my knee where I sit in the back to paddle — both times my sons saved me. They kept calm. They turned round with their machetes and hit him in the head; the first time it was Alfredo, my first-born, and the second time it was Bernardo. Old Joaquín Conde, who went with the Frenchmen to the source of the Orinoco — his son was eating close to the river when the anaconda stole him.'

'He won't bother us,' said Galvis. 'There are too many of us.'

'It's braggarts like you who get killed,' said Chimo.

Galvis shrugged.

'Besides,' said Chimo, starting to eat his fish soup, spitting out bones with professional ease, 'it's not just the anacondas. What about jaguars? I've seen many jaguars in my time. And why do you think I'm still alive, eh? It's because I know what to say to them. It's simple – the first time you see a jaguar you must really shout at it – you must call it *almost* all the bad words you know. *But not all of them.* Because it's the second time you meet the same jaguar – the next day, round another bend of the river, *that's* when a jaguar is really dangerous. Then you must shout at it again – but if it's already heard all your bad words, it will know them. And then it is not afraid. And then it will kill you. It will bite you in the head; and carry you off about a hundred metres; and eat you.'

Galvis laughed outright.

'Okay,' said Chimo, 'if you're so smart – why do you think jaguars round towns are so dangerous?'

'No idea,' said Galvis.

'Because that's where they've already heard all the bad words there are to know,' said Chimo, triumphant.

By dawn the rain had stopped and we left under a thick grey sky. Lagoons became less frequent; the river narrowed still further; and, rounding a bend, we surprised a bushdog, standing four-square, squat in the shallows by the bank. He turned and swam beside the bongo for a few yards, watching us with quick black eyes, and then he scampered up a muddy incline on his short legs, stopped to shake a puff of water from his stiff fur, and trotted off behind a clump of ferns, waggling his stumpy tail.

'Bushdog!' I shouted, wildly excited. 'Perro de monte!'

'Perro de agua,' said Chimo firmly. 'It was an otter.'

'He had a tail,' I muttered, disappointed. 'That was a tail, not a rudder. That was a bushdog.'

'It's your word against Chimo's,' said Simon, with a nasty grin.

At midday Chimo and Pablo ran the bongoes onto the shore by a small lagoon and Galvis passed round bowls of manioc and made coffee on his primus, set in a biscuit-tin at his feet. Through the binoculars I watched a Muscovy duck, with fifteen ducklings in tow, make her way anxiously across the middle of the little lake. On its

far side, a pair of Greater yellow-headed vultures flew heavily round
and down in tightening circles over the trees. Big and black, the
vultures of deep forest, they were obviously hunting by smell,
homing in on something rotting in the branches or on the jungle
floor – and, with the cloud so low, I reflected, they would probably
be able to poke their yellow-skinned heads into the carcase of the
monkey or deer or tapir and eat in peace, their descent unmarked by
the even larger King vulture which, on a sunlit day, hunting by sight
high overhead, would follow them down and drive them off their
finds.

Several hours upriver we disturbed a coatimundi on a branch on
the right bank. Furry black-brown, probably a solitary male, he was
foraging along the bark, thrusting his flexible snout into clumps of
bromeliads, rootling for insects. Seeing us, he sat back on his haunches,
his forelegs limp, and looked at us for a second or two, his long
black-ringed tail hanging down into space – and then, whisking it
straight up into the air behind him, he galloped back to the main
trunk and disappeared.

'Baria!' announced Chimo, waving at the main stream ahead. 'Yatua!'
he added, swinging the canoe into a river flowing in from the east.

'Reymono,' he said, unzipping his penis and making water to
starboard. 'Here the Pasimoni becomes the Yatuá and the Baria.
Tonight I will take you to a little hill. Tonight Chimo will show you
Neblina. We will watch him from a long way off, from as far as a
man can see.'

Two hours later, the cloud lifting steadily, we came to a long,
sloping shelf of brown granite and pulled up the boats.

While the others began to make camp and Galvis to prepare a
curassow stew, Juan, Simon and I followed Chimo along the shore.
Humming to himself, his pipe in his left hand and his machete in his
right, he turned sharply into the undergrowth along a gulley in the
rock, swiping at the few low bushes which obstructed our passage.
A pair of small, very dark nightjars fluttered about us. They flitted
and twisted from rock to rock, settling for a moment between the
sparse, wiry bushes and tufts of razor-grass, their feathers richly
mottled black and grey with a scattering of white at their necks; and
they looked at me almost as intensely as I looked at them before
flicking away again, *tchick tchick tchick*-ing as they went.

'Come on Reymono,' said Chimo, starting to climb the next hump of wet, slippery rock, 'they're only Aguaitacamino negruzco.'

He left his pipe and machete in a crevice and went up on all fours, his massive buttocks as round against the sky as the rock itself. At the summit we were no more than two hundred feet up, yet, beyond three tall palms and two emergent forest giants in front of us, whose darker green tops stuck up above the canopy, the forest stretched away in almost all directions beneath the grey sky, the light greens of the foreground shading gradually away into the blues of distance. To the north tall trees obscured the country towards the Casiquiare: from the bare top of a dead tree a hawk with a grey back, a brown-and-white barred chest and a fearsome bill whistled at us, shrill and clear. But to the immediate south-east Cerro Avispa, Wasp Hill, curved gently above the jungle; and on the furthest horizon to the south, east of a line of small tepuis, a great mountain rose sheer into the sky, long and grey, high and flat-topped at its eastern end, broken in the middle, lower, flatter and longer to the west. We were gazing at Neblina.

Channel-billed Toucan

6

Back in the camp shelter I identified the nightjars (Blackish nightjars) and the hawk (a Hook-billed kite) and then turned to my photocopy of Spruce: it was as I suspected – we had been standing on the hill which he had marked 'cerrito' on his sketch-map and which he had climbed on his way back from a botanical collecting trip up the Pasimoni. He called Avispa Tibiali and Neblina Imei but there was no doubt that he had seen the same mountains: he, too, had been 'astonished at the magnificent scene that burst on me ... especially Imei in its entire length'. But after camping amongst the trees behind this very same sloping shelf of granite he and his paddlers had made their way back to San Carlos. Tomorrow we would enter the Baria. From there I would have to say goodbye to our last shadowy companion, Richard Spruce, and, in a sense which probably mattered only to me, I would be alone.

I was distracted from such morbid thoughts by a loud buzzing, as from a gigantic bumblebee, and looked up in time to see a Humming-bird hovering in front of the knot with which Galvis had tied his fancy red hammock-rope to the frame of the shelter. Dark green on its back with yellow stripes running down its head and a long curved bill, it was perhaps a Green hermit, but whatever it was, it realised that the rope was not a flower, and whirred away.

*

It rained with sustained ferocity all night; but in the morning the sun gradually drew the mist off the surface of the river and up the trunks of the trees to the canopy; and by the time we regained the confluence of the Yatuá, the Pasimoni and the Baria, the sky was as blue and the heat as merciless as it had been on the Casiquiare.

We turned into the Baria, Chimo saluted it in his habitual fashion, and, for several hundred yards, five or six dolphins played about the boats. The suck of air at their blow-holes sounded like gasps and gurgles of pleasure; and their grey backs surged up at regular intervals all around us in fast and graceful curves, as if, in the black-brown water, from the surface of the river to its bed, they were looping the loop. The most primitive of dolphins, they are closely related to Squalodon (which became extinct fifteen million years ago), but little else is known about them: they live in small family parties; they hunt fish (including piranha); they rootle about the bottom with their beak-like snouts for mudfishes and freshwater shrimps; and they stick together in muddy water by touching flippers as they swim.

In our narrowing strip of sky, between the closing trees, we caught glimpses of circling Greater yellow-headed vultures, and of the occasional pair of Great black eagles; and, just above the canopy, we saw our first Swallow-tailed kites, a group of three, the most elegant of all the birds in the air, their heads, stomachs and the leading edge of their long wings an unblemished white in the sunlight, their primaries and long, tapering, forked tails a glossy black. They stayed with us for a minute or two, wheeling and gliding, dipping and turning without apparent effort, hunting the swarms of flying termites which rose in dark columns from the trees.

Flights of Blue-and-Yellow macaws screamed and cackled overhead, swearing down at us as they crossed the river, and, from both banks, we were accompanied by the incessant whistle of the Screaming piha. Now and then we passed flocks of Mealy parrots, clucking and babbling in a fruiting tree; and later in the day, perhaps because I was only just beginning to be able to distinguish particular notes in the cacophony, I noticed a new sound, a yelping like a pack of beagles on a scent.

'Piapoco!' said Chimo, pointing ahead at a lone manaca palm on the right bank. Five toucans were bouncing about where the bunches of fruit hung grape-like beneath the fronds. Through the binoculars I watched one calling from the topmost stem, bobbing its head, jerking up its tail and throwing its absurd bill from side to side with each note. The bill itself was black and its black curve was continued down the bird's back and tail, but from the base of the bill to the stomach its colours ran blue, white, yellow and red, in that order.

I flipped Schauensee open at the familiar plate of my Oxford fantasies: they were Channel-billed toucans. We closed with the base of their tree and they decided, one by one, that we were not to be trusted: a jump off the frond, a few quick flaps, and they were seemingly towed down and across the river by their bills, missiles following their nose-cones, each bird entering the foliage on the opposite bank in a low, mad glide.

It was time to make camp and Chimo, who could tell the hours and half-hours infallibly when the sun was visible (and almost as well by the quality of the light when the day was overcast), made for a small rocky bluff on the left bank.

Simon, too absorbed to speak all day, suddenly flung *War and Peace* down on the tarpaulin in front of us.

'Finished!' he said. 'Bloody marvellous. *I'm in love with Natasha.*'

'Of course you are. And all this effing and blinding. It doesn't fool me – you're really quite a cultured gangster.'

'I'm about as cultured,' said Simon, 'as a Kentucky Fried Chicken.'

We tied the dugouts on long ropes to a tree, climbed the sloping ramp of granite which led to the little cliff and made a shelter in the forest behind it. Huge flies with zebra-striped rear ends zigzagged everywhere and landed on everything; and tiny, yellow-brown flies settled all over our hands and faces, crawled into our eyes and nostrils, and clustered at the edges of our mouths. Sweat bees, said Juan, and for some reason both bees and flies exasperated Simon. But I was merely pleased that unlike the long-legged mosquitoes and the green horseflies, neither species was after our blood. The zebra-stripes merely lusted for rotten piranha-flesh and Chimo's hammock; the Sweat bees seemed to want nothing more than a lick of sweat, tears, saliva and snot.

To mark our arrival on the Baria, and to keep the Sweat bees at bay, I unpacked the pipes which I had bought at Savory's in Oxford and presented one to each man together with a tin of Balkan Sobranie tobacco apiece. Chimo put the gifts into his shirt pocket without a word and carried on hauling in piranha; Galvis left his cooking-fire and bore his off to the medicine-chest in the bongo; Culimacaré and

Pablo stuffed their pipes with the smoking mixture, lit up, took Chimo's gun, cast off in the little fishing canoe and, puffing like a twin-stack tramp-steamer, disappeared upriver. Old Valentine, however, sat on the edge of his hammock for a while, stroking his new pipe, running a scarred, broken and badly re-set forefinger round and round the outside of the smooth and polished bowl.

'Thank you Reymono,' he said. 'I've always wanted a pipe. I've always wanted a pipe just like the one that Charlie gave to Chimo.'

There was a pipe left over – and as I re-wrapped it in two spare socks and placed it halfway down a kit-bag of medicines, dressings and bandages, I wondered who I would give it to: a Yanomami headman? the Chief of an uncontacted tribe living quietly in the uncharted delta of the Baria? or just to Yamadú, the great demon, the spirit responsible for all the unexplained noises of the forest and for every misfortune which occurs within it?

At that moment Simon was sauntering across the open space of the incline behind the little cliff, carrying *The Brothers Karamazov* and going to join Juan who, as usual, was writing up his carbon notes from the morning's dig, and sitting by the river. My thinking of Yamadú obviously summoned the god from more serious duties, for Simon suddenly yelled with pain, dropped his book, and then dropped his trousers.

Chimo, Valentine and Juan cheered and clapped Simon as he danced, his ankles yoked together.

'Bastards!' said Simon, pulling a large bee out of his pants and stamping on it. 'You shouldn't laugh at people in pain. *It's not funny.*'

Juan got up and inspected the corpse.

'It's only a bee,' he said.

'It's a wasp,' said Simon, shaking with anger. 'We have wasps in England. It's a wasp.'

'You have wild bees in England, too,' said Juan, bridling.

'There are no wild bees in England,' said Simon flatly. 'I should know. I live there.'

'I am sorry,' said Juan, suddenly, going back to his notes. 'You are in pain. I am mistaken.'

Simon picked up his book, hobbled to his bergen, found his Anthisan and covered his right buttock in cream.

'You savvy sod, Slim,' he said, 'now I know why you tuck your trousers into two pair of socks.'

'Of course there are bees in England,' I said, laughing.

'Thinks he knows everything,' said Simon, climbing heavily into his hammock – and then leaping out again with a genuine scream.

He scrabbled at his neck with both hands.

'Help me!' he shouted.

The largest ant I had ever seen, jet-black, at least an inch long, was clamped into the back of his neck; I pulled it out and ground it into the leaf-litter with my boot. Ants were running along the shelter cross-pole, down Simon's hammock-ropes, and in all directions over the inside of his hammock.

Valentine, serious-faced, sympathetic, flicked them onto the ground and hit each one hard with the flat of his machete.

'The veinte-cuatro,' he said, 'their bite hurts for twenty-four hours. Their poison makes a man faint. Only the catanare, the fire-ant, is worse.'

'No kidding,' said Simon, sitting on a manioc tin. 'I want to go home.'

Culimacaré and Pablo came back with a curassow and Chimo a pile of piranha; and, in honour of his wounds, Galvis cooked Simon fried corned beef and rice.

I rubbed greasy Autan into everyone's hammock-ropes to dis-courage the ants, and we prepared to go to bed by the orange light of Chimo's fire and the green lights of cruising fireflies.

As I took off my wet, day-time trousers and hung them on the parachute-cord line, the little Indian figure fell out of my pocket and landed beside Simon's hammock.

'What the hell's that?' said Simon, shining his torch at it.

'An Indian carving,' I said. 'I found it a few camps ago. I'm going to take it with me. I'll take it home, if we ever get home. I'll put it in my cork-lined fetish room.'

'Fetish room?' said Simon, alarmed, leaning out of his hammock as I put on my dry trousers, retrieved the figurine, wrapped myself in the groundsheet and manoeuvred myself beneath the mosquito net.

'It's the real thing,' I said. 'It's full of junk and bits and pieces. And over the window it's got double black velvet curtains and a big black leather sheet like an archaeopteryx wing.'

'What sort of bits and pieces?' said Simon, forgetting the pain in his neck.

'Bird's eggs. A stoat and a weasel and a partridge that I stuffed as

Indian rock drawing.

(*above*) A gap in the trees above the Baria.   (*opposite*) The bongos.

Simon. A pause on the climb to the waterfall.

(*above*) The huts of the Siapa Yanomami.   (*opposite*) Pablo with piranha.

(*above*) Jarivanau
in his hammock.

(*left*) Jarivanau with
his bow and arrow

(*opposite*) Off to
hunt peccary.

Juan.

a boy. Bull's horns. Precious books. My first bird books. My first shotgun. And a friend's foot in a Maxwell House coffee jar.'

'You what?'

'Douglas Winchester. He was a friend of mine at school. We were in the same house and we were rivals in the same biology set – and we used to go poaching rabbits with his ferret in Savernake forest and gathering fungi all over the place. We'd try the fungi on Forbes minor first. He soon learned the difference between a Shaggy ink cap and a Death-cap – in fact he became a real expert in no time at all. I took Douglas out on my 250 Royal Enfield Crusader one prep-time to drink at a little country pub and to buy beer and cigarettes. The contact-breakers went as we came back past the gates, and we were caught by the woodwork master as we tried to push the bike back to its hiding place behind the gym. The housemaster flogged us for breaking all the rules at once. He loved that sort of thing. He wore baggy flannel trousers, and when you bent over you could see his dick thrust up in the folds. Anyway, after school we made our way round Europe on an old BSA 650 Flash with an outsize sidecar and then we went up to Oxford together. Douglas was supposed to be reading physiology, but he inherited some money and left because he thought he wanted to be an artist. We shared a house – he liked painting bulls best of all, then dead foxes, then young naked girls like everybody else. He would go to the slaughterhouse and scrounge a severed head and bring it back and paint it. I remember turning off the lights in his room one night when he'd gone off somewhere. *Click, click, click* went something in the darkness. So I switched the light back on and checked all the plugs for an electrical fault, a short somewhere. I checked the paraffin stove. Then I happened to glance at the bull's head. Maggots were bursting out from its eyeballs, *click, click, click*, and falling on to a sheet of stiff drawing paper on the table.'

'Let's talk about something else, shall we?' said Simon, disappearing beneath his mosquito net. 'Let's talk about something *wholesome* for a change, eh?'

'He married and had a child and grew obsessed with his own decay and how ugly he was and how pointless it all seemed on a grey day at three o'clock in the afternoon, so he rode his Egli Vincent to Holland Park, walked to a place he liked in a copse behind one of the ponds, scraped up a pile of leaves, doused it and himself with five gallons of petrol, lay down, and lit a match. Then his post-dated letters arrived for me, telling me all about it, how sorry he was, how he'd gone to make space, so he said. So Belinda and I went to the park. The warden was from Ceylon. He'd seen Buddhist monks burn themselves to death. They all tried to crawl away at the last moment, apparently, but Douglas had just lain there, straight out. So I found the place and picked up a piece of charred flesh, about where his foot would have been. I've got it in my Maxwell House coffee jar; and I've got two other, identical jars waiting beside it — just in case any more of my friends are thinking of doing the same thing.'

'Look!' said Juan, equally engrossed in his own concerns, jumping out of his hammock on the other side of me. 'I've caught a firefly.' It shone with three bright green lights, one on either side of its thorax and one on its abdomen.

'Chimo!' he called, moving on down the line of hammocks with his prize, 'Look at this. What do you call this?'

There was a pause in the darkness. And then, 'You crazy bastard,' said Simon, 'you're not having my foot.'

Bushdog

7

The Baria is not the easy waterway which Spruce imagined it to be. Four days into its dendritic delta it seemed the most difficult place on earth. The yelping toucans, the big Amazon parrots, the paired flights of macaws, the rattling cry of the Ringed kingfisher, the giant herons, the anhingas, the Swallow-tailed kites — all the birds of the open river had long since disappeared. Even the big blue Morpho butterflies and the bats, the tiny grey bats that fluttered in flocks like blown woodsmoke from one dead branch to another as we approached — even they had gone. The trees in the labyrinth met overhead, knotted together with lianas, their foliage thickened with epiphytic orchids and umbrella-leaved bromeliads. The sun only reached the black-water channels of the Baria when a storm or old age or a collapsing bank had felled a tree and left a gap in the canopy.

Woken at four-thirty in the morning by the one clock still functioning, a cheap Classa alarm which I kept in a plastic bag, I shone my torch across the leaf litter and carefully noted the positions of two scorpions. Small, mean and black, with a serious-looking whip-over sting, there would be a scorpion, I had calculated, under every eleventh leaf. They, too, caught by the rising water, had to camp with us on islands that were never more than ten yards by twenty. We had to share these small outcrops with all the refugees from the jungle floor. I changed fast out of my dry clothes, made a brief tick check by torchlight, pulled on my wet clothes and steeled myself for the first personal trauma of the day. In my own utopia I would elect to shit only in a lead-lined chamber half-a-mile underground, safe from enemy radar. Shitting two yards from Simon and five yards from Chimo was, I found, difficult. I hung on to a sapling with one hand, switched off my torch, took down my trousers and squatted over the black, swirling water.

'Don't look,' I said.

'Who's interested?' said Simon, leaning out of his hammock and pointing his torch straight at me.

'Push!' yelled Chimo.

'Bit runny today,' said Simon.

Dawn filtered down. Frogs and cicadas began to call. The mosquitoes scrambled. And, as we folded up the wet tarpaulins, there came four loud blasts on a whistle, followed by a noise of sucking, then clickings of disapproval.

'Viudita carablanca,' said Chimo, putting his fingers to his cheeks, drawing in his breath, and making sucking and clicking noises in his turn. There was no reply. Somewhere up in the green tangle, a troop of White-faced sakis were watching us.

Chimo, Culimacaré and Pablo cut fresh poles and we set off, punting the heavy canoes slowly forward. It was not easy to find a purchase for the ten-foot-long poles – the channels, although never more than six to fifteen feet wide, were far too deep for us to touch bottom – so we pushed against submerged branches or roots on the soft bank. Most of the time we could not punt at all, but pulled the boats forwards, standing on submerged branches up to our waists or necks, easing the hull over fallen trees, hacking a way through their dense, upstanding, lateral shoots.

At such times, when standing out of the water, the main discomfort was the ants, not the dangerous veinte-cuatro and catanare who seemed to confine themselves to well-marked territories on shore, and not the army ants, but just thousands of ordinary biting ants (I counted fourteen different species) which went for your head and neck and fastened onto your back inside your shirt. 'Hormiga! Hormiga!' Culimacaré would shout when he struck a particularly ant-rich bush, but there was not much you could do to avoid them. At other times we would crouch low, easing the dugouts beneath larger trees which had fallen, but which were still supported lengthwise above the ground and the river by their broken branches, forming bridges for leaf-cutter ants. I grew fond of these fundamentally non-homicidal insects, fully engaged in their perpetual harvest: neatly clipped leaf-sections, held upright, jerkily processed above our heads.

One species of wasp and one species of hornet, in small separate colonies, hung their nests from twigs or fixed them to the backs of leaves suspended over the water. As we cleared a passage with our machetes it was impossible to spot their yellow-brown upended cones. One tremor along a branch, one near cut, and they ejected through the entrance at the base, coming for us with extraordinary speed and concentration. A cry of 'Avispa!' really galvanized your limbs: wherever you were, you dived for the water and held your hat across your face to protect your eyes. A wasp sting on the back was tolerable, one on the neck was very painful; five wasp stings on the back equalled one hornet sting on the back. Simon, who disliked the cold, black water on principle and tried to keep his clothes dry for as long as possible each day, moved a fraction slower than the rest of us and, as the last available target, was often stung on the back of the head.

At water-level, there were a surprising number of hunting spiders, no bigger, in total extent, than the palm of your hand, which jumped across the surface. Tiny tree frogs, a bright, translucent green as if fashioned in glass, some with little red eyes and feet, dislodged from the foliage as we passed, would fall into the boat or the current, and, pausing to collect themselves, hop or swim to shore; and about twenty times a day we would see the cazadora, the hunter, the long, thin Green vine snake, its slim head raised above the water, towing its Vs of ripples.

At normal eye-level, we edged past the bases of a seemingly endless variety of tree species, their trunks wrapped with lianas and furry with lichens, their bark smooth or ridged or ringed with spines, and supported on the ground with mats of root fibres, or buttresses, or prop roots like wigwam frames or birdcages, or, occasionally, they were themselves dead or imprisoned in the grasp of a buttressed, hollow, parasitic fig tree which grows from a seed wiped from a bird's beak on some high branch, puts down the slow roots like giant fingers, and throttles its host.

About two hundred yards downstream from our campsite, after

an hour-and-a-half of travelling, we met our first serious obstacle: a trunk across the channel which was so large its mass descended some two feet below the water surface and rose about four feet above it. But the tree was big enough, and had fallen recently enough, to open a clearing in the canopy. In the sudden warmth, our clothes began to steam slightly. A Screaming piha was calling, unseen, as it did all day, every day.

'And that's another thing,' said Simon, lying back on our shared thwart against our packs under the tarpaulin, stretching in the sun and putting his hands over his ears, 'just when that moronic bird stops going *hum hum hum up your bum* all night, this bloody idiot starts whistling.'

'It's sex,' I said, 'they're telling the girls they've got their patch.'

'Leave it out,' said Simon, 'you're going soft in the head.'

Pablo brought the second dugout up and Culimacaré started clearing the mass of shoots and shrubs from one end of the tree trunk, whilst Chimo and Pablo laboured at the other.

A tiny blue-black Humming bird, perhaps a Fork-tailed Wood-nymph, suddenly appeared above us; it whirred to and fro like a dandelion seed in a thermal and then hovered purposefully, obviously curious, repeating the manoeuvre, drawing closer.

'Quick, Simon, where's your camera?' I said.

Simon drew the body with the long lens on it out of a plastic bag beneath the tarpaulin, and the bird flew off like a bumblebee.

'Mira!' yelled Chimo, pointing at the leaves in front of him. 'Mira! Mira!'

Pablo and Culimacaré stopped cutting. It was a startling picture. It was a full frontal. It was a short, dangerous, angry Coral snake, banded bright red and black to warn its predators, a pattern which even at night tells everyone how deadly it is: and it hung down from its twig-coiled tail, its head up, its white mouth open, hissing.

'For Christsake, take that!' I said.

Simon thrust himself right back against the tarpaulin, his camera clutched across his chest for protection.

'I ain't taking no fucking pictures of no fucking snakes,' he shouted, *'they give me the creeps.'*

Valentine ran forward and knocked it into the river with a punt pole.

Culimacaré, Pablo and Chimo took it in turns to axe through the tree. I went ahead with my machete and hacked at the easy vegetation. I felt eaten up inside with little white maggots of rage.

Two hours later, sitting together down a clearish straight stretch, Simon reached into another plastic bag and drew out his tape-recorder diary. He clicked down the record button and put the machine to his mouth: 'Dateline May 14th. Place: Baria river. What's new? I ask myself. No rain today, *that's* what's new I tell myself. Hear that' – he held the machine over the side of the boat – 'Right? No endless thundering buckets of piss crashing down on my head all day. Well, you can take it from me, Angel-drawers, the whole ghastly business will start again tomorrow. Up-to-the-minute report: only three wasp stings this morning. No more than 10,000 ants. No hornets. Blissikins, you might say. Oh yes – one more thing before I mosey on out to my favourite pub: Fatso's got the right needle with me just because I wouldn't take a picture of some frigging horrible snake. And how do I know Fatso's got the right needle with me? I know Fatso's got the right needle with me cos he hasn't spoken to me for *two whole hours*.'

The rage eased. I laughed. I must fight this anger, I thought; such feelings were as dangerous as they would be in a prison cell. It was an effective weapon, that recorder. I rather wished the mould had grown in it as thoroughly as it had colonised his cameras. I only half-treasured the memory of part of last night's entry, for instance, on which I had eavesdropped from my hammock whilst pretending to be asleep: 'In all honesty, Angel,' I heard him say, *sotto voce*, 'to be perfectly frank with you, Redmond is a selfish bastard. He pretends he likes it here. The Indians, of course, poor geezers, don't know any better. And that Juan is just a nasty little dago who treats me like a moron. Good night. I bite your bum. I miss you. Simon.'

The normal dank, rotting smell of the river bank – or rather the endless series of little islands and interflowing creeks – was displaced by the powerful, musky odour of otter scent and droppings and urine. We passed a muddy patch of firm ground, big enough to camp on, which had been entirely cleared of its undergrowth of shoots and of the usual plants with thick pointed-shovel-shaped leaves; it was a piece of Giant otter advertisement which we met three or four times a day.

'The pong those guys make,' said Simon. 'It's about as close as you get to comradeship around here. There's not a lot else on offer, not so as you'd notice.'

We rounded a bend and came to a small pool where four little streams met, and there, barring the way, were the otters themselves. Five large, dark-brown, tightly furred heads, flattened on top, stuck out of the water in a line.

'Ha! Ha! Uh! Uh! Oof!' they said.

Chimo imitated their chatter and they grew agitated, looking at each other, at the boats, then diving and surfacing right beside us.

'Jesus,' said Simon, 'knock it off, will you Chimo? They're huge. There's no room in here. *I don't want my nuts nicked off.*'

They had small, laid-back ears, large brown eyes, blotches of white on their big chests, and efficient-looking teeth. Drops of water slid off their long side-whiskers.

'Go on boys,' said Simon, waving his arms at them, 'piss off and scrag a fish.'

The otters submerged and re-appeared in a creek to the left.

'Christ,' said Simon, getting his cigarettes out of the plastic bag.

'They grow to six-foot-long,' I said.

'Surprise me,' said Simon, inhaling.

'They're just curious,' said Juan, laughing, 'they've never seen people.'

'That's why they thought we were fish,' said Simon.

We ate our manioc-and-water on a strip of sandy mud beneath another sudden gap in the canopy, where a legume tree lay across the stream: it must have fallen in the storms of the last few days because its outsize, broad-bean-like seed-pods were still fresh. Everyone except Simon gathered handfuls, brushed off the ants and opened the long, green, knobbly cases with a thumb; we sucked the sweet, white, protective fur from each bean, spitting out the bean itself.

'No wonder you've got the shits,' said Simon, turning away to pee on the sand.

Several round-winged, yellow butterflies settled on his slightly steaming urine; and almost at once they were joined by a solitary Kite swallowtail which jostled its way to the centre of the patch: its triangular wings were a filmy white translucence, edged with black, and striped across their veining with black lines of varying lengths, some fringed with scarlet, some with a light green, some running from the leading edge to the scalloped rear and continuing down the long blades of its two sword-like tails.

'Bit like you,' said Simon, sitting on a fallen branch, rubbing the scabs on the back of his neck, and watching the butterfly with distaste. 'Looks all right to start with — you'd never guess it had such nasty habits. You'd never think it would eat bird-gut soup with froth on top, piss, anything.'

The swallowtail pumped up the warm liquid in its proboscis at one end and jetted it out again, in little spurts, from its anus. It was so exposed, so obvious a target for any passing antbird or gnatwren or tanager that I wondered idly if its warning colours were a copy of some poisonous, plant-feeding species; perhaps it was a party to that Darwinian bluff, Batesian mimicry, which Bates had discovered on his travels in the Amazons to the south.

Culimacaré, Pablo and Chimo, working in relays, took an hour to axe through the legume tree and clear our passage back into the dark tunnel ahead of us. And three trees later, in the early evening, as Chimo looked in vain for an island in the black maze of streams which might be large enough to camp on, we emerged, without warning, into an open river.

'Told you so!' said Chimo, lying through his gums and so pleased with himself that he forgot his ritual greeting. 'The Maguarinuma!'

Released into space, sky, clouds, a land with horizons, we were silent, allowing our eyes to roam. A pair of Swallow-tailed kites were gliding low over the palms of the left bank and eight black vultures were stacked above us, wheeling overhead, the highest only just visible. We laid our poles down the edge of the tarpaulins; Chimo and Pablo tilted the hitched-up engines back into the water, pulled their strings and opened up the throttles. We rounded a couple of bends — and there, straight in front of us, were the dark, lowering, canyon-sides of the mountain, three-quarters wrapped in cloud.

The light began to fade; the bushes and then the trees on the bank darkened. The clouds, hanging like slow eruptions of steam from the great peaks to our right, turned pink along their undersides and spread their reflections across the water. To our left the high cliffs and the gullied slopes beneath them grew purple, seemed to increase in size and, as night fell, moved towards us until their shadow finally engulfed the jungle and the river in a massy blackness.

Blue-crowned Motmot

8

Culimacaré switched on Chimo's big torch and waved the dug-outs into a landing-stage on the right bank. There were wooden steps; there was a handrail; we had reached Charlie's old base-camp.

The canoe rocked wildly. A big stomach, looming up behind over the cargo, knocked me onto the duckboards. Chimo grabbed his torch from Culimacaré and heaved himself up the steps as if stung by a flight of hornets.

'There'll be food!' he yelled. 'There'll be food from North America!'

Simon threw his cigarette into the water, jumped ashore, and ran up after him.

'Wait for me!' he shouted.

'Thank God and the Holy Virgin!' called Chimo from the darkness, 'I'm not waiting for anyone!'

Reaching the top of the steps I could see Chimo's torch waving about in an open shed to the right. When I joined him the beam had steadied and he and Simon were admiring a line of tins and packets on a shelf – perhaps two days' supply of food.

'Vegetarian Menu Number Four,' said Simon, adding the bag to a personal cache on the table behind him.

'Sausages,' said Chimo with deep satisfaction, studying their por-trait on a can.

The others arrived and pushed round us. Old Valentine put his hand on my arm.

'Charlie brought us here in helicopters,' he said proudly. 'We worked for the North Americans. We built the huts. We ate well, Reymono, and we were dry every night. *We were treated like scientists.*'

'I was the cook,' said Galvis, reaching into a packing case and handing out spoons, bowls, mugs and three tin-openers. 'I cooked for everyone.'

But there would be no need to cook that night. Chimo had the lid off his tin already. He waved two pale, bendy sausages at me and then eased them both into his mouth at once. Culimacaré and Pablo were bolting palmfuls of sweetcorn. Simon was speechless with pineapple chunks. I took a tin-opener to a can of Italian tomatoes. Galvis, his mouth full of baked beans, unhooked a row of ten kerosene lamps and lit them all. An owl hooted, a steady *booo booo booo*, but I was too busy to care.

Eventually, feeling ill, distended with sweetcorn, baked beans, tomatoes, frankfurters, marrowfat peas and several tins of sardines apiece, we picked up a lamp each and followed Chimo on a tour of inspection. Three long huts with corrugated iron roofs, raised floors of saplings laid side by side and half-walls of saplings tied upright, were set parallel to the river. The hut nearest the forest was clearly the field laboratory. Rough tables, with chain-sawed sections of tree-trunk for stools, ran down its sides. A board hanging from a support-post announced 'AMER. MUS. NAT. HIST. DEPT. HERPETOLOGY — BIEN-VENIDOS'. The roof had buckled in places where small branches had been blown down on it but the contents of the hut seemed remarkably dry — and remarkably attractive. Every corner was stuffed with abandoned equipment: plastic sheets and bags, plastic containers of chemicals for preserving specimens, killing jars, pins, specimen boxes, cast-off clothes and shoes, piles of paper (graph, ruled and plain) and new yellow gum boots. Even the brown plastic mugs looked desirable.

'Mira!' said Chimo sharply, holding up his lamp fully so that it shone into the corner of the far chamber.

A large spider, fangs up, reared above her egg-ball on top of a plastic sheet. Hundreds of tiny offspring, just hatched, were scattered around her.

'The Monkey spider,' said Juan. 'Stay here. She is very poisonous. She jumps at you.'

Chimo darted forward, seized the near corner of the sheet and, in one smooth movement, tossed it out of the door-opening. We clapped, and resumed the pillaging. Culimacaré climbed into a pair of torn Levi jeans and a jacket to match, both some ten sizes too big: he found a pair of gumboots that fitted and strutted about in them, watching his bright yellow feet strut too. Chimo put on a pair of enormous waders and did his little dance, bouncing about on the sapling floor-boards and shaking the hut. Even Old Valentine, slower than the rest, discovered some boots that pleased him. Galvis, scrabbling about in a jumble of boxes, whooped with excitement, and began pocketing bars of soap.

'It is an honour to be here,' said Juan, suddenly overcome with emotion. 'This is a very famous campament. Thank you, Redmon. Much good science was done here. The zoologists and ecologists from the American Museum of Natural History went to the top of Neblina in Charlie's helicopter and collected hundreds of new species . I will dig many pits for charcoal – and perhaps Charlie will think well of my work, perhaps he will publish my results in his *Journal*.'

We fetched our packs from the dugouts and slung our hammocks in the sleeping-huts, from firm posts, in the dry, in a place entirely free of hornets, wasps, scorpions, ants, mosquitoes, blackfly, horseflies and ticks.

In the morning I looked out of our hut, through a gap in the tall trees, at the high outlying arm of the Neblina massif opposite; the brown, sunlit river was immediately below us, and beyond the tall, light-stemmed palms and forest giants (one spreading its branches out above the canopy like a monkey-puzzle tree) was the great grey bulwark of rock. Through the binoculars I could see that it was much further off than it at first appeared: the lichens on the lower slopes were trees; and the tiny yellow-white streak like a bird dropping down the centre of the high cliffs was a waterfall. When we have rested, I told myself, we will go there. It was obviously the place where we might expect to find the pure white bird ('High rain forest on the slopes of the tepuis,' said Schauensee) which Wallace dreamed about, the White bellbird, with a three-inch-long black wattle hanging from the top of its beak and a ringing call which you could hear a mile away.

I bundled up my wet trousers and shirt and went down the long flight of steps to the river for a swim and a clothes-wash. To the right of the deep water by the landing-stage there was a small island close inshore, and between it and the bank proper there was a beach of white pebbles and a stream, diverted by the island from the main river and flowing through a bed of rounded stones. Little brown butterflies with dull red hindwings flew rapidly between the splashes, from one wet boulder-top to another and back again. A lustrous green heliconid and a big butterfly, black and turquoise above, flecked yellow, brown and orange underneath, with odd crenellations on its rear wing margins as if someone had nibbled it from behind, flitted about the drier pebbles. Charlie had chosen the right place for his base camp.

Over the next four days, except when the rain was falling so hard that it was painful on the back, I repeated my early-morning routine; and then, while Simon read *The Brothers Karamazov* or played Patience in the laboratory hut, and Juan and Pablo dug pits for carbon and Chimo went hunting, I walked with Culimacaré to one or other of the small hills rising over the jungle at the back of the camp.

We would set off across the large cleared area where the helicopters had landed (Charlie had made his first touch-down on the beach), and past the pile of empty orange fuel drums, each one stencilled 'KEROSINA CHARLES' down the side, and which, expanding in the morning heat and contracting in the evening chill, made a sound like cannon-fire all day and kept automatic guard over the camp.

In the high, rich, *tierra firme* forest we surprised a deer with a brown coat, a black nose and two little spikes for antlers. He waggled his big ears, flipped up his scut (white as a rabbit's underneath), skipped off for fifteen yards, stood still, and watched us until we disappeared. I decided he was a Brown brocket. We found the nest of a Scarlet pigeon (two fledglings sitting bemused and friendly on top of a broken tree stump); ocelot tracks at the side of a large puddle; several curare vines; and, as we walked up the slope of a hill which was so thickly forested with laurels and legumes and ferns and lianas that no view out was possible, Culimacaré's stomach rumbled at every step and his large intestine made a noise like a basinful of water on its final exit down the pipe. No, he said, he had not got diarrhoea, it was giant worms moving in their burrows beneath us: each one thick as an egg and as long as your arm and good to eat when times were bad. As a storm approached, we disturbed two small black monkeys with long tails walking cat-like along a branch above our heads. Yellow-handed titis ('Viudita!' whispered Culimacaré), they peered down at us with worried little black faces, a contrasting band of white fur at their throats seeming to emphasise their fear. We crept away.

In the evenings, with Pablo in the stern and Culimacaré in the bow, Simon and I would take one of the dugouts and let the current drift us gently downriver. There was no noise but the muted whirring and croaking of cicadas and frogs on the banks, the yelping of Channel-billed toucans, the whistle of the Screaming pihas and the occasional splash of Pablo's paddle – until we found the local Olive oropendola, a crow-sized bird, yellow-olive and russet, who was usually perched on top of a manaca palm and who, on seeing us, would hold his sharp beak open, make a noise like castanets, put his head down as if being sick, glug like a carafe of wine suddenly turned upside-down, rustle his feathers, and regain his composure as if nothing had happened.

Among the flocks of identical-looking, round-winged, fast-flying green parrots it was some comfort to be able to pick out a pair of a smaller species, black against the sky: the Dusky parrot. And on the stems of dead trees whose crowns had been ripped away by the storms that swirl round the base of Neblina, big black Crimson-crested woodpeckers foraged, climbing jerkily up and round the stubs and pausing occasionally to drum a loud double rap on the bark. As dusk fell, Pablo would start the outboard motor and we would return to camp, putting the anhingas to flight from their roosting-perches.

'Easy-peazy,' said Simon, looking at the distant waterfall through the binoculars. 'Of course I'm coming.'

The Blue-crowned motmot, Chimo's favourite bird (the huduri, he called it), the most beautiful bird in the forest, with a turquoise head, yellow breast, green wings and a long brown racket-tipped tail, sang its soft early morning call from somewhere low in the undergrowth nearby, *hoo-doo, hoo-doo, hoo-doo.*

We emptied our bergens of everything except medicines, a set of dry clothes each, and our hammocks and mosquito-nets; Culimacaré and Pablo fitted bark headstraps round the tops of two empty rice-bags; Simon shared out three days' worth of spam and manioc; Chimo motored us across the river; and we set off to climb the mountain.

The thick foliage of the bank gave way almost at once to the high gloom of primary *tierra firme* forest. Culimacaré walked at his usual fast and easy pace, lopping the odd branch of a sapling or shrub as he passed, marking the trail. I tried to stay close behind him, just out of machete-range, pausing only to gulp water from one of the bottles at my belt and to wipe the sweat off my glasses with my shirtsleeve. Simon, attended by Pablo, followed some distance behind. We crossed many streams in flood, and then the country began to rise.

'Marimonda!, Marimonda!' hissed Culimacaré, stopping and pointing up into the canopy.

Four large, black, Long-haired spider monkeys, spindly as gibbons, all arms and legs and tails, looked down at us, fascinated. The monkey immediately over our heads held a bunch of leaves aside to get a better view; he clasped an adjacent branch with his other hand, one to the rear with both feet, and wrapped his three-foot-long tail around another branch above his head.

'They're good to eat,' said Culimacaré, longingly.

The spider monkey moved his head from side to side, studying us with bright black eyes and twitching his broad black nose: his nostrils were set at its side, opening outwards. We were Old World primates, catarrhines (with nostrils close together and opening downwards); he was a New World primate, a platyrrhine. I was glad we had left the gun in camp.

Pablo arrived, alternately grinning and pointing by pouting his lips at a gap in the bushes behind him. There was a rustling in the leaves above us; the spider monkeys, one after the other, dropped twenty feet into the branches of the next tree along and swung away, hand over hand.

Simon appeared through the gap, his nostrils flared like a platyrrhine, his face yellowy-white and covered in sweat. He leant against a tree; his whole body shook as he drew in great draughts of humid air.

His breathing gradually became more regular, his contorted features slowly re-set themselves, and he began to look very cross indeed. Eventually, when he could speak, he turned on me.

'After this,' he gasped. 'I want you to understand – I'm not coming with you anywhere, *nowhere*, never, *not ever*, okay? Is that plain? NOT ANYWHERE.'

'I'm sorry. I was just trying to keep up with Culimacaré.'

'You don't half have some wacky heroes,' he said, pausing to cough up a string of fluid and reaching for his cigarettes. 'Toy soldiers; a bunch of dead geezers rabbiting on about fuck-all a hundred years ago; that fascist Charlie Brewer, maker of the Hitler knife; and now this mob of Indian hit-men who just do what they like with you.'

'We'll go slowly. We'll have lots of rests.'

'And you can tell those maniacs in the SAS, while you're at it, that their bergen's a bummer. They've *got* to be into SM to carry a thing like this. Unquestionably. It wrenches you round the neck and the straps do a half-nelson on your arms and every time you move it puts the boot in your back.'

A pair of Marbled woodquail, hidden on the ground somewhere, suddenly erupted into their antiphonal alarm-call. *Coro-coro-coro*, screamed the male, *vado* added the female, *coro-coro-coro* screamed the male, *vado* repeated the female, the noise seeming to swell all around us.

'Sounds like an air-raid siren,' I said.

'If there's an air-raid,' said Simon, inhaling deeply, 'I want to join the aircraft.'

Six slow hours later we made camp, high up, by a little stream. We knelt on the stones, holding our heads in the tumbling water to wash away the sweat; Pablo and Culimacaré built a small fire to keep off the jaguars; we ate our spam and manioc and, without waiting for nightfall, collapsed into bed.

There came a loud, high-pitched *meeeayow*, like a cat on the wrong side of a closed door.

'Gallito de las rocas!' said Pablo, sitting up in his hammock and pointing. 'Reymono – el macho!'

But Simon and I turned too slowly to see it.

We were not to mind, said Culimacaré from his hammock beside the fire, there was no need to come here, to the ends of the earth and the big mountain, to see the Cock-of-the-rock. His brother kept one as a pet, and the best place to find them was round the rock of Culimacaré, across the river from his house. There were many alligators, too, in the Lago Culimacaré, and a jaguar had killed two pigs in his village only last year. His mother grew sweet and bitter manioc, pineapples, plantains, cashew nuts; and she kept hens, ducks, pigs, but no cows. There were no cows in Culimacaré. I fell asleep.

*

Leaving our packs behind, we began the climb again at first light. We made our way up between large blocks of sandstone, rounded on their tops, fluted down their sides, weathered away into shallow caves at their bases, the whole surface covered in dull green lichen. The trees, many of them with white trunks irregularly ringed with brown, like silver birches, grew thinner and shorter. Lianas became rarer and a bracken-like plant replaced the broad-leaved shrubs.

It became noticeably colder, we sweated less, and the trees began to clothe themselves in moss. They shrank further, hunched themselves, their trunks gnarled and twisted down as if dragged towards the rocky ground by the hanging curtains of thickening moss. Low palms and ferns replaced the bracken and the canopy lowered itself again, until it was no more than fifteen feet above our heads. The jungle grasses gave way to deep carpets of dark green moss and we climbed over the tops of great boulders swathed in moss: I followed Culimacaré closely, copying his every foot- and hand-hold as he pulled himself up the small trunks of trees which snaked towards the light, flat against the walls of wet moss and rock. The leaves on the trees grew tiny; purple and dark red epiphytes sprouted in every cranny; and where the moss had died and turned brown it was speckled and streaked with silver-green lichen. In places, when Culimacaré, small, light and lithe, had crossed a gap without difficulty, his yellow gum boots moving in front of me like a pair of dancing-shoes, my heavy, awkward feet pushed through the moss fibres and the roots of epiphytes, and, through the hole made by my boot, I looked down into black chasms that seemed to drop forever. It would not be sensible, I thought, to break a leg so far from home; but just as I was deciding to call it off, telling myself that at least I had seen the Cloud forest, and that our main purpose was to find the Maturaca, not to disappear into a moss-hidden crevasse, Culimacaré turned to his left, I followed, and we emerged onto bare rock in the open sunlight.

We stood on a lip of stone beside the course of the waterfall, just under the high fringing cliff of the plateau. To the south-west, six thousand feet below, the Brazilian jungle stretched away unbroken to the far horizon. In the foreground, directly opposite, the sharp ridges of the southern arm of Neblina gathered themselves up towards the ten-thousand-foot peak, half obscured in plumes of cloud. Slightly to the west of the massif, in the middle distance, a small tepuis jutted above the flat expanse of forest; and behind it there lay a still dimmer shape, the outline of the Sierra Amori: somewhere in that vast otherness, hidden beneath the trees, the Maturaca made its secret way to the west of the small tepuis and then swung east, passing between the extreme southern flank of Neblina and the northern slope of Amori, before turning south again to flow into the Cauaburi river. It looked so much easier, so prettily man-made, on a map. Huge cumulonimbus clouds moved across the sky towards Neblina; they pulled their shadows after them and, as they passed, they plunged hundreds of square miles of light green forest into momentary darkness.

I turned round to look for Culimacaré – he was climbing the gully towards the thousand-foot fall of white water, and to give himself a better purchase on the wet rocks he had taken off his yellow gumboots, tied them together, and slung them round his neck; I decided that only a barefoot Curipaco or Sir Edmund Percival Hillary in crampons could make a serious attempt on that angle of slope.

Here and there small laurels with dark-green leaves were growing from debris caught in the wide, steep ramps and steps of stone. Pink flowers with floppy petals sprouted directly from their stems. At the margins of the watercourse, before the moss-forest began, tall, purple and red orchid-like flowers were scattered, and a grass like a burr-reed was in yellow bloom. Where the stream itself foamed down the centre of its flood-bed the purple-grey rock was stained sulphur-yellow; and at the edges of the pools enormous frog or toad tadpoles were grazing on the algae. Thick mist began to billow down from the rim of the plateau above us, enveloping the waterfall, rolling slowly into the top of the gulley.

There was a mighty shout from below. Two hundred feet down Simon stood on the rocks, one arm around Pablo's shoulders, the other raised in a closed-fist salute of triumph, his sufferings forgotten.

'Magic!' he called up. 'Magic, old mate!'

Back in camp Chimo was skinning a small Brown brocket deer which he had shot in the forest that afternoon. Juan, Valentine and Galvis had just returned from a charcoal-dig and were standing by the mess-table drinking coffee.

'Redmon, there is trouble,' said Juan the moment he saw me, before I could say anything, before I could tell him about the Spider monkeys, the moss forest, the mountains. 'The Indians want more food. They say they are starving. There is not enough to eat.'

'There's lots of food,' said Simon unexpectedly, barging forward before I had a chance to reply. 'There's megatons of disgusting food. There's enough for fifteen days.'

'They don't believe you,' said Juan, moving back a pace.

'They can take a flying fuck at a rolling doughnut,' said Simon. 'And so can you. I'm in charge of the stores. I packed them myself. It's all written down in my notebook.'

'You must show them how the stores will last. If you speak the truth, you must show them. Galvis and Valentine are not satisfied. They wish to return to San Carlos.'

'Then they can walk,' said Simon, taking off his bergen, sitting down on it, and getting out a pack of Venezuelan cigarettes. That's the spirit, I thought, proud of him.

'I have been thinking,' said Juan. 'We should go back.'

'Come on, Fats,' said Simon, standing up again. 'We'll lug the whole lot up from the boats and bung it in bags. Fifteen bags. Fifteen days.'

So with help from Chimo, Pablo and Culimacaré we carried all the sacks and Charlie's storage tins up to the camp table, and Simon began dividing our remaining spam, flour, rice, coffee, sugar and manioc into piles.

Everyone gathered round. 'I say there's not enough,' said Galvis, 'and so does Valentine. What if we have no food? What if we are weak when the Yanomami catch us in the Maturaca? Eh? What then? Everyone knows they kill you. We are all getting thinner.'

It was true. Only Chimo was undiminished.

There was a long silence.

Chimo glanced at me, winked, and turned majestically to the assembled company.

'We're men aren't we?' he said. 'We can hunt.'

'So far,' said Galvis, 'you've killed just enough food to feed a couple of dogs.'

'Galvis is a woman,' said Chimo, taking the pipe out of his shirt pocket, 'but the rest of us are men. Galvis will cook us two fried flour-cakes each for breakfast every day. We will have an hour for lunch. We will stop at three o'clock every afternoon and make camp so that I and my nephew and Pablo have time to go hunting and fishing. We will keep our promises.'

'We'll go up the canyon tomorrow,' I said, the warm release from anxiety seeming to sweep down my vertebrae. 'And then we must leave at once for the Maturaca.'

All night long a storm raged, the thunder moving away and then returning from another direction, the rain hitting the corrugated iron roofs like gunfire; and before I fell asleep I counted five separate series of explosive cracks, followed by a long, confused sound of sporadic smaller reports and muffled tearings, as big trees toppled over in the forest.

In the morning the river had risen to cover the butterfly-beach but the day was clear. We ate two flour-cakes each and a mess-tin full of boiled venison and manioc; we emptied Chimo's dugout of everything except three-days'-worth of stores; and we set off up the Maguarinuma into the heart of the canyon.

We passed several islands and long beaches of rounded stones; we upset a pair of Yellow-ridged toucans (smaller than Cuvier's, with an orange-yellow band across their rumps) perched in a manaca palm. They croaked instead of yelping. A flock of about fifteen little Mountain swifts wheeled together close above us, showing off their white throats and notched tails, and making a noise like the winding-up of fifteen alarm clocks.

For the first three rapids we simply jumped in up to our waists and dragged the boat up the shoots of boulders; but the fourth was a real cataract both sides of an island, and looked impossible — too shallow on one side and far too powerful on the other. Chimo considered it carefully and then issued directions: Pablo and Culi-macaré took the long bow-rope, waded up wide, looped the rope over an over-hanging branch at the top of the sluicing curl of river, took a firm grip on the end of the rope, anchored their feet against an underwater boulder and, leaning backwards, pulled with their whole weight. The rest of us, up to our chests in the white water, brushing against the overhanging foliage, heaved on the gunwale. Looking up to ease a crick in my neck I saw a big black eagle, perhaps a Solitary eagle, suspended above us, and appearing, with his abnormally small head and short white band of a tail, to be almost bodiless, a great spread of black wing adrift between the black canyon-sides, which echoed with his brief, piercing screams.

The next moment six hornets injected their venom into my shoulder-blades and I screamed myself. I dived forward without thinking, submerged, let go of the dugout, and was swept backwards under-water into the massive, rubbery coils of a waiting anaconda: coils which transformed themselves, as I broke surface, into Chimo's out-stretched right arm and leg. By some chance my glasses were still on my face and Chimo held my hat. Everyone laughed.

'Serves you right,' said Chimo, handing back the hat. 'You should help to look after the bongo. This is my bongo. There are plenty of eagles in the sky, Reymono, but Chimo has only one best bongo.'

We warped the boat up the next rapid in the same way, but just before we reached the top Chimo pointed ahead at the clear water.

'Mira! Danta!' he called. 'Culimacaré – get the gun!'

Culimacaré was clamped to a rock one end and to the rope at the other and in no position even to turn round; so the tapir, its light-grey head and rounded ears and long snout held at an angle above the water, reached the bank unmolested, scrambled ashore with surprising agility, and disappeared.

'No man is a hunter until he has killed a danta,' said Chimo solemnly. 'Culimacaré is my own nephew but he has never killed a danta. He only came with us, Reymono, because I said he could hunt a danta. There is no other meat so good.'

Five sets of smaller rapids later, beyond a stretch of river from which two squat, fortress-like outcrops of rocks rose above the plateau-line of cliffs ahead of us, Chimo brought the dugout into a boulder-strewn beach.

'This is my city,' he announced, stepping ashore. 'Charlie named it after me.'

He took his blue helmet off, ran a large hand through his hair, put his helmet back on again, took his pipe out of his shirt pocket, filled it, and sat heavily down on a stone.

'One day, when the time is right, I will found Puerto Chimo properly,' he said, inhaling half a bonfire of Alligator Brand. 'Its protector, Reymono, will be the Blessed Virgin – and I shall build my house there' (he waved a hand at a cleared space a few yards higher up the bank) 'and to the right of my front door, there, I will found the brothel, and to the left of my front door, there, I will found the bar. I will remember, every morning, to turn first to my right. And you can take a word of advice from Chimo who knows these things – a bar is a lot of use to a man after a brothel, Reymono, but a brothel is no use to a man after a bar.'

*

Looking out at the river, which was now no more than thirty or forty yards across, we ate our lunch of boiled venison and manioc. In the middle of the eddies and waves of fast-flowing water stood two high rocks, strata lines running almost vertically across their jagged crests. Part of one of the oldest rock-formations in the world, the Guiana shield, they had perhaps last been horizontal, undisturbed, when South America was still joined to Africa, the Niger was the upper Amazon, the Amazon flowed through its present mouth to its tail, the continents had not yet begun to move and so the bow-wave of the Andes did not yet exist.

Galvis and Valentine took the bucket of remaining venison, paddled Chimo's bongo to the side of the rocks and spread the strips of meat to dry in the open sunlight; Culimacaré shouldered Chimo's gun and set off to hunt in the forest.

'Come on, Simon,' I said, 'let's walk up the canyon.'

'You can walk till your nuts drop off, for all I care,' said Simon, slinging his hammock, 'but I'm not coming with you. Not ever. I meant what I said. From now on you go walkies on your own. I'm going to read. And when you get back I'll give you a ribbon to tie on your hampton, a toy-soldier campaign ribbon – that's what you're after, aren't you?'

Pablo and I clambered over the boulders by the river for half a mile or so, clouds of tiny butterflies with bright yellow, black-margined wings fluttering about our feet. Even here, almost at the head of the canyon, the water was dark brown like a very old claret. The streams that feed the Maguarinuma, draining from the soggy, cloud-covered plateau by a thousand waterfalls, had already run through enough jungle (technically a Sandy-belt forest) to absorb so many tannins and phenols and all the other poisonous chemicals with which trees growing on nutrient-poor sandy soils protect their leaves against predators, that its waters were almost as dark as those of the Rio Negro.

The wet pebbles shone with flecks and blotches of green and pink like Dunlin's eggs, and here and there they glistened with fragments of encrusted mica. Small pieces of driftwood, sculpted and sand-blasted by the river, lay jammed between boulders and cast up along the shore.

In the surprisingly high, liana-rich forest we frightened a reddish-brown squirrel. It dashed across the leaf-litter in front of us, undulating its bushy tail, and disappeared up and round the back of a buttressed tree. We stopped to fill our shirts and pockets with piles of yuco, a large, yellow-brown, hard-cased fruit which lay scattered for twenty square yards beneath a yuco tree (whose branches began so far up towards the canopy that I could not even make out the shape of its leaves). Pablo split some open with his machete: inside was a big fibrous nut covered in fleshy, orange-red pith: you eat the pith, which takes sweet and creamy and butterscotchy at first, until, by nut three, you realize that some chemical is removing the skin from your lips, the surface from your tongue, and a layer of tissue from your throat. It is then time to stop.

When we reached camp it was raining doggedly. Chimo and Valentine had caught a land tortoise with black-and-yellow legs and a small river turtle with pink legs, roped them up with creeper to a frame of four sticks and hung them from the end of Simon's hammock-post.

'Fatso,' said Simon, 'if it's the only time you ever manage to tell these people what to do – get them to set those poor little bleeders free, for my sake. Okay?'

'I'll ask in the morning,' I said uneasily, changing into my dry clothes. 'I can't do it the moment they've caught them. Not after all that talk about hunting.'

Culimacaré, very wet, emerged from the trees carrying a Black curassow. As big as a turkey, glossy purplish black, it differed from our normal prey, the Lesser razor-billed curassow: its belly and thighs and under-tail coverts were silky white, the base of its bill and its cere (the waxlike membrane behind the bill) were yellowy red; and the short feathers of its crest, curling forward, as if back-brushed, stretched all the way over the top of its head to the back of its neck.

Valentine began pounding the yuco fruits with a stick in the water-filled cooking pot, and Galvis started to pluck the curassow.

'Holy Mother!' said Chimo suddenly, looking at the river. 'The deer meat!'

Great black waves were tossing past us, thrown down from some storm on the mountain, breaking into rising semi-circles of foam against the two rocks. Pablo, Chimo and Culimacaré jumped into the pitching bongo, grabbed their paddles, and swung out alongside the

107

fast-disappearing rock where the strips of venison lay. At either end of the see-sawing boat Pablo and Culimacaré clung on to ridges in the strata, while Chimo, in the middle, scrabbled the meat back into the bucket. Thrown sideways to the current for a moment, filling with water and almost capsizing, they brought the bongo back to shore, baled it out, and roped it fore and aft to two big trees. We moved our stray bags and tins and punt-poles off the narrowing beach, and hoped that the forest was as genuinely tierra firme as it looked.

'Redso,' said Simon that night as we fell asleep to the sound of crashing water, 'here comes the biggest wet dream of your life.'

But in the morning, although the rain still fell with a persistence unvarying in its rhythm, the river level had fallen slightly. We ate boiled venison and mingao de yuco, yuco sludge, which I thought was as thick and sweet as porridge and syrup; and which Simon said was as frigging disgusting as everything else.

Juan and Valentine rigged up a tarpaulin to shelter themselves while they dug for carbon. Culimacaré went hunting. Knowing that it was our last day at Puerto Chimo and hoping that the rain might ease, I set off with Pablo to walk upstream as far as we could.

We wore our capes and I trudged for three hours behind Pablo's white plastic back through the forest beside the river, the canyonside lost in cloud.

Then, 'Reymono,' he said, turning round, 'tell me — what is it you think you'll see? Your birds and animals are in their holes and we, too, when the rains come like this, we also should be in our holes.' A thought struck him and he grinned. 'But then perhaps you want to see the pez buey swimming in the trees, eh?'

I had an absurd vision of the manatee, the sea-cow, the ox-fish, dragging his ten-foot blubbery body out of the river, standing on his hind-flipper in the rain, browsing on the sapling leaves with his blunt and bristly lips, chewing up the vegetation with his renewable molars (the whole tooth-row moves forward at a rate of one milli-metre a month) and swallowing the minced pieces of foliage into his 150-foot-long intestines.

Further on, Pablo pointed with his lips at the jungle floor: bean-sized seeds, bright red and black as if each one had been hand-painted, were scattered across the decaying leaves. We gathered two pocketfuls each ('for our girlfriends,' said Pablo) and made our way back to camp.

And on my return I did receive a ribbon of sorts, although not from Simon. 'Here you are,' said Chimo, as big and benign as a manatee and holding something on the flat of his palm. 'It's a bird — for you. It's a bird from Puerto Chimo.'

A small piece of drifted hardwood, eroded into the form of a tail and two upbeating wings held a fragment of knotted stick that served as a head and a beak. I wrapped the precious gift up in a sock, enclosed it in a plastic bag and placed it in my bergen. The old man smiled.

Culimacaré came back empty-handed; but, even so, Chimo agreed to release the tortoise and the turtle. With one of Juan's thick felt-tip marker-pens Galvis wrote 'EXPEDITION MATURACA INGLESES VENE-ZOLANOS COLOMBIANO' across their shells and placed the tortoise in the undergrowth and the turtle in the water.

Just after nightfall, as we lay in our hammocks, a low, booming cough reverberated eight times from the other bank of the river.

'That,' said Chimo quietly, 'is the grandfather of all jaguars.'

He got to his feet and piled armfuls of driftwood onto his fire until the flames leapt up; by their light we could see that he was concentrating hard, his eyes half-closed, and that he was muttering, very fast, some kind of incantation to himself.

Giant Otter

9

Ten days back into the Baria, we were making camp on a small island, a patch of dank mud barely raised above the floodwaters in the interconnecting tunnels, the mesh of streams. A Nocturnal curassow called, starting its song earlier than usual, *hūm hūm hūm hūm de hūm hūm.*

'That bird again,' said Simon hanging his hammock and then pausing to light a cigarette from his last packet. 'I can't bear it.'

'It's all right,' I said. 'Tomorrow we will find a stream flowing to the south. We're nearly there. We're going to do it.'

'About bloody time. I've been working it out – I've been stuck in here thirty days. But if it's five down the Maturaca, five down the Cauaburi, three in a big boat down the Rio Negro – I could be in Manaus in thirteen days. Straight to the airport. A day's flight. I could be in London with Liz in two weeks. In two weeks I'll eat beef and yorkshire and peach melba and drink claret and roger her stupid, all ways.'

'We must be in Brazil by now. You promised you'd come up the Purus.'

'You've *got* to be joking.'

Simon was now much thinner, and appeared haggard and red about the eyes. I was worried that sometimes he had a distant, empty look that I had last seen in Douglas's face, a few weeks before he

110

killed himself. And lately he had begun to share something else – his movements were either tense and fast, stiff and violent, taut as a stretched wire, or unnaturally relaxed. In the evenings he had taken to lying in his hammock, saying nothing, not moving, staring into the trees.

I sat on a manioc tin beside him, blowing the occasional very small mosquito, a blanquin, out of my mouth or nose, and plucking a guan.

'It's disgusting, watching you do that,' he said, leaning against a tree, smoking. 'It turns me up. It really does.'

'What's wrong? You eat chicken, don't you?'

'I buy it ready-wrapped. And then I give it to my cats. I get my meat at the best butcher in West Drayton.'

'So what's the problem? You must have plucked and pulled a chicken in your time, paunched the odd rabbit?'

'Pull your plonker. Have I hell – yes, that's me, that's Simon, cold bath first thing, skin a rabbit, roll with the under-matron, nothing I like more. Look here, *old chap* – how many people in London do you think have plucked a chicken? I suppose you just take it as per normal that everyone goes hurling round town ripping fur off rabbits, lobbing guts out of windows, sticking their little ears in flower pots? Eh? Nearest I ever got to a rabbit, *old bean*, was when I worked down the Playboy Club, skinned a few of *them*. Cut the elastic on *their* furry tails.'

'On a rabbit,' I said, 'they're not called tails, they're scuts.'

'Butts, scuts, who cares?' said Simon, lighting another cigarette, scratching the bites on the back of his now swollen, scabby neck. He turned away, put his arm up against the tree and leant his head on it, staring down at the water where it rustled past amongst the leaves. 'This place is the pits,' he said. 'This place is the arsehole of the earth.'

The next morning, Valentine, cutting a fresh punt pole by the bank, dropped his machete into the deep, black, cold water. Galvis, who was loading the cooking-pots and mess-tins back into his dugout, stripped to his pants, stood on the bow, and dived in: bubbles surfaced and then he emerged, triumphantly holding the machete in his outstretched right hand.

'Well done Galvis,' said Chimo, grudgingly.

Four fallen trees later we turned right into a channel some four

111

feet wider than the lattice-work of waterways we had travelled in that week.

'Maturaca!' announced Chimo, grinning with pride and unzipping his fly.

Simon, overcome with sudden *joie de vivre*, picked up his machete and joined us in the water as we balanced on the submerged branches of a dead tree, hacking at the vegetation. Slitting through a liana in the middle of the stream I dislodged a small woven basket of plant fibres, which was hanging by its looped handle from a twig: the nest of the wren-like Black-headed antbird, it contained two purple-olive eggs, like nightingale's eggs. They were warm to the touch so I edged along a branch and re-hung the basket from another liana-shoot drooping over the water, strong enough to hold a family of antbirds but too flimsy, I hoped, to bear the slide of a snake. And a little further on, a sure sign, I thought, that at last the endless dank maze was about to open up and fall away behind us, we passed under a rough platform of sticks, like a woodpigeon's, the nest of a Green ibis laid on a small forked branch some four feet above the centre of the stream. The bird herself sat tight until we were directly beneath her, and then flew off between the lianas making her gobbling alarm-call, *kullakullakulla*. Two half-grown chicks peeked their faces over the edge of the nest. Considering us carefully, first with one eye and then with the other, they waved their long curved bills, very seriously, from side to side.

We axed a way through two more trees and came out into a clearish, winding stretch. Poling round one of the bends I found myself staring into two enormous yellow eyes. A buzzard-sized owl sat on a low branch some fifteen feet away, unexpected, self-contained, pure white against the dull green of the glaucous leaves, a black mask of feathers round his eyes and bill exaggerating the force of his stare. He looked at us for a moment, then stood up straight on his feathery legs, turned round as if every movement was an effort, and slipped easily away through the undergrowth on his brown, rounded wings.

'It's an owl,' I said, stupidly.

'White man no speak with forked tongue,' said Simon.

'Lechuzon de anteojos,' said Chimo, pointing at his own eyes with his forefinger and nodding his head.

I took Schauensee out of the waterproof bag: there he was, a mere schematic representation of the real thing, outlined on Plate IX, a juvenile Spectacled owl, not yet equipped with its 'chocolate-brown upperparts and broad breast band'.

The dugout came to a standstill. I looked up. Culimacaré had run the bow into the bank. Chimo was resting on his punt pole, staring ahead. Simon suddenly clasped his arms to his head and bowed his body right forward between his knees.

'Oh god, oh god', he said, beginning to rock himself back and forth, 'dear god.'

We had come out into another channel. But there were axe marks everywhere. It had been cleared. The vegetation had been cleared right down the stream. Someone had come here before us. We had been forestalled. It was all too late. I felt cold down my back, dull and blank in the head, weary, old.

'Who is it?' I said.

'Who is it?' repeated Simon with a strangled chuckle. 'Who is it? It's us, you idiot. *We did it.*'

A little way down to the left I recognised the bole of a big red hardwood.

'It's all right,' I said, 'we've just come in a circle. We'll go back and try again.'

Simon flung himself back against the tarpaulin.

'We're lost,' he said, pounding his pack with his fist, 'it'll take months. *We're lost.*'

The second dugout came up. Galvis shouted his habitual formulaic greeting.

'Simon! No problema!'

'Bloody big problem,' muttered Simon, unsmiling. He stared at the duckboards, plucking at his forehead with his right hand, as if he was scraping a cobweb off his face. 'You've got to let me go, Redmond. I don't trust myself. *I shall do something terrible.* You've got to let me have their dugout and get back to San Carlos. Galvis will come. He can't stand it either. And Valentine — he's so old he should never have come in the first place.'

'Pull yourself together,' I said, at once feeling absurd. 'You'd never make it without Chimo. And anyway, we must have two boats to get through the Maturaca. What if we smash a boat on these logs?'

Simon shut his eyes, lay back on the tarpaulin, and turned away.

Refusing to speak, Simon sat and looked at the water slipping past the gunwale. We poled quickly and silently down our old track: we drew almost level with a young otter eating something at the bank edge before he looked round, thick-set on his short legs, considered us and then scampered off between the thin trees. Culimacaré punted the bow in and picked up a dead paca. A large fruit-eating rodent, about two-and-a-half feet long, it had rat-like front teeth, long whiskers, long toes, and an orange-brown furry coat covered in white spots and lines like a baby fallow deer. Its belly and chest were white; there were two teats between the front legs and two between the back. The broad nose and mouth were covered in foam: the paca had obviously died by drowning, the otter catching it from the river and keeping its face underwater. The otter had begun to eat at the back of the neck.

'It's a gift from god,' said Chimo, 'and bad luck on the perro de agua.'

We stopped early at one of our own old campsites, an island at a junction of two narrow, deep channels. We started a fire, placed water on to boil for scalding the paca skin, and put up our shelters and hammocks from the ready-made posts and cross-pieces. Pablo took Chimo's gun and paddled off on a hunt in the curiara.

Simon retired to his hammock. Down to his last two cigarettes, he had nearly finished the stock of paperbacks, too; tonight of all nights, I noticed, he was finally going to confront *Heart of Darkness*.

Frogs peeped like chaffinches, quacked like mallard, cawed like rooks. I had a swim, fully dressed, in the cold water, washing myself and my clothes at the same time. I then dried myself under my mosquito net; dusted my crutch in zinc-talc anti-fungus powder (Juan, who had spurned such an un-macho indulgence, now had difficulty walking); put Anthisan on the bites of the day, Savlon on the cuts, Canesten cream on my badly rotted feet. I re-covered myself in sticky Jungle Formula everything-repellent and thought with admiration of Humboldt and Wallace and Spruce who had had none of these fetishistic comforts.

There was a shot from some way off — although it was difficult to judge the distance of a noise in such a landscape where even the sound waves from an explosion were broken up, stilled and smothered almost at once. Valentine and Chimo laid the paca on a bed of palm leaves, poured boiling water over it, scraped off the fur, slit open the stomach, threw the guts in the water and jointed the meat. The bladder drifted slowly away, bobbing up and down, pulled from below by piranhas.

I took out my maps again: CODESUR thought the entrance to the Maturaca was to the north-west of us; Charlie's diagram thought we were in the right place; the Operational Navigational Chart I had bought in London made a wild guess in heavy blue, put a large swamp to the north, but had sound advice for pilots flying to the east of Neblina: 'ABRUPT CLIFFS REPORTED IN THIS AREA – HAZARDOUS FLYING UNDER 13000 FEET.'

I was saved from my perplexity by a happy shout. Pablo appeared, the little canoe half-swamped by the weight of a huge cayman. We hauled it out and measured it: almost exactly six feet long. Its back, knobbed and ridged, was the exact colour of the brown-black water, its tail was mottled with light patches like dim spots of filtered sunlight. We laid it down on the muddy ground, white belly uppermost. Chimo felt about in the middle just up from its back legs and pulled a slim white penis out of an armoured pouch flush with the curve of the underside. Personally, said Chimo, he could do with an arrangement like that himself round here. It would make life a lot easier. It would make swimming a pleasure. We all agreed. Chimo pointed to the cayman's front right foot: he'd lost all his claws, probably in a fight with an otter when he was a young man. Really big cayman were more likely to go for you than an alligator was, said Chimo, and they were much quicker in the water.

Valentine began to build a platform for smoking the meat; Galvis had almost finished preparing the paca soup. Pablo and the otter had temporarily dispelled the perpetual anxiety about finding food: maybe we could still find the Maturaca, despite everything. Perhaps Simon would recover in a week or two. We turned the cayman over and Pablo opened it up with axe blows along its backbone: unlike alligators and crocodiles, caymans possess an interlocking series of bony plates which protect their stomachs. We cut out the dense flesh in sections and laid it on Valentine's platform; Charlie's knife no longer seemed quite such an excessive instrument. I slit open the distended stomach and released an appalling stench.

'Jesus,' said Simon, who, unnoticed, had come to watch.

I peeled back the lining and pulled out something that was covered in fur and slime. It was a small monkey with big circular eyes; it was intact apart from its tail, its little hands and feet still in place.

'No, no,' said Simon, stepping against a tree, holding the back of his hand to his nose. 'Just promise me, Redmond. Just promise me *you're not going to eat that as well.*'

'Mono de las noches,' said Chimo.

It was a Nocturnal or Owl monkey – first described by Humboldt – the only truly night-living monkey in the world, which comes out fifteen minutes after sunset, safe from every predator except the Great horned owl and, it seemed, the cayman. It is monogamous; mother and father and the babies (one a year, and they leave home when they are two and a half years old) move about together foraging for fruits, insects, nectar and suitable leaves. A lonely male searching for a mate will hoot like an owl, but only when the moon is full. What had happened? Had a two-year-old fluffed its jump? I threw the tightly furred little body into the water.

Galvis announced that paca soup was ready. And he had also cooked Simon's rice and put out a tin of spam.

'Come on, Galvis,' said Simon, banging his mess tin with his spoon, 'it's the eighth day – where's my tomato ketchup?'

Juan translated.

'Galvis says it is in the boat,' said Juan. 'And it is only the seventh day. You divided the stores. It is your rule. You must stick to it.'

'It's the eighth day,' said Simon, doggedly, still banging his tin, 'and I want Galvis to get my tomato ketchup.'

'Why don't *you* get it?' I said.

'Just keep out of this,' said Simon.

'It's only a bottle of tomato ketchup,' I said.

'*Precisely*,' said Simon.

'You listen,' said Juan, shaking with rage, his sharp chin and beard thrust forward, 'here we are, lost in this swamp. Everyone is trying to be cheerful, even when we are all afraid. We are lost. We have no food but the paca and the cayman and your rice and tins of meat which were meant to be for all of us to stop us from starvation, but which now are almost gone – and you complain about your sauces.'

'Steady,' I said.

Simon turned on me, his eyes wild, his face taut.

'I'm going to kill this little shit,' he said, 'I warn you. I'm going to bust his teeth in.'

'Not here,' I said, suddenly exhausted. 'Fight anywhere else if you must, but not here. Just for my sake.'

'Dear god,' said Simon, throwing his mess tin and spoon to the ground and bringing his right fist down on the side of his thigh with a convulsive spasm.

Hunched forward, he walked to the edge of the island, by the black, still-rising water, and he looked up into the dark overhang of trees. Then he threw his head up and back, like a dog.

'Where's-my-tom-ato-ketch-up?' he screamed into six million square kilometres of jungle.

There was no echo from the soft leaves.

Tapir

10

For five days and nights the rain fell without a pause, the monotony of its drumming on the canopy and its splattering through the leaves broken only by a series of thunderstorms. Chimo, uncharacteristically quiet, his pride hurt by his failure to find the Maturaca, the reputation of the greatest navigator on the Rio Negro at stake in front of his peers, insisted that we retrace our route and check every possible wrong turn, investigate every stream whose current seemed to move to the south. But the water had risen over so many islands, so few knolls of land still showed their muddy tops above the moving blackness that a different current seemed to swirl and eddy and flow back on itself between each pair of trees.

After three days of such searching, Chimo decided to make camp on the highest piece of ground we could find; and, taking the gun and Culimacaré as protection against anacondas, he paddled off each day at dawn to look wherever his instinct led him. On the sixth day the rain eased and then stopped; the Screaming piha reasserted itself; the runnels of water cascading down the trunks of the trees gradually slowed and dried up.

We had long since finished the thick white meat of the cayman (a blend of halibut and chewing-gum); and now every day Pablo fished until he had hauled in fifteen or twenty piranhas. That morning Juan and I happened to be squatting next to him, gutting the fish, when something wide and pale, wide as the eagle's wings in the canyon, loomed up in the shadows at the end of his line; Pablo gave an involuntary yelp of fear or surprise; the shape undulated once from wing-tip to wing-tip, and subsided back into the darkness.

'Stingray!' shouted Juan, in my ear. 'They hit you with their tail, Redmon, and drive a poison spike into you. The wound becomes infected. It takes months to heal, sometimes a year.'

'He's eaten my hook,' said Pablo gloomily, pulling in the severed line.

After a silent lunch of boiled piranha and manioc, Valentine and Pablo perched on empty storage tins whittling with their machetes at two new, half-made paddles; Galvis reclined on a root with his copy of the *Reader's Digest*; Juan sat at his place in Valentine's bongo, away from the mosquitoes, indulging himself with a little light escapist reading, the second edition of T. C. Whitmore, *Tropical Rain Forests of the Far East* (1984); and Simon and I climbed into our hammocks, he with *Heart of Darkness* and I with Humboldt.

'Why the hell didn't you bring more books?' said Simon. 'We could have brought a *kit-bag* of paperbacks.'

'How was I to know you'd read so fast? I thought you'd stick a finger under each word and mouth it.'

'You bastard,' he said, with real conviction. And then, 'I can just imagine you living out here for ever. Noshing people. Bunging the odd boat-race up on a stake.'

'Boat-race?'

'Boat-race. Face,' said Simon, bringing the conversation to a close.

His book, which he held up in front of his eyes as he lay on his back, registered the slight shaking which had begun in his hands, perhaps an effect of nicotine withdrawal. Looking at him as he suffered in his hammock, reading *Heart of Darkness* for the third time, I suddenly felt immensely fond of him and then, equally quickly, guilty, remorseful. The promises I had made came back to me, as if from another world: the chance to change his life and career, the fun we would have, the prize-winning pictures of birds he would take.

'I'm sorry,' I said. 'Perhaps it's not as much fun as we expected. We didn't imagine it quite like this.'

Simon sat up as if stung in the back.

'You bloody con-artist,' he said, staring straight at me, showing the whites of his eyes. 'I read your Borneo book. You said that was fun and I believed you. You said this would be fun and I believed

119

you. Well, I can't even *imagine* fun any more, not anywhere. *Not anywhere at all.*'

He threw Conrad to the bottom of his hammock, lay down, and closed his eyes.

As night came, Chimo and Culimacaré returned in the fishing-canoe.

'It's hopeless,' said Chimo, clambering ashore. He picked up a smoked piranha and peeled a strip of flesh from the bones. 'Reymono, don't you worry,' he said, between mouthfuls, 'we will find you other problems. Last year a Chori came to Solano. If we could find that man — and we think he lives on the Siapa — he might lead us to the Choris who live in the centre. We might be able to go up the Emoni. We might go where we have never been.'

'It's a good offer,' Juan said to Simon and me. 'They call them Choris, which means friends in Yanomami, because everyone is frightened of the Yanomami. They are a naked people. Very dangerous.'

'They whack you on the head with poles,' said Simon.

'Think of the pictures,' I said.

'Sod the pictures,' said Simon.

That night I was visited by the recurrent dream which had troubled me ever since I had realised we were lost. I was back, eight years old, on another family expedition to the Avon. We carried the two-seater canvas canoe through the archway in the ancient, ochre-stone farm-buildings, across two rough fields with worn wooden stiles set into their hedges, and lowered it into the stream. My mother, as usual, went for a swim in the pool above the weir and my elder brother began to fish for pike with his new short rod and spinner. My father sat in the back of the canoe and I sat in the front and we paddled upstream with our double paddles. A moorhen fussed across in front of us, its head jerking, its white tail flicking, and disappeared into a clump of water plantains. At the fourth bend a pair of teal sprang into the air. At the fifteenth bend the unreachable railway bridge came into view through the gap in the stand of bullrushes, unimaginably far away from the landing-stage and the picnic basket behind us. We turned back and, as always, I felt immeasurably disappointed. Somehow, if I could only get to the bridge, if I could just see what lay beyond it, I might be safe in a hidden kingdom of my own — I might be free of the smell of new polish and my rug all alone at the end of a dormitory bed; of the cold plunge every morning; of cricket balls I could not hit and figures I could not divide and ropes in the gym I could not climb; and above all I might never again have to look up at Mr Macrae, the Headmaster with the little flat board of his own design which he kept in his cane rack solely for use on the under-tens.

Three days later we emerged by our old course onto the Pasimoni, where, just past the mouth of the Baria, dolphins began to play about the boats, and we saw our first swallow, a Black-collared. We put into our old campsite, now virtually unrecognisable because the river had risen some thirty feet to cover the rocks and lap against the top of the bank. Culimacaré took the fishing-canoe and Chimo's gun and paddled diagonally across the river, intending to make his way upstream, cross over and, drifting silently down on our side, shoot a curassow for breakfast. The rest of us ate piranha and manioc soup, slung our hammocks, changed into dry clothes, and were preparing to go to sleep when we heard five shots in succession, followed by a distant shout for help.

'He's been attacked by Indians!' said Galvis. 'He's killed someone.'

'He's killed five peccaries!' said Chimo. 'I shall have one to myself!'

Everyone except Simon and Galvis got into the boats, and we motored upriver until Chimo spotted the empty curiara moored to a tree.

Juan stayed in the dugouts while the rest of us jumped ashore. The water in the forest came up to my waist. We found Culimacaré, in the dusk, in a swamp, holding his gun out of the water, wildly excited, with a tapir floating dead at his feet.

'He! He! Lo maté!' he was shouting. 'Hey! Hey! I killed it!'

'Well done,' said Chimo, putting an arm round him, calming him down. 'Well done. Tonight we'll cut it up and salt it down and then we'll have enough meat to feed everyone in your village *and* mine.'

Compact and streamlined for pushing through thick undergrowth, six or seven feet long but very heavily built, it took Chimo, Pablo, Culimacaré, Valentine and me to lift the tapir out to the river. Large, dull green ticks were feeding all over his belly, neck and genitals. His penis was equipped with a cross-piece, like that of a rhinoceros. The largest mammal in South America, the tapir is also one of the oldest in the world, even older than the dolphins in the river, its skeleton unchanged since that of its fossil ancestors of twenty million years ago; the tapir, like the rocks of Puerto Chimo, had its place in the ancient continent of Gondwanaland.

We butchered the carcase, ate the liver, put our entire stock of salt over the strips and square of meat, sealed them in our biggest storage drum and, at four in the morning, under the Southern Cross, we set off for the village of Culimacaré.

Matamata

11

At Culimacaré our one-room guest-hut with its palm-thatch roof and mud-and-wattle walls seemed to be the height of architectural sophistication: it was luxurious to sling a hammock from cross-beams and listen to the afternoon storm splashing into the puddles and runnels in the mud outside. In an absurdly euphoric moment I even imagined that a three-day spell in the dry might kill the algae and fungus growing on our shirts and trousers and hammocks, and so release us from the intimate and constant stench of decay.

When the rain eased we went down to the muddy slope which served as a landing stage beside the sweeping bend in the course of the Casiquiare, and manhandled our last full petrol drum and the rest of our equipment out of the canoes and back across a corner of the square to our hut. Small black flies swarmed everywhere; they hung across the surface of the water in clouds, they drifted up and down in the small currents of air beneath the eaves of the huts, they swirled inside every time we opened the netted door. It was at first hard to believe that anything so tiny and gnat-like could possibly deliver a bite so painful. My hands began to swell with clusters of large bumps, each one with a blood spot in the centre.

'You will become accustomed,' said Juan. 'I am now going to take a bathe in the river naked. I wish to become strong like the

Indians. These flies – they are *jejenes*. You, I believe, call them blackfly. They hatch in May and in June.'

'More bloody lectures,' muttered Simon, sitting heavily down on his hammock, swinging his legs in, the boots still on his feet, and turning his face to the wall. 'It's lectures, lectures, round here. All bloody day long.'

'I like lectures,' I said, 'and I like like Juan.'

'I could strangle him,' said Simon.

'You'd like to kill me too,' I said, rummaging in my bergen for a fresh bottle of insect repellent.

'You're too fat to strangle,' said Simon.

Chimo and Pablo, driven inside by the blackfly, set up our primus in a corner of the hut and began to boil the strips of tapir meat. I drew up a log stool to the ex-mission table, and decided to comfort myself by imagining that all biting flies were still at a decent academic and historical distance. A passage in Humboldt had once seemed amusing. Relatively free of mosquitoes while travelling on the black-water rivers, he and Bonpland had discovered that 'our sufferings recommenced as soon as we entered the Casiquiare'. And in general:

> Persons who have not navigated the great rivers of equinoctial America, for instance, the Oroonoko and the Rio Magdalena, can scarcely conceive, how without interruption, at every instant of life, you may be tormented by insects flying in the air, and how the multitude of these little animals may render vast regions almost uninhabitable. However accustomed you may be to endure pain without complaint, however lively an interest you may take in the objects of your researches, it is impossible not to be constantly disturbed by the moschettoes, *zancudoes*, *jejens*, and *tempraneroes*, that cover the face and hands, pierce the clothes with their long sucker in the form of a needle, and, getting into the mouth and nostrils, set you coughing and sneezing whenever you attempt to speak in the open air.

And it was reassuring to remember that even Spruce had been temporarily oppressed on this very river. As he wrote to Sir William Hooker from San Carlos on 19 March 1854:

I calculated on spending a month in the voyage up the Casiquiare, but after passing the mouth of Lake Vasiva mosquitoes began to be so abundant that my Indians became very impatient of stoppages. So long as we continued in motion, comparatively few mosquitoes congregated in the piragoa, but when we stopped to cook or gather flowers they were almost insupportable, and the cabin especially became like a beehive. You will easily understand that, however much my enthusiasm as a naturalist might conduce to render me insensible to suffering and annoyance, I could not help occasionally participating in the feelings of my sailors....

Driven out by the droplets of meat-vapour saturating the already hot and humid and sweat-laden air, I went for a stroll round the village and decided to send Simon with Juan and Chimo to San Carlos on a two-day journey to collect fresh stores; to use the time myself to search for cock-of-the-rocks across the river with Culimacaré, and, when Simon returned, to journey up the Siapa and Emoni rivers to find the unvisited group of Yanomami.

Early next morning, in the dark, I crept out behind our hut to the yucca plantation for a shit; flicking on my torch, I did my usual cursory erogenous zone-check – and then I looked again. In the cold dawn, the secret nightmare had finally clasped me: the Great Fear had come to stay. My penis had turned green. To the touch it felt like a hanging cluster of grapes. Swollen tapir ticks, as big as the top of a thumb, were feeding all down its stem. 'Keep calm,' I repeated out loud; and then I scrabbled at them, pulling them out, dropping them on the ground, popping them under my boot, yelping with pain. They were all over my crutch and the tops of my thighs; I ran with dribbles of blood. I covered myself with half a tube of Savlon from my belt-pouch, and as I walked back to the hut, all sphincters jammed tight with shock, I squelched slightly in my pants.

Yes, said Chimo, laughing over a breakfast of meat and manioc, everybody knew, tapir ticks always climbed up a man's trousers and squeezed in sideways between his belt and his stomach – they went where every women that he, Chimo, had ever known, in sixty years of service, always wanted to get her fingers. The ticks were used to it. That was where they lived. That was the one place on its body which no tapir ever rubbed on a tree.

After breakfast I went for a stroll round the village. The ground was steaming slightly, and in the clear sky high over the Casiquiare a King vulture was soaring, its white belly and the leading edges of its wings catching the sun, its black primaries spread. Near at hand, small boys were trying to blowpipe dickcissels (chattery, sparrow-like birds with yellow throats) out of a palm tree; and, in the centre of the rough square, their elder brothers were already playing football with some sort of gourd. Three girls, probably Culimacaré's sisters, were watching the game from a bench by the doorway of his hut on the far side. Everyone was dressed in shorts, tee shirts and gym shoes, bought in exchange for bundles of palm fibre cut from the jungle (and later made into brooms) at the Colombian trading post beside the junction of the Casiquiare and the Rio Negro.

An old woman, her back bent under an enormous basket full of firewood, her head and neck pushed forward almost parallel to the ground against the weight of her headband carrying-strap, mumbled a greeting as she passed. She disappeared into a large hut near the landing stage, its walls made of reed-slats.

Galvis, scattering a flock of chickens, appeared from behind a hut next to our own quarters.

'Reymono!' he shouted in his squeaky voice. 'Quick! Come and look at this! It's a matamata!'

He unhooked a wicker basket from a support-post under the low eaves of the palm-thatch roof and lowered it, with obvious effort, to the ground. Something large and brown stirred faintly inside. Culimacaré's puppy, Rombo, a Collie-Retriever-South American cross, crept up behind me and began to copulate with my right leg. Galvis untied the lid of the basket and tipped out its heavy cargo: a turtle from prehistory, its neck was massive, hanging in wattles of skin at either side, creased with immeasurable age, laden with colonies of warts. Its shell, perched well back, rose in three separate ridges, each crowned with four contorted peaks; two tiny eyes were set, widely spaced, above the rim of a growth-encrusted mouth, and, between them, there projected a snout like a short worm. Very slowly, the animal straightened its back legs, raised its shell, and began to paddle forward across the mud. Rombo, breaking off in mid-orgasm, fled into the plantation.

Juan joined us, back from his long swim, dressed only in shorts and with his towel slung over his right shoulder. Every exposed bit of his body was covered in white weals, as if he had been hit with a cat-o-nine-tails.

'You're crazy,' I said, 'you'll give yourself a fever.'

'The pain is now very bad,' said Juan, 'but it will be gone already in one hour. I will have only spots of blood. I will now dress. And then' (he gestured at two notched poles beside the hut) 'to distract myself, and if you wish it, I will explain to you the making of manioc.'

'You mad scientist,' I said, 'I would like that very much.'

'In that case,' said Juan, turning to go, 'we will discuss also the fruits of these people. We will ask Chimo.'

'He treats us like children,' muttered Galvis in Spanish, as we recaptured and re-caged the matamata and struggled to hang it back on its peg beneath the eaves. 'He thinks he's so bloody special. Just because he's been to university and gone to North America and learnt to speak English and studied everything. He's still just a Colombian. He should cross the river and go back to his own country. He wants me to dig holes for his carbon. I said *you* are the chief, not him. *You* employed me to cook; I am not a digger of holes! I will not be told what to do by a little Colombian who has no business here! I will return to San Carlos!'

Juan came back and Galvis strutted off, kicking up flecks of mud with his shoes as he went, the crisis unresolved.

'So tell me about this,' I said, running my hand down the worn, notched side of a large, chest-high post. A matching post stood some ten feet away with a vertical series of holes, rather than notches, cut in its side.

'This is an interesting story,' said Juan, picking up two long poles which lay on the ground. 'This is a sebuean. It is not possible to imagine how the Indians made the discovery of manioc. The root of one of the species of yucca they use is poisonous. It is full of cyanide. It kills you – in order to eat it you must soak it and peel it and grind it and mix it with water. You then take that' (he pointed to a long, tightly woven, tapering cylinder of wicker-work with loops top and bottom, which was hanging on a peg) 'put in the wet, ground yucca root, push one pole through the top loop and into the top positions on the two posts, thread the other through the bottom loop and into a hole one end and a notch the other, and then, with all your strength, push down from notch to notch, squeezing out the poison. It drips from the basket into a bowl and you must throw the contents of that bowl well away, where the chickens and the dogs cannot drink it. It is very effective. If cows drink it, they die. You then take the pulp from the basket and roast it, to drive off the remaining poison. Come and see. Come with me. The people here will not mind.'

We walked round to the front of the hut, startling a Yellow-rumped cacique in a wicker basket by the door. Inside the hut, a single room, it was dark and smoky and insufferably hot. As a protection against blackfly and mosquitoes there were no windows. In one corner a large flat pan was raised on stones over a fire. Two girls knelt beside it, one easing logs into the heat, the other constantly spreading and turning a rough sawdust of chips and flakes of manioc in the pan.

'The yucca is ground on this,' said Juan, picking up a thick board from beside the mud-block wall, 'the root is rubbed and rubbed against these little stones set into the wood. This is a poor example, but sometimes they are very old. Sometimes the stones make patterns, pictures of animals from the beliefs and stories of these people.'

As my eyes adapted to the murk I noticed an older woman, very thin, wedged into the far corner, still, watching us. Two little boys, one clutching a midget bow and arrow, played with a lizard on a string at her feet.

'She has malaria,' said Juan. 'Chimo told me. We must tell the student-doctors in San Carlos. They will help.'

Another fire was smouldering to the right of the door, the smoke rising through a reed platform on which lay the neck, the tail, and three legs of a cayman. Against the right-hand wall stood a reed-lattice table piled with a heap of cotton tee shirts, shorts and skirts. Two terrier-like puppies were asleep beneath it.

'We will now see the fruits of these people,' announced Juan, nodding goodbye to the girls. 'We will find Chimo.'

Chimo was sitting on the stool where we had left him, lost in his own thoughts in the fetid guest-hut, lifting strips of tapir meat, with a stick, out of our salted oil-drum container, dropping them into a cauldron of boiling water, and transferring the scalded pieces into a second drum.

'If you touch raw meat with your hands,' said Chimo, confidentially, in the stench of decay, 'it goes bad.'

'Come on,' said Juan, 'you've nearly finished. Come and tell us about the plants.'

Chimo turned off the primus and joined us outside.

Beside the yucca plantation and dotted around the square behind the huts there were coconut trees, and mango and cashew-nut and breadfruit and guama and orange and lemon and plum trees; there were manaca and pijiguao palms; there were pepper bushes, and poma rosa and tamarind and gauva and cucura bushes. Behind the guest-hut itself was a small bristly bush whose leaves, Chimo said (blowing his nose out onto the ground with a finger against each nostril in turn), were ground and boiled, and the resulting infusion used to give the new-born children of the village their first bath. In the plantation of the hut nearest the landing stage, by a reed-cane and palm-thatch chicken coop, was a dark green, chest-high bush, some kind of legume called a varsvaco whose leaves in solution were used to poison fish; a small square of straggly maize (Juan said the soil of Culimacaré must be exceptionally rich); a laurel whose stems were used to make the manioc sieves; a tree whose bark was good for stopping holes in dugouts; and a camasa, a marrow-like plant whose ripe gourds were made into water containers.

Beside Culimacaré's house (a four-room hut, the largest in the village) there were ahuyama, cucumber-like vegetables; a grass-like citronella, a herb used for stomach pains; tupiro plants, for salads; and an onoto bush hung with fruits like young curled-up hedgehogs, whose seeds produce the bright red dye used to paint faces and bodies and baskets and cloth. Culimacaré's mother (big and cuddly) was roasting manioc in a huge budare, a yard-square baking pan, raking the grains back and forth with a wooden spatula; she worked, over her fire, in an open shelter, well away from the house.

'It's safer that way,' said Chimo. 'But she feeds her family, and also she feeds the mosquitoes and zancudos. She bakes manioc and she gives blood.'

By the back door of the house there hung a small wicker cage and in it sat the bird for which we had searched in vain on the climb to Neblina: a young, olive-brown, bright-eyed male cock-of-the-rock, his crest only a quarter developed but already distinctive, springing from an arc spanning from the back of his head to the front of his eye and falling forward over his bill. Soon he would turn bright orange, like the bird which Wallace admired in a thicket on the Brazilian side of the Rio Negro in 1850, 'shining out like a mass of brilliant flame'.

'Chimo, where did they find this?'

'The birds live here,' said Chimo, his large wizened face breaking into his semi-toothless smile. 'They live across the river round the big rock. Culimacaré will know where.'

That evening, sitting on benches in the guest-hut, eating manioc and tapir stew, we made plans. Culimacaré and his brother agreed to take me to see wild cock-of-the-rocks in the morning. Simon (himself eating our last tin of spam and part of our last packet of rice) agreed to take Juan and Chimo and six hundred pounds in small-denomination bolivar notes to buy stores in San Carlos, one day's travel away. We decided that we needed coffee, sugar, salt, cornmeal, oats, spaghetti, rice, tins of meat, cooking oil, tomato ketchup, cans of dried milk, cans of margarine, torch batteries, lighters, cartridges, motor oil, kerosene and petrol; and, in the unlikely event that we should actually find the Yanomami, lengths of red cloth (no other colour would do), boxes of No. 12 hooks, fishing line, combs and mirrors; and (Chimo insisted) for the Curipaco of Culimacaré (and himself) we must provide extraordinary quantities of beer, rum and aguardiente for the farewell party, before we all went to our deaths.

We fell asleep to the gentle burr of cicadas in the plantation, the *peeep-peeep* of small frogs around the landing stage, and the patter of rain on the palm-thatch roof.

The next morning, the temperature seemed to have dropped two or three degrees, the sky was dark grey with low cloud and a fine mist hung in the air, unmoving.

'It's an aparo day,' said Chimo, as we carried our two outboard motors down to the dugouts. 'The aparo is a frog who takes his young on his back. Today we are cold because the aparo is moving from the south to the north. Next month, once again, we will be cold, because the aparo will be moving from north to south.'

'Can we find one?' I said.

'No,' said Juan. 'No one ever sees the aparo. He is a legend of these people.'

'When I was young,' said Chimo, 'we could have asked the old men about the aparo. But now they are dead. Now no one can tell where the aparo goes.'

Chimo, Juan and Simon set off down the Casiquiare, bound for the Rio Negro and all the delights of San Carlos. Simon, overwhelmed by one of his sudden accesses of *joie de vivre*, waved until he was out of sight. A pair of startled Orange-winged parrots crossed the river from right to left, flying very fast and staying close together, each rapid, stiff beat of their rounded wings flashing a patch of orange-scarlet through the drizzle.

Culimacaré, his younger brother and I fixed the small Yamaha to our second dugout. Culimacaré took the helm, resplendent in newly-scrubbed tee shirt and trousers, and we made our way across and slightly downriver towards the Great Rock on the opposite bank.

We landed by a little path which led up to an open-sided palm-thatch shelter.

'We rest here when we come to gather palm fruits,' said Culimacaré, pausing to discuss the route in Curipaco with his brother.

The path wound up, over and between moss-covered boulders, to the base of the cliff. The rock had been worn smooth by millions of years of rain storms and marked by odd, dirty-white, cascading stains. From a ledge halfway up its swelling mass two birds with bright chestnut stomachs were hawking insects. Thrush-size, with heavy bills, they flew like small falcons on long, tapering wings, making quick dashes out from the rock face and returning to the same perch; I recognised them from their distinctive presence in the otherwise distressingly similar ranks of flycatchers in Schauensee: Cliff fly-catchers. And if you were going to be a flycatcher, I thought, as I scratched my blackfly bites (each one now with a blister on top), then this was certainly the right place to set up a practice.

We climbed further, among the ferns and small palms, the path twisting past great blocks of stone, themselves hung about with a woody rigging that had grown down from the thick-leaved arums clustered on their tops – which must be, I realised, the very plants which Spruce found here 'in such quantities that it is scarcely possible to thread through their pendulous roots'.

Culimacaré's brother stopped beneath an enormous overhang of thick rock. The recess was framed, as one looked out, by flutings of stone, inverted crenellations, upside-down battlements worn by water falling unevenly over its edge. The ground was bare and, compared with the spongy mass of leaves and rootlets outside, almost dry. To one side was an odd, greenish, seat-high stone, polished smooth and with a hand's-width ringed channel worn in its centre. The brothers spoke in Curipaco, and then Culimacaré turned to me, his left hand half-clenched and jigging up and down, his index finger crooked and pointing forward.

'This is a very old place,' he said. 'Other Indians lived here before

131

we came. Look at this' — he pushed the curved end of his long machete blade into the ground with his right hand and trowelled up the soil — 'see — we find their pots for cooking on the fire.'

I bent down and, sifting the small pile of disturbed earth, found two heavy fragments of thick pottery. I pocketed them, to add to Juan's collection.

Higher up, we came to a fissure at the back of the main rock and, to its right, another cave-like overhang with a drop of thirty or forty feet, in front of it, to more boulders below. Culimacaré's brother squatted down quietly and pointed into the gloom. We followed, peering at the rough back wall. High up, as my eyes adjusted, a rock-coloured mud nest formed itself, seemingly stuck straight onto the granite. Two glinting spots of reflected light peered back at us. Above them was a short dull crest, and at the back of the nest a dark, squared tail projected.

'Come on,' whispered Culimacaré, grinning with toothless triumph, 'my brother will find another one.'

Swinging on hanging roots, scrambling over the broken rocks with extraordinary agility, the two Curipaco disappeared into the fissure. I followed as best I could, knocking myself against the tight sides, glancing apprehensively at the irregular jumble of rocks jammed in the canyon itself and, high above our heads, lodged across its upper rims. Eventually, much bruised, we emerged onto a small open platform above a semi-circular cliff. A thin palm, its fronds just above our heads, reached up from the ground below. Its trunk was about five feet away, just out of reach. The Curipaco sprang out onto it, one after the other, without looking round, and, gripping in an orderly and alternate fashion with hands and feet, lowered themselves to earth. Remembering that at such moments thinking about things in general is not supposed to help, I jumped. The tree braced itself, swung on its axis, and punched me in the crutch. The rocks danced round the edge of my field of vision. The ground came up and kicked me in the buttocks.

'Keep quiet,' hissed Culimacaré, looking quite angry, 'we want to see the bird.'

I stood up, put a hand down a pocket to check that I was still intact, and followed the others. My boots flapped as I walked. Already rotting, they had both split along the insteps. I congratulated myself on having brought a spare pair in one of the kit-bags.

In a cave to the left there was another nest. It, too, was stuck high up on the back wall, but there was more light and we could edge closer. The bird was agitated, probably as upset as I was by my treatment from the palm tree. Dun-coloured, she clacked her yellow-brown bill as we approached.

'Will we see the male if we wait?' I whispered.

'No,' said Culimacaré, 'the macho is a bad husband. He plays in the forest. He never comes near the house.'

We withdrew quietly, without forcing her to fly off the clay and palm-fibre and cock-of-the-rock-spit nest, and climbed into another fissure, slightly wider than the first. Almost at once bats began to hurtle past us; one of them, confused, presumably, by the strong echo-location signals bouncing back to its receivers from the granite walls to either side, crashed into my jaw. Dazed, he clung for a moment to my shirt front, his fur black and thick, rich and shiny. He was much bigger than the small grey bats, our companions on the Baria river.

'Hold your arm in front of your face,' said Culimacaré. 'Here the bats have a big village.'

Pausing in front of a black hole in the rock, Culimacaré's brother lobbed in a small stone. Before it had stopped clattering down, the air was full of bats zig-zagging out of the entrance and down the fissure, the beating skin of their wings, as they passed us, sounding like loose canvas in a high wind. We made our own way out through a smaller crack, climbed over the boulders and, by the thick growth of the riverside, past the thorn-ringed trunks of palms and the flanks of buttressed trees, beneath the interlocking coils of lianas twisting up to the light and across the spongy clumps of surface roots, we emerged where our boat lay moored.

That evening, after a supper of tapir meat, I lay in my hammock and re-read parts of Charlie's photocopy of Napoleon A. Chagnon's *Yanomamo, the fierce people* (1968). I liked the alarm which George and Louise Spindler's foreword generated:

> This is indeed a book about a fierce people. Yanamamo culture, in its major focus, reverses the meanings of 'good' and 'desirable' as phrased in the ideal postulates of the Judaic-Christian tradition. A high capacity for rage, a quick flash point, and a willingness to use violence to obtain one's ends are considered desirable traits. Much

of the behaviour of the Yanomamo can be described as brutal, cruel, treacherous, in the value-laden terms of our own vocabulary. The Yanomamo themselves, however ... do not all appear to be mean and treacherous. As individuals, they seem to be people playing their own cultural game, with internal feelings that at times may be quite divergent from the demands placed upon them by their culture.

I must remember to remember, I thought, when lying on the jungle floor, porcupined with six-foot arrows (as the curare is telling the muscles of the diaphragm and the heart to relax, to take it easy after all these years) that the individual Yanomami did not really mean it. And anyway, no warning could be clearer than Chagnon's summary:

> The thing that impressed me most was the importance of aggression in their culture. I had the opportunity to witness a good many incidents that expressed individual vindictiveness on the one hand and collective bellicosity on the other. These ranged in seriousness from the ordinary incidents of wife beating and chest pounding to dueling and organized raiding by parties that set out with the intention of ambushing and killing men from enemy villages.

I also had with me Charlie's photocopy, in English translation, of Jacques Lizot's very different but equally impressive (and equally disturbing) account of Yanomami life and myth, *Le cercle des feux: Faits et dits des Indiens Yanomami* (1976). Lizot, unlike Chagnon, keeps himself well clear of his anthropological descriptions. And it was the sinister resonance of the explanation for this silence which reverberated in my skull: 'I could of course have evoked my own experience of life among the Indians, but I wanted to speak of other things, for strictly personal reasons: I am not yet ready to speak of the terrible shock that this experience was for me ... perhaps I will never be able to speak of these experiences, for I would have to evoke so many harrowing things that touch my inner being....'

Well, whatever the terrible shocks that Lizot experienced may have been, I thought, the Indians have suffered worse. Humboldt's account of the exploits of the missionary of San Fernando could stand for them all, before and since. In 1797 this monk set out with

his converted Indians on a soul-saving expedition to the banks of the
Rio Guaviare, where they found

in an Indian hut a Guahiba mother with three children, two of
whom were still infants. They were occupied in preparing the flour
of cassava. Resistance was impossible; the father was gone to fish,
and the mother tried in vain to flee with her children. Scarcely had
she reached the savannah, when she was seized by the Indians of
the mission, who go to *hunt men*. The mother and her children
were bound, and dragged to the bank of the river. Had the mother
made too violent a resistance, the Indians would have killed her,
for every thing is permitted when they go to the conquest of souls
(*à la conquista espiritual*), and it is children in particular they seek
to capture, in order to treat them in the mission as *poitos*, or slaves
of the Christians. The prisoners were carried to San Fernando in
the hope, that the mother would be unable to find her way back
to her home by land. Far from those children who had accompanied
their father on the day in which she had been carried off, this
unhappy woman shewed signs of the deepest despair. She
attempted to take back to her family the children, who had been
snatched away by the missionary; and fled with them repeatedly
from the village of San Fernando, but the Indians never failed to
seize her anew; and the missionary, after having caused her to be
mercilessly beaten, took the cruel resolution of separating the
mother from the two children, who had been carried off with her.
She was conveyed alone toward the missions of the Rio Negro,
going up the Atabapo. Slightly bound, she was seated at the bow
of the boat, ignorant of the fate that awaited her; but she judged
by the direction of the Sun, that she was removing farther and
farther from her hut and her native country. She succeeded in
breaking her bonds, threw herself into the water, and swam to the
left bank of the Atabapo. The current carried her to a shelf of rock,
which bears her name to this day. She landed, and took shelter in
the woods, but the president of the missions ordered the Indians
to row to the shore, and follow the traces of the Guahiba. In the
evening she was brought back. Stretched upon the rock (*la Piedra
de la Madre*) a cruel punishment was inflicted on her with those
straps of manatee leather, which serve for whips in that country,
and with which the alcades are always furnished. This unhappy
woman, her hands tied behind her back with strong stalks of

mavacure, was then dragged to the mission of Javita.

She was there thrown into one of the caravan-seras that are called *Casa del Rey*. It was the rainy season, and the night was profoundly dark. Forests till then believed to be impenetrable separated the mission of Javita from that of San Fernando, which was twenty-five leagues distant in a straight line. No other path is known than that of the rivers; no man ever attempted to go by land from one village to another, were they only a few leagues apart. But such difficulties do not stop a mother, who is separated from her children. Her children are at San Fernando de Atabapo; she must find them again, she must execute her project of delivering them from the hands of Christians, of bringing them back to their father on the banks of the Guaviare. The Guahiba was carelessly guarded in the caravansera. Her arms being wounded, the Indians of Javita had loosened her bonds, unknown to the missionary and the alcades. She succeeded by the help of her teeth in breaking them entirely; disappeared during the night; and at the fourth rising Sun was seen at the mission of San Fernando, hovering around the hut where her children were confined. We pressed the missionary to tell us, whether the Guahiba had peacefully enjoyed the happiness of remaining with her children; and if any repentance had followed this excess of cruelty. He would not satisfy our curiosity; but at our return from the Rio Negro we learnt, that the Indian mother was not allowed time to cure her wounds, but was again separated from her children, and sent to one of the missions of the Upper Oroonoko. There she died, refusing all kind of nourishment, as the savages do in great calamities.

The following evening, as I sat outside our hut, covered in insect repellent, smoking my pipe and reading Chagnon, Culimacaré broke off the game of football he was playing with his brother and three sisters.

'There's a motor coming,' he said, pointing to the west. 'They're coming back.'

Half an hour later I heard the noise myself.

Simon, transformed, sitting upright and eager in the middle of the dugout, was shouting even as Chimo brought the boat to shore.

'We've got almost everything! I had the best evening of my life!'

'So what happened?' I said, as we unloaded crates of Brazilian aguardiente and rum and beer, and all kinds of foods which suddenly seemed equally rare and exotic and exciting, like porridge oats.

'Well, we bought food from the Guardia,' said Simon, his features looking less taut beneath his straggling beard, his eyes less sunk and haunted. 'We've even got vegetables, potatoes and *onions*. And there are two new student-doctors in the dispensary in San Carlos. And they speak *English*. And one's a girl. And she's the most beautiful girl I've ever seen. And they asked us to supper. And we sat on chairs and ate real chicken and drank beer and listened to *music*. Bach and things. All kinds of music. And I talked and talked *to other people*.'

'What did you talk about?'

'About you,' said Simon, with a sudden grin, 'about how mad you are.'

After dark, when we had distributed the last of our tapir meat to every family in the village, we held a party in Culimacaré's house. The biggest hut, it had an extra room for receiving guests, bare and bleak, with a table in one corner and benches round the walls. I lined up our bottles of aguardiente, according to Chimo's instructions, in the middle of the table: they gleamed evilly in the light of our paraffin-wick lamp, their labels proclaiming CANINHA TATUZINHO, red on yellow, beneath a black, stylised coatimundi, who was winking, and sticking his snout into a clump of sugar cane.

The Curipaco slipped into the room, out of the darkness, the men sitting on the bench nearest the door, the women beside the entrance to the inner room. I filled our mugs with aguardiente and the Indians passed them from hand to hand, everyone, including the women, taking urgent gulps at the clear spirit. Chimo, huge, stately, benign, the pipe I had given him clamped between his gums, sat in the centre of the main bench, his legs apart, his left hand retaining a cup for his own use, his right passing on the communal mugs, from which he also drank.

Culimacaré fetched the enormous cassette player which he had bought in the Colombian shop with his advance payment for the journey, and inserted his only tape, a Venezuelan pop song. To its rhythms, Galvis and Culimacaré's youngest sister led the room in a jigging waltz-shuffle dance. Chimo, pulling two spoons out of his pocket, stood up, put one leg on the bench, opposed the spoons in one hand and beat time between his knee and his free palm. I danced first with the old woman who had passed me with her crushing load of firewood. Her back bent even when at rest, her hands, in mine, as rough and ridged and calloused as a cayman's skin, she glanced up, once, a great grin cracking across her wrinkles.

'Chimo,' I said, as we started on the second crate of aguardiente and the tape spun itself out for the fiftieth time, 'are there any Curipaco songs?'

'Not here,' said Chimo, red-eyed, blowing his nose with one hand, shaking the snot to the floor, and drying his fingers by running them through his frizzled hair. 'The Curipaco in Colombia may know some songs; but here they are all forgotten.'

Simon, I noticed, was not dancing. He sat apart, his head between his hands, staring at the floor. Culimacaré, noticing too, went and sat beside him.

'This is *my house*,' said Culimacaré, 'you are welcome here,' and then he lay down on the earth floor and was easily and copiously sick. His sisters at once stopped dancing and carried him into the back room. Simon got up and left.

The Curipaco were taking a rare holiday from themselves, sliding into oblivion, falling asleep in corners. I, too, decided it was time to leave, and made my way back across the mud of the square through a violent rainstorm.

Inside the guest hut Juan was sitting on a bench, looking agitated. Simon lay in his hammock, a bottle of rum open beside him.

'I thought we were preserving that for our nightly tots,' I said, 'to keep our courage up as we approach the Yanomami. To stop us thinking' (and, on the drunken spur of the moment, this seemed excruciatingly funny) 'of our proper place, in the mornings, in the Yanomarmalade, and, at tea-time, in the Yanomarmite.'

'God,' said Simon, without a smile, 'what a stupid fifth-form joke.'

'I have bad news,' said Juan to me, 'you have made a mistake. You gave these people alcohol. They do not know how to use it. They get sick. We agreed not to tell you, but now it is my duty. When we were in San Carlos the son of Pablo came to see us. He is fourteen. His sister is twelve. They are starving. They have no food. The money you gave Pablo for half his wages when the expedition started – you remember, Redmon, he spent the night before we left until he was so drunk he lay on the ground and then his friends rob him. So now we gave enough money to keep his son and daughter alive and spent less on your stores. Right now, again, Pablo is drunk. He lies in the mud outside. He offers to fight us all and then he cries for his wife.'

'His wife?'

'He often cries for his wife. Sometimes he talks in his sleep. You do not understand these people. They are children. They do not fight misfortune. His wife — he always cries for his drowned wife when he is drunk. Pablo cannot adjust. He is a strong man. A good worker. But all his work goes to drink. And Valentine — he is like-wise. The reason too is drink and his wife. He beats her when he is drunk.'

'Okay,' I said, 'so I won't do it again. They can recover tomorrow, and the next day if they need it, and then we'll head up the Siapa and there'll be no more drink. Anyway — we've only got two bottles of rum and a crate of beer left. We'll soon be with the Yanomami, blasted on nothing but yoppo.'

'It is well known,' said Juan, 'that yoppo is a drug that damages the brain.'

'You're welcome to it,' said Simon suddenly, with extraordinary vehemence, sitting up in his hammock, the rum bottle clutched in his hand. 'I won't be there. I won't be coming.'

'What?' I said, my stomach seeming to tie a knot in itself.

'Why the hell should I? Why the hell should I put up with all this? That's what I want to know! You tell me! I can't stand it. Why should I? Why should I be stung by ants and wasps and hornets and bees all day? I've been thinking about it. It's nothing but rain and mos-quitoes and the same bloody awful trees and endless rivers and disgusting food and being wet all the time. There's no comradeship. There's no wine and no women and no song and nowhere sensible to shit.'

'I'm sorry,' I said, 'you'll think differently in the morning.'

'No I bloody won't,' said Simon, his eyes white in the murk, 'oh no I bloody well won't! I've been thinking about it *for four weeks*. And when I had that supper with the doctors in San Carlos I realised exactly what I was going to do. I only came back to tell you properly. It's not that I'm frightened. It's not really your fault. *It's just that I can't bear to go back in there*' (he waved the bottle in the direction of the landing-stage and the uncut jungle) 'and why the hell should I?'

'Do you think you are so unstable already,' said Juan, in his most precise way, his beard outlined in the light of the kerosene lamp, pressed forward in interrogation, 'because of the sudden withdrawal of drugs and alcohol on this journey?'

'You stupid dago,' said Simon, exasperated, 'how the hell would I know?'

'Don't do it,' I said. 'You'll feel bad about it later. About deserting me.'

'Redmond,' said Simon, relaxing, 'I'll handle all that with the first pint of cognac.'

'Don't be silly. You'll never forgive yourself.'

'Oh yes I damn well will. I have already. Redmond – I've cried four times in my adult life. Once when my father died; once when my wife left me; once when Pinky my cat was run over in front of me; and every night when we were lost up that stinking pitsville of a swamp.'

'What about the Yanomami? What about your pictures?'

'I don't want to see the Yanomami. *I can't stand all the poverty.* These people are bad enough. *They don't own anything.* And anyway, my cameras are totally, but totally full of mould and gunge and parasites, and the odd fish too, I shouldn't wonder. It's the pits. I can hear the films turn to soup as I wind them on. But I've worked it out – I'll leave you the manual Minolta I haven't used, in the sealed bag; the small zoom; the flashgun; and all the remaining black-and-white rolls. Then with your Nikonos as well you'll be ready for anything. It's different for you, all this. You've got no taste-buds at all. You think everything's wonderful. You wouldn't know a good meal if I shoved one down your throat. You're a fat brute. You're about as sensitive as a rhinoceros. And there again, you're manic on top of it. You get excited every time you see a new bird. Whereas me, in all honesty, Redmond, to be totally frank with you, I just think, well, *there goes another fucking bird.*'

'What will you do,' I said, suddenly envious, 'when you get home?'

'I will drink *top-class* wine,' said Simon, '*in huge quantities.* I'll take Liz and the kids to Portugal for a holiday. And when we come back we'll have pork and beef, on alternate Sundays, for family lunch. But I'll always do the potatoes because Liz never gets them quite crispy enough, just round the edges, know what I mean? In fact, now I come to think of it, I'll damn well marry her. We'll buy a decent house together, *well away from you.* And I'll go back to the casino and graft like a shitcake and never ever complain about anything ever again.'

The next afternoon, when they were sober enough to walk, Chimo and Pablo took Simon downriver to the army post at Solano, whence the resident marines gave him a lift to San Carlos.

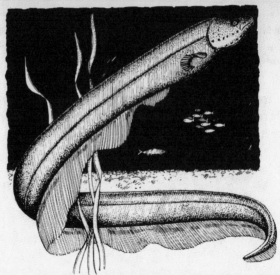

Electric Eel

12

Watched by a flock of forty-eight cattle egrets (pure white and absurdly clean) who would flap laboriously into the air when alarmed, circle low, and drop down again at some forty yards' distance, we spent a further day skulking near the plantation, creeping between the yucca plants, squatting amongst the pineapples, hiding behind bushes whose names were temporarily of no interest whatever, retching at the mouth and at the anus, our intestines driven to violent and constant peristalsis by bad tapir meat or good aguardiente or both.

The day after, still weak but already half-cured by Imodium, we repaired the leaks in the two dugouts, stuffing pieces of two of my rotted shirts into the lengthwise slits in the wood and caulking them over with Chimo's pitch, watched by the women who came to wash their clothes in the river and to scrub them on a rough board by the landing-stage; by four little boys who came to swim; and, from a wicker basket half-submerged in the shallows, by three young mata-mata, two baby chipiro (ordinary-looking turtles with red streaks on either side of the head) and two tortuga (ditto, with yellow streaks).

The following morning we linked the dugouts together, loaded the stores, waved goodbye to the assembled Curipaco, and set off upriver to search for the Fierce People.

*

'I am sure that one day we will arrive to the Yanomami,' said Juan, sitting beside me between the two mounds of tarpaulin-covered cargo in the centre of Chimo's dugout. 'Chimo will know how to help us. We will see Gabriel, his friend. Gabriel is a *caboclo*, a settler from Brazil. He has a hut and a small clearing at Porvenir, and he trades with the Yanomami on the Siapa. We will make our campament with him.'

Galvis sat opposite us in the other boat, still making his way through an ancient copy of the *Reader's Digest* in Spanish; Valentine and Culimacaré perched as lookouts in the two bows; and Pablo, wrapped in his blue plastic waterproof cape, fell asleep by the other, unused motor. Chimo, the veteran inland sailor, bound for a river whose upper reaches were unknown even to him, took the helm, hour upon hour without a rest, his pipe clenched in his gums, its bowl stuffed from his fresh supply of Alligator brand Brazilian tobacco, the strongest mixture known to man.

Even under the drab sky of an *aparo* day, the Casiquiare seemed extraordinarily beautiful. We were on the move again. The small wake from the puttering motor spread out behind us on the sluggish, dirty-brown, flood-swollen waters.

We kept close to the bank to avoid the central current, and every three or four miles we would disturb a solitary White-necked heron perched low down beside the water.

Halfway through the morning Culimacaré suddenly shouted and pointed high up into a tree ahead. Chimo slowed the engine and brought the boats to a standstill, hanging in the current. 'Pereza!' he said.

I trained the binoculars where everyone else was looking. A scraggy, grey-green clump of leaves seemed to be on the move near the crown of foliage. But the bundle appeared to have white stripes on its underside and eventually, a small, wide, black face with a bulbous nose and a white streak on its forehead came into focus.

'It's a sloth!' said Juan. 'It's a Three-toed sloth!'

'Quiet!' I said. (The toes I glimpsed looked more like meat hooks).

The animal stretched itself front and rear and, in a surprisingly short time, gained the cover of a large tuft of bromeliads, in a fork of the tree, and disappeared from view.

In the early afternoon we rounded a bend and swung into a straight stretch of river: there, halfway up, was Gabriel's settlement. Boldly marked 'Porvenir' on our CODESUR map, it was nothing but a small landing stage (to which two dugouts were tied), a shelter, a hut and two outbuildings.

Gabriel, his wife (I think), his son, his daughter, and four attendant children came out to greet us. Five mealy parrots (large, green, resentful), two dogs (whippet-like, wounded, abject) and one Red-and-green macaw (scarlet, blue and friendly) completed the population of Porvenir.

We unloaded our stove and cooking pots and one box of stores.

'Gabriel,' said Chimo, 'tonight we make a fat supper. We have many things to discuss.'

Gabriel was about sixty, his face cragged and very dark, his body squat, his speech and movements slow. I dug about in my bergen, found the last bottle of rum which I had hidden from Simon (and everyone else) and presented it to him. He ran his big hands over the bottle, held it up against the light as if to check its colour, and bore it off round the back of his hut. His wife followed him. The hut itself was a curious construction: palm thatched on the roof and down the walls, in layers across a palisade of stakes, which were driven in so close they pressed against each other. It was without windows and its hinged front door was likewise thatched; it was mosquito-proof.

We sat on lashed-pole benches outside and chatted to Gabriel's daughter and his son, Clemente. The two dark-skinned boys stood close up against their mother's knees.

'These are my children,' she said. 'My husband left me, so I came back here to live with my father. These' (she nodded towards the two light-skinned, bright eyed boys – perhaps five or six years old – who stood slightly apart from her) 'are Choris. The Yanomami, the Siapateris, brought them to us. Their parents are dead. They were not wanted. Gabi will look after them. They help in the canuco.'

A dog sniffed my trousers and I stroked its head. Gabriel's daughter, in one smooth movement, picked up a log and brought it down on the dog's back. The animal howled terribly, and hobbled off to lick itself.

Gabriel and his wife returned, she carrying a bowl of manioc and water, he holding two freshly killed chickens by their necks.

'Tonight we will eat like the King of Spain,' said Galvis, taking the scraggy birds and beginning to pluck them. 'We will have chicken and rice and spaghetti.'

'And lao-lao,' said Pablo, pointing with his lips at a pile of cylindrical wooden floats. 'Reymono must try the big catfish.'

'You take Chimo and Pablo for the fishing,' said Juan to me, 'and I will take Culimacaré and Valentine and go to dig for carbon beyond Gabriel's conuco. But if you find the giant catfish, Redmon, be careful. It can grow two metres long and when it is in the river no one takes a bath far from the bank. It drags children to the bottom of the river and there it eats them.'

We passed round the big wooden bowl of manioc, swilled in a mouthful of sawdust solution each, loaded the floats into the dugout, took some rotten piranha from Clemente's bait-store in his own canoe (in exchange for a promised lift to his downstream fish trap later) and set off upriver. Pablo sat in the bow, a bark-paper cigarette in the corner of his mouth, unravelling the lines on the floats, cutting the piranha into sections and impaling the pieces on the enormous hooks. Two miles upstream Chimo swung the dugout over to the left bank and we then travelled right across the river, Pablo throwing in one of his lines every twenty yards or so. The floats bobbed in the choppy current, their silver-painted ends glistening. We motored a little way upriver, moved into the centre, and shut off the engine.

The boat turned broadside gently, the water lapping against its hull. A Screaming piha called.

A Ringed kingfisher, crossing the river low and straight and fast, altered course to have a look at us, banking over the boat, the late afternoon sun briefly catching his chestnut stomach before he flew off, blue and white.

We drifted down to Porvenir, where Clemente was standing on the landing-stage, waving. Chimo started the engine and we retrieved the floats; almost all the baits had gone.

'Nothing but piranha,' said Pablo, imitating sets of nibbling teeth with his fingers. 'The big fish are asleep.'

We picked up Clemente (who was carrying a fine-mesh wicker basket full of palm-fruit and a long harpoon with three barbed prongs) and motored downriver to his fish-trap. It was set well in to the left bank beneath the thick overhang of branches and dangling lianas. Fish swimming upstream, drawn by the smell of rotting fruit, would be edged out from the bank by a long fence of stakes, channelled into a wooden corral, and admitted, via a narrow gap, into a large semi-circular holding pool on whose surface ripe moriche palm-fruit lay invitingly, their red leathery scales half rotted away, their cheese-like flesh exposed.

Clemente climbed carefully onto a wooden ledge, made of lashed poles, which ran round the wall of stakes about two feet above the water. He pulled a small stake-door across the gap, held onto the structure with one hand and his wooden harpoon with the other, and, leaning out, prodded the opaque pool. The trap came to life. A long, sinuous, grey-brown shape rose up from beneath and seemed to uncoil across the whole surface at once.

'Wheeeee!' sang Chimo, 'temblador! Hold your pinga, Clementine! You fall in – you'll never fuck a pig again!'

Clemente grinned, crooked one leg around a stake and stabbed the harpoon into the water with both hands. He finally connected amidst a violent splashing, transfixing the electric eel behind its head. Then, with great difficulty, his muscles bunched, he hauled it out. It hung straight down from the end of the harpoon, as thick as a leg and about five feet long, its eyes tiny, its body a slimy cylinder with an anal fin running from the tip of its tail to its throat. Clemente handed it to me, still attached to the harpoon, over the fence of stakes; its open mouth was dark orange inside. I passed it to Chimo in the stern; he lowered the body into a bush on the bank and detached the harpoon with a sharp pull.

Clemente emptied his basket of palm-fruit into the pool and, still clutching the basket, jumped in and disappeared. He surfaced bearing two half-chewed piranhas.

'The temblador has eaten our supper,' he said.

Diving again, he brought up two limp, electrocuted but intact piranha, a pavón, and a bocachico.

Back at Porvenir, we sat round Galvis's cooking fire beneath the open shelter. We ate fish soup and manioc and rice and spaghetti; and then we ate chicken soup and manioc and rice and spaghetti.

'Looks like we see the Yanomami tomorrow,' said Juan. 'A group of Siapateri has been here. They bring their baskets to Gabriel to trade for machetes and they help him in his plantation. They left three days ago. They have a big heavy bongo which they paddle very slowly. They stop whenever they see a palm in fruit or hear the peccary in the forest. They are not in a hurry. Their idea of time, Redmon, is different from ours. We will catch them tomorrow.'

'And then what?'

'Then Gabriel says you must give them food and your presents of beads. And Jarivanau, the chief of this little group, he will take you to the people in the centre, far away, beyond the Emoni river.'

'What if they kidnap us?' said Galvis.

'No one would kidnap you,' said Chimo, 'your tits are too small.'

'They kidnapped my aunt,' said Gabriel's daughter, matter-of-factly. 'Her name is Helena Valero. They took her away for twenty-two years. She had four sons. It is well known. But now we have no news of her.'

'It's true,' said Juan. 'An Italian professor wrote a book about it. If this expedition ever returns, if I ever see Caracas again, I will find you the reference.'

'Cheer up, Juan,' I said, putting my hand on his shoulder. 'What do you think they'll do to you?'

'Do not patron me,' said Juan, tensing, his eyes flashing, pushing my hand away. 'Just because you've been to English Borneo, you think you know this jungle! Yes you do!' (He was almost shouting.) 'You are ignorant! The real, untouched Yanomami are not your English gentlemen. You think it's easy. You say we will do this Juan, we will do that Chimo, we will find the Yanomami. We will give them presents. Why should they want your presents? You know nothing! In Brazil, the poor white settlers take their land. They hunt the animals in the forest that belongs to them. They kill the Yanomami like wild pigs. And now, on the Cauaburi, some Brazilians have traded shotguns to the Yanomami. The trappers shoot at them. The missionaries kill their culture. So now the Yanomami shoot back. They hide on the banks of their rivers and they shoot at the trappers. They shoot with curare arrows and with shotguns. And why not? This is not a kind country. My own country is not a kind country. It never has been. Here, Redmon, the Yanomami have only two friends – Jacques Lizot and Napoleon Chagnon. And the Yanomami on the Emoni do not know either of them – and there are no nice fat policemen from England on their bicycles, with whistles, and little sticks in their belts.'

There was a pause. I was silent.

'I am sorry,' said Juan, getting up. 'I am angry. I will go and sling my hammock in Gabriel's room. I will finish my supper in Gabriel's house.'

The banquet broke up. Chimo, Valentine, Galvis and Culimacaré slung their hammocks from the post of the shelter, around the central fire. Gabriel picked up my bergen and led me to his hut. Stopping outside he took my arm. The bright, skewed rectangle of the Southern Cross was extraordinarily clear.

'Listen to me,' he said. 'You will be all right. Jarivanau is a good friend of mine. I know the Siapateri well. They visit me, and they visit the mission at Esmeralda on the Orinoco. They were once Emoniteri, but they quarrelled in the tribe. There was a great fight over women and many men were killed. Jarivanau and his relations moved down to the Siapa. They were too few to fight any more. You must say you know Gabi. You will be all right.'

In Gabriel's hut, in his front room, Juan was already half-asleep in his hammock. An oil lamp burned on a small table in a corner. The stake walls were covered in hundreds of pictures, cut from magazines, every one a photograph of the Pope on his visit to South America. On the earth floor there was a pile of curious baskets, dull red, decorated with black roundels. Some were shaped like helmets, others like shallow fruit bowls.

'What are those?'

'The Yanomami make them,' said Gabriel. 'They weave them from the mamure vine. They split it with their teeth. They trade with me for axes and machetes. My brother brings me many things from Brazil in his covered bongo, and in exchange he takes the baskets.'

Gabriel showed me where to hang my hammock and then withdrew through a narrow strip-curtain doorway to join his family in the inner room.

I blew out the light, climbed into my hammock and fell asleep; and I dreamed, all night long, or so it felt, that I was running through the jungle pursued by the Yanomami, each one armed with an electric eel.

Black Scorpion

13

I woke to the sound of heavy rain; and I was greeted outside by Galvis who was sheltering under the palm-thatch eaves.

'I will stay here,' he said. 'This journey will be very dangerous. It is not sensible. In San Carlos I love my son and I love my daughter and I am fond of my wife, too; I wish to see them again. Gabriel's brother will take me back when he comes in his bongo. And besides, I do not wish to dig for carbon. I do not want to work for Juan.'

'Okay. Forget the carbon. Will you come for my sake?'

'Of course not,' said Galvis.

'500 bolivares?'

'Done,' said Galvis, shaking me by the hand.

The parrots were wet and miserable; the macaw was wet and miserable; we were wet and miserable. We crowded inside the cooking hut and finished our fish soup, packed the dugouts and set off, hunched under our plastic capes.

After two hours the storm passed; the white, puckered surface of the river regained its normal brown swirl; and we turned into the Siapa. Chimo celebrated in his usual way.

'Tomorrow,' he said, 'I will surprise you Reymono. I have been talking to Gabi. I will show you something by a lake.'

149

'A lake?'

'You wait,' said Chimo, packing his pipe.

As we made our way slowly upriver, clinging close to the left bank (the Siapa near its mouth is almost as wide as the Casiquiare) the clouds of blackfly became denser. Individually so small they were almost invisible, their numbers were such that they formed a continuous, oscillating, dark-grey band about two feet above the water surface.

'No man could paddle on this river,' announced Chimo, spitting insects out of his mouth and turning up the throttle.

An hour or so later, three Swallow-tailed kites appeared briefly over the trees beside us. Wallace's big-bellied palms grew at intervals along the banks.

We rounded a slow bend into a straight stretch and Culimacaré immediately pointed ahead to the right.

'Choris!' he said.

'Mother of God,' said Chimo, 'there they are.'

Through the binoculars I could make out a large bongo with a cargo of naked people; two men paddled at the stern and two at the bow. As we gradually closed with them, the men stood up.

'Whooooo!' they yelled, a high-pitched shout of tremendous force.

'Choris!' said Chimo, when we were twenty yards away. 'Jari-vanau?'

'Jarivanau!' shouted a thick-set man in the stern, pointing at his chest with a jabbing finger and waving us alongside. His head was close-shaved, and, as he bent forward to hold our gunwale, I saw that the top of his skull was ridged and indented with four or five enormous scars.

In their boat, the most decrepit bongo I had ever seen, there were nine men, eleven women, ten children, eight dogs, one cat, one parrot and the rear right leg of an armadillo. Two old women sat in the middle of the dugout weaving baskets; in our honour, they each put on a khaki-coloured man's shirt (probably traded from Gabriel), leaving it open down the front. The younger women squatted with an arm round one or more children; almost everyone had a wadge of tobacco stuffed in the space between the lower gums and lip, distending their mouths, giving them a misleadingly Neanderthal-like profile. They were much lighter-skinned than Pablo or Culimacaré or Valentine or Chimo, much fairer, indeed, than I at first thought; looking closely I realised that they were covered in tiny blood-spots.

They had suffered so badly from the blackfly that there was not a space left anywhere on their bodies for a fresh bite.

Several of the men had drawn black lines and circles on their forehead and cheeks and one of them wore four-inch-long wooden plugs through the holes in his ears. The old women had rouged themselves with red onoto-seed dye. As well as his bow and two arrows, Jarivanau was clutching a narrow reed-cane pipe which was about two and a half feet long and had a small black nozzle at one end. It was, as I recognised from Chagnon's description, a yoppo pipe, a device for blasting a fearsome dose of hallucinogenic stuff up one's nostril.

I pointed at it and mimed holding the nozzle to my nose. Jarivanau grinned and nodded.

'You take that,' said Chimo, as we lashed our dugouts either side of theirs, 'and you'll be one mad Englishman.'

'It damages the brain,' said Pablo.

'The next thing you know,' said Chimo, 'you'll be tying your pinga up with string.'

'Looks that it's very bad,' said Juan, 'it's addictive.'

Jarivanau flashed me an enormous smile and smacked his forehead with his free hand. There was nothing wrong with *his* teeth.

Pablo and Chimo started the two engines and the new convoy, three abreast, moved slowly upriver. The young women near the prow of the bongo passed Galvis a large cooking pot and he filled it with manioc and river water. All the Yanomami drank and then offered the remains to me. It was impossible to refuse such a draught of sawdust and friendship; usually careful to drink only from one of our chlorine-pilled water-bottles, I wondered, irrationally (because we were far from any settlement) just how many parasite eggs I had invited to a hatching in my gut.

'Jarivanau,' said Chimo, pointing at a woman suckling her child in the stern of the boat and miming love-making by moving his pelvis forward and back, 'is she your wife?'

Jarivanau shook his head and put his arms round a young woman and a girl, who could not have been more than ten years old, sitting in front of him. He then stood up (he had on a pair of ancient black trousers, probably Gabriel's, several sizes too big for him and cut off at his ankles) and pointed into the middle of the boat. A woman we had not noticed lay there, half-propped up against a carrying basket, emaciated, listless, her brown eyes huge in her sunken face. She tried to smile at us, but coughed instead. She turned her face away.

'It's malaria,' said Juan, 'and probably TB also; when we return, we'll take her with us.'

Every time we passed a manaca palm in fruit the Yanomami would point and shout, and their dogs would yelp; but Chimo and Pablo motored on regardless.

'We'll take them a good long way,' muttered Chimo, 'and then double back. There are too many people. If we camp together we'll lose everything. They'll have your trousers off you as you sleep, Reymono.'

I nodded at the two old women next to me. They nodded back. They were, on balance, I decided, a great deal cleaner than I was.

Some time later Chimo, realising, I suppose, that he had an entirely new audience, stood up and repeated his pissing trick. The Yanomami yelled their approval.

'Whoooo!' they sang.

'It took me a long time to learn that,' said Chimo, pleased. 'No one else can do it. I taught myself.'

'I'm glad to hear it,' I said.

'I'm going to leave them here,' said Chimo, running all the dugouts into the foliage overhanging the invisible bank.

The Yanomami bongo, several feet longer than ours, ploughed first and furthest into the bushes, dislodging an unseen wasps' nest. Their two prow-men, with shouts of pain (and laughter from everyone else), dived into the water and held their hands over their heads. We ducked and put our hats over our faces to protect our eyes. It was good to know that we shared the same wasp-attack routine.

When the insects had dispersed Chimo pointed at the sun, gestured its going-down and its rising and mimed our return the following day. Jarivanau and the three other men resignedly took up their paddles, and Chimo and Pablo motored us swiftly downstream.

After half an hour's search we found a small piece of bank which was just high enough to allow us to make camp.

'Manaca,' said Chimo, pointing to a tall palm in fruit a few yards back from the bank, 'Culimacaré, up you go.'

'I hate this job,' said Culimacaré, resolutely taking his machete, yanking a length of mamure vine down from a neighbouring tree, cutting a piece, knotting the ends, folding it into a coil and placing his feet inside the loop. Holding his machete between his teeth he embraced the tree with his arm and his vine-linked feet and alternately pulled and pushed himself up the trunk into the sky.

'Hormiga!' he yelled, with a strangled shout, his mouth full of machete, squirming as the big red ants bit him, unable to pick them off his skin. About sixty feet up he reached the manaca, and we all clapped. Attached by a thick stalk, bunches of twigs hung down Weeping-willow-like, each twig beaded along its length with dark red, damson-sized fruit; Culimacaré grasped the tree with his knees and hacked through the stalk, shouted a warning and dropped his machete, and then slid to the ground in a cascade of dislodged fruit, bearing the heavy bunch in his left hand.

As we cleared the area of small saplings and cut uprights for our hut, Valentine stripped the manaca fruits from the twigs and tossed them into a cooking pot half-full of water; he then pounded them with the end of a punt-pole to break off the small surround of pulp which lies between the skin and the hard kernel. There would be manioc in bitter manaca juice for supper.

The blackfly gyrated about us in thick clouds, biting wherever the sweat washed off the Jungle Formula; they flew into my mouth; they crept up my nostrils and fed on my nasal linings; they clustered on my eyelids. Juan unpacked his face-net and the Indians wrapped spare shirts over their heads. Realising that the Siapa was far worse than the Casiquiare (and made the insect life of the Baria seem almost impoverished), I distributed the last of our repellent, three precious bottles to each man.

'This place is insupportable,' said Galvis, pouring paraffin on his pile of cooking-fire sticks and adding leaves to make smoke, 'we cannot stay on this river.'

'It gets better further up,' I said, airily.

'How the hell do you know?' said Juan.

'Spruce says so,' I lied.

'That Spruce of yours,' said Galvis, 'he, also, was probably mad.'

Chimo, seemingly unmoved by a mere half-million blackfly round his old head, stood calmly by the bank, throwing his catfish-baited line and hauling it in, time and again, with a piranha on the hook. The rest of us put up the shelter.

Spreading a groundsheet at my end of the line of hammocks (so that incoming ants and tarantulas could be spotted), I happened to brush the leaf-litter with my hand. A sudden, fierce pain travelled up my arm and seemed to lodge in my armpit. I stood up and kicked the leaves aside with my boot. A small black scorpion crouched on the ground, its claws up, its sting arched forward over its back. I stamped on it.

'Jesus,' I said, 'do these things kill you?'

'No,' said Juan, glancing up from unfurling his hammock, enjoying the scene, 'but in my country, in Colombia, we are not like the English. We do not feel we have to shake *everything* by the hand.'

There was a neat puncture-hole just below my wrist. An odd tremble, like the fast fluttering of a sparrow's wings when they are begging for food, ran up and down inside all my limbs.

'It will hurt for several hours,' said Juan, 'like the bite of the veinte-cuatro. It sends some people into a big shock.'

I felt shocked at once.

'Cheer up,' said Chimo, abandoning his fishing and coming over to inspect my hand, 'it's only a scorpion. Tomorrow Culimacaré and I will take you for your big surprise.'

We slung our hammocks and then chopped up enough rotten logs to keep the fire burning all night, waiting until darkness fell and the blackfly disappeared before ladling out our piranha soup and manioc and standing round the cooking pot.

'We thank God and the Virgin for this food,' announced Chimo suddenly.

'Chimo,' I said, 'do you believe in God?'

'Of course not,' said Chimo, spitting out a mouthful of piranha bones, 'but up the Emoni we'll need all the help we can get.'

'Oh yes?'

'Oh yes, my friend. Even for me it is not easy. On your map it is a small river. But your map is not true. It is a long river, believe me. Four years ago I was the motorman for sixteen Italians who came to study our trees. We turned back. Seven years ago I was the motorman for the Government, for the Ministry of Mines. We, also, turned back. I am the best motorman in Venezuela. You can ask anyone, Reymono, and that is what they will tell you. But still we turned back.'

'But this time will be different. We have a guide. Jarivanau will come.'

'Jarivanau,' said Chimo, running the fish-covered fingers of his right hand through his frizzled hair, 'maybe he will come. And maybe he will not come.'

The twin green lights of fireflies drifted among the trees. *Peeep-peeep-*

peeeep sang the tiny brown frogs by the riverside. *Waaaark-waaaark* sang some other species. It was time to go to bed.

In my hammock, remembering that Simon might be, even then, sitting with his mistress at a cool, dry table in a London restaurant free of mosquitoes, halfway through a jeroboam of claret, I turned quickly to Chagnon's *Yanomamo, the fierce people*. Having actually seen some Yanomamo head scars, I wanted to re-read Chagnon's description of how they were acquired, a description which, in Caracas, had seemed impossibly exotic and remote — and only half believable.

On a graduated scale of violence, chest-pounding duels are the friendliest formal exchange. Chagnon witnessed one such contest between two rival Yanomami groups:

Two men, one from each side, would step into the centre of the milling, belligerent crowd of weapon-wielding partisans, urged on by their comrades. One would step up, spread his legs apart, bare his chest, and hold his arms behind his back, daring the other to hit him. The opponent would size him up, adjust the man's chest or arms so as to give himself the greatest advantage when he struck, and then step back to deliver his close-fisted blow. The striker would painstakingly adjust his own distance from his victim by measuring his arm length to the man's chest, taking several dry runs before delivering his blow. He would then wind up like a baseball pitcher, but keeping both feet on the ground, and deliver a tremendous wallop with his fist to the man's left pectoral muscle, putting all of his weight into the blow. The victim's knees would often buckle and he would stagger around a few moments, shaking his head to clear the stars, but remain silent.... After each blow, the comrades of the deliverer would cheer and bounce up and down from the knees, waving and clacking their weapons over their heads. The victim's supporters, meanwhile, would urge their champion on frantically, insisting that he take another blow. If the delivery were made with sufficient force to knock the recipient to the ground, the man who delivered it would throw his arms above his head, roll his eyes back, and prance victoriously in a circle around his victim, growling and screaming, his feet almost a blur from his excited dance. The recipient would stand poised and take as many as four blows before demanding to hit his adversary. He would be permitted to strike his opponent as many times as the latter struck him, provided that the opponent could take it.

The next stage is one degree nastier:

> The side slapping duel is nearly identical in form to chest pounding, except that the blow is delivered with an open hand across the flanks of the opponent, between his rib-cage and pelvis bone. It is a little more severe than chest pounding because casualties are more frequent and tempers grow hotter more rapidly when a group's champion falls to the ground, gasping for wind, and faints.

On this occasion 'one of the more influential men was knocked unconscious, enraging the others. The fighting continued for just a few minutes after this, but during these few minutes the men were rapidly changing the points of their arrows to war tips: curare and lanceolate bamboo.' Warfare proper was only just avoided. But in the general course of things:

> Club fights represent the next level of violence. These can take place both within and between villages ... The clubs used in these fights are, ideally, 8 to 10 feet long. They are very wiry, quite heavy, and deliver a tremendous wallop. In general shape and dimensions, they resemble pool cues, but are nearly twice as long. The club is held at the thin end, which is frequently sharpened to a long point in case the fighting escalates to spear thrusting, in which case the club is inverted and used as a pike.

> Most duels start between two men, usually after one of them has been caught *in flagrante* trysting with the other's wife. The enraged husband challenges his opponent to strike him on the head with a club. He holds his own club vertically, leans against it and exposes his head for his opponent to strike. After he has sustained a blow on the head, he can then deliver one on the culprit's skull. But as soon as blood starts to flow, almost everybody rips a pole out of the house frame and joins in the fighting, supporting one or the other of the contestants.

> Needless to say, the tops of most men's heads are covered with long, ugly scars of which their bearers are immensely proud. Some of them, in fact, keep their head cleanly shaved on top to display these scars, rubbing red pigment on their bare scalps to define them more precisely.

Jarivanau had everything except the red pigment.

A Nocturnal curassow was calling. And I was trembling slightly, but whether because of the bite of the scorpion or the mere thought of the Yanomami, I could not decide.

14

I was woken in the dark by a pig-like rootling and snuffling; something large and eager was clattering about amongst our mess-tins.

'Quick!' hissed Chimo, from the fastness of his huge hammock. 'Cachicamo! Pablo's got my gun!'

'I'm here,' whispered Pablo. 'Put your torch on, you old idiot.'

The hammock heaved. Chimo found his big torch, switched it on and pointed the beam at the noise. The armadillo, grey and heavy-looking, bunched itself and bundled for cover. Pablo fired; the animal slumped in its run, lay down, its short legs slowly kicking, and then became still.

'My gun is a good gun,' said Chimo. 'Now we will have something to give the Yanomami.'

'It's a bloody awful gun,' said Pablo, inspecting the carcass, 'but I'm a good shot.'

Chimo switched off the torch and we went back to sleep.

At dawn, squatting behind a bush, I did not at first notice that I was under attack. But then I felt tiny darts of pain all over my face and buttocks. Two species of mosquito, both new to me, had obviously decided, as the main thrust of their symbiotic evolutionary strategy, to wait two million years, twenty yards back from the bank of the

Siapa, for the first man to come and shit. One type, large and silent but with white ends to its legs, was tilting slowly from side to side as it angled in at my head. The other, large and noisy but difficult to spot, came in two feet from the jungle floor targeted on my bum. It was impossible to protect both ends at once.

Retreating, I disturbed Old Valentine behind another bush.

'To hell with everything,' he said. 'The zancudos are even worse than the jejenes. We must not stay in this place, Reymono.'

The Nine-banded or Common long-nosed armadillo was about two and a half feet long, with a tail of almost the same length again. He had a long snout and head covered in a mosaic of bony plates; small eyes, a thin beard under his throat, and two large sticking-up, oval ears. His body was tightly enclosed in a beautifully patterned carapace of roundels of horn, broken in the middle by plates arranged in nine rings along the head-to-tail line. His legs were short and thick, ended in curved claws and, like his tail, were protected by rings of bony squares. When we turned him over, however, his underside was soft and grey and vulnerable and clothed in nothing but hair.

Chimo and Valentine laid three large palm leaves on the ground, placed the armadillo on top and began the skinning and jointing. The armour came off in one piece, yellow-white underneath. Having no spare salt with which to preserve it, we left it where it was. Big green flies began to gather.

'Chimo, did you dream of anything last night?' said Galvis, boiling up the first lumps of armadillo meat.

'Of course,' said Chimo, still cutting, 'I always dream. I am a man who likes his dreams. Last night I dreamed that I was back in San Carlos. Two of Valentine's daughters and the daughter of Machado, who lives next door, were trying to pull down my trousers. "Don't be silly," I said, "I'll please you one at a time, in the garden at the back of Valentine's house." But then a nun came along and ruined everything. "What are you doing to this poor man?" she said.'

'I had the same kind of dream,' said Valentine, coughing.

'Of course you did,' said Chimo, 'because you're only a youngster.'

'I dreamed I was marrying again,' said Valentine, 'but it was *two* girls. How would I pay for it? I was very worried. After all, it was bad enough the last time – and then I only married one. But the fathers came to see me: "Look here," they said, "you may not have any money but you're such a good lover that we'll pay for *everything*." And then all the relations came from everywhere and we had the biggest party that San Carlos has ever seen. And one of the girls turned into my former wife, Olinda, and I was so happy to have her back I cried; and the other girl was Gabriel's daughter – I could have her every night of my life. And before the party was even over they were fighting each other, to decide who would be first. And then I woke up; and I found that there was nothing here but mosquitoes.'

'So, Culimacaré,' I said, 'what did you dream about?'

'I dreamed I saw a lot of Choris,' said Culimacaré, pausing from dismantling our shelter, 'I cut down trees, to make a bridge, to reach the Choris – but I couldn't get there.'

'I dreamed,' said Pablo, grinning, 'that I went out with a terrible old gun to hunt an armadillo. And when I woke up – there it was.'

'I only asked,' said Galvis, moodily ladling out half-cooked bits of armadillo into our mess tins, 'because I had the worst dream of all my life. I arrived back in San Carlos and there was no one to greet me. No happiness. The house was dark. So I walked down a small track at the side; and I found my wife and my brother sitting in this darkness in my back room. "While you were away," said my brother, "your wife burned little Jean-Paul until he died." "How is this?" I said. "How can this be?" And I hit my wife full in the face. I was going to hit her again, but I couldn't, because at that moment we all began to change. We began to change into those cockroaches that live in the hut where we go to shit in the garden. The ones that you find on the walls when you open the door and which run so fast to hide down the hole. And that's what we were doing when I woke up. We were living down there and eating old, black shit. So what does it mean? Eh? What does it mean?'

'That's enough of that,' said Chimo, standing up and putting his hands where his hips would have been if he had not been shaped like a barrel. 'It means you're a nasty little beetle with a squeaky voice. It doesn't mean a damn thing. And when we've finished our breakfast you can help Juan dig a hole for his carbon; and Reymono and I and Culimacaré will go and find a chenchena.'

'A chenchena?' I said.

'Yes, ' said Chimo, 'the bird you're always wanting to see. The one you bother me about. The one in the book with his feathers in his hat and a bad smell.'

*

About a quarter of an hour downriver Chimo swung the dugout into the overhanging branches of the trees by the bank. He pulled the curiara, which we were towing, tight up to the stern, and we took out the paddles. But there was no bank. We slid easily over the tops of bushes; we passed slowly and silently just beneath the crowns of the trees, pulling ourselves forward under lianas, from one trunk to the next, the hull rustling over submerged branches. Suddenly the eerie quiet was broken by the sound of a thousand wet, suckling kisses.

'Mono chucuto!' hissed Chimo, pointing with one hand and, sucking air into his mouth, waggling his cheek with the other.

A flurry of little black monkeys, Black uakaris, disappeared to the right from just above our heads, running on all fours along the branches, taking great leaps from tree to tree.

'Every time you make their words,' said Culimacaré, from the bow, to Chimo, 'you frighten the life out of them.'

The foliage grew thicker, forcing Culimacaré to stand up and use his machete, and then it parted and ceased, giving on to a large, oval lake, the Yacuta lagoon. The expanse of water was glassy calm in the sunlight. The great trees standing around its flooded sides seemed to plunge their tops as far into its depths as they rose out of it into the sky. The unrippled surface was broken only by the outlines of Giant turtles, basking at its fringes (through the binoculars I could make out the small domes of their heads, then a gap, then the great domes of their shells); and it was disturbed only by the brief splash, swirl and gurgle of dolphins rising to blow. About forty Giant egrets perched impassively amongst the trees on the far shore.

'Keep quiet,' whispered Chimo, as we paddled round to the left.

Some three hundred yards further, Culimacaré stopped and held his finger to his lips. At first I heard only the drip from my paddle resting on the gunwale; and then, intermingled with the plop of palm-fruits falling into the water beyond the bushes beside us, there came the sound of twenty or thirty old men, fast asleep, snoring amongst the trees.

Chimo pulled the curiara alongside and motioned to Culimacaré and I to climb in; I sat, very still, in the bow, the slightest movement in the tiny dugout threatening to tip me into the lake. Culimacaré paddled gently, sending us slipping in among the tree tops. There was a rasping and a hissing noise; something began to thrash the leaves all about us. And then I saw a hoatzin right above me – it was pheasant-sized, chestnut and orange-white, with spread wings and fanned-up tail, moving awkwardly on a branch, tipping back and forth and swearing. There were perhaps fifteen to twenty of them in the surrounding trees; they peered down at us with their red eyes and blue faces, a crest of spiky feathers standing straight up from their skulls; and then they would hurl themselves away at the next tree, crashing into the leaves and branches without restraint, all feathers spread. Their wings were large but badly assembled: you could see strips of light between the primaries.

I looked about for a chick, for some prehistoric downy reptile clawing its way across the twigs, but there was no sign — perhaps they had already escaped by dropping into the water and diving to safety. Culimacaré pointed out an empty nest, a simple platform of sticks like a woodpigeon's nest.

'You can't eat them,' he said, 'they smell like Chimo's hammock.'

Jarivanau's hut

15

We broke camp early, set off upriver, and, late in the afternoon, rounding a bend into a straight stretch, we were astonished to see a large plantation on the right bank. Two rectangular huts were set close by the shore, their windowless, thickly-thatched roofs sloping right down to the ground on all sides. A haze of smoke diffused from the thatch into the sky.

A few large palms were still standing, but over several acres all the trees had been axed and burned, their great scorched trunks lying black and twisted among the new yucca plants and the young plantains. We tied the boats up by the Yanomami bongo at the muddy landing-stage and went ashore through clouds of blackfly. There was a rustling noise low down at the end of the hut nearest us and a thatched door, about three feet high, was thrown back. Two of the young women who had been in the bongo the day before emerged, blinking in the sunlight and putting on their shirts. They stood looking at us, slapping themselves as the blackfly bit their arms and legs. Their glossy black hair was cropped short at the back of the neck and hung in a fringe across their foreheads. They were thick-set and square-shouldered but no more than four and a half feet tall; transverse black lines, drawn across their faces, rippled as they smiled. The younger, Jarivanau's new adult wife, had a matchstick poked into a hole just below the centre of her lower lip, the ignitable end towards us. It wiggled up and down as she talked, ceaselessly, her own emphatic language. She had also, I noticed, deep round holes at the corners of her mouth. We stood there, talking together, enclosed in our different languages and enclosed, too, in our very own columns of furiously swirling blackfly, columns which tapered to a point above our heads.

Chimo, perhaps tiring of being bitten, mimed that we would go now and make camp upriver, returning when it was dark, with food for them, and to have a fiesta. And 'tengamos la fiesta en paz,' he added to himself, 'let us have no trouble.'

On our way upstream Culimacaré pointed and shouted, 'Picure! Picure!'

An agouti, rat-like, about two feet long and with large, rounded ears which stuck up above the water, was swimming fast across the river. Chimo manoeuvred the boats alongside and Galvis killed it with one cut of his machete to the neck, pulling it on board by its long back legs. Its copious, coarse hair, instead of the usual brown and gold, was black on top and white underneath.

'We'll put him in the armadillo soup,' said Chimo, looking pleased and farting with anticipation.

Clearing a small patch of undergrowth for our shelters with my machete, I came across a pineapple. The fruit was no bigger than a cricket ball, ripe, and as desirable as any fruit could be.

'Juan!' I said, 'I've found a pineapple! There must have been a plantation here!'

'Don't make a stupid,' said Juan, wandering over to look, 'this is where they come from. The pineapple lives in the Orinoco lands.'

'Everyone will have a little piece,' said Chimo, bending down, cutting it free and picking it up.

It burst in his hand.

'Fuck a nun,' said Chimo, 'it's rotten.'

'Everything here is rotten,' said Galvis, filling a bowl with rice, 'and soon we, too, will be rotten.'

'Galvis, you must eat more,' said Chimo, 'the bigger a man is, the happier he gets.'

Juan and I unpacked the big army kit-bag which we had filled with presents. We took out enough mirrors, combs, fish hooks and line for thirty people; and several hundred of the intricately patterned, hand-painted beads of all sizes which I had bought in Oxford.

'We leave the rest for the real Yanomami,' said Juan.

'Aren't these real? What's wrong with them?'

'Everything,' said Juan. 'The Yanomami are not a river people. Normally they make nothing but square canoes of bark. You would never think they float; and they only go downriver. They do not grow manioc, only plantains. They are hunters, not farmers. The men walk for many weeks in the forest. And they make the great house, the shabono, a ring with a plaza in the middle. These are here because they wish to trade with Gabriel. They copy everything from him. You'll see.'

'They look genuine enough to me,' I said. 'I think we should go hunting with them. I think we should hunt the peccary. I want to see them use those arrows.'

'No Redmon. The báquiro is dangerous. He is not like your wild pig. The báquiro walks in tribes, many, many together. Sometimes they turn on you. Many men die like that – you climb a tree but still you are not safe. The báquiro gather at the bottom and they take down that tree with their teeth. They have their revenge.'

As night fell we unloaded our ordinary stores from Chimo's dugout and, leaving Valentine on guard, we set off downstream with the presents, with bowls of manioc, ready-cooked spaghetti, and – the centrepiece – our giant pot full to the brim with agouti and armadillo risotto.

Jarivanau came out to greet us and helped carry our cargo as we crouched low through the tiny door into the hut. Several small fires were burning on the mud floor on either side of the tall building, and Chimo hung up our two kerosene lanterns, but it still took time for our eyes to adjust to the thick murk. Each family had a segment to itself, stretching from the angle where the roof met the floor to the central support-posts, in which short and narrow split-vine hammocks were hanging. A flimsy platform of long poles ran around the edge, high up, on which baskets and baskets-in-the-making were stored, and from which hung a few pots and the odd plastic bag. A narrow entrance at the back of the main hut led to a second, almost as large, in which many of the family spaces were empty of hammocks: obviously a part of the group was away on a journey. Three dogs – whippets-cum-terriers – smelt my ankles and growled softly.

The two old women who had sat opposite me in the big dugout squatted in a corner, hacking up yucca tubers with machetes. The younger mothers had painted themselves with red onoto-dye, in lines across their faces and, with thicker strokes, in scallops and circles which ran from their shoulders, around their heavy, splayed-out breasts, to their waists. They wore strips of vine tightly tied around their legs, just below the knee. They sat on the floor around us, unsmiling, waiting, their babies on their laps or held firmly against their bodies with a cross-sling of red cloth. The men leaned against the support-posts.

Feeling big and awkward I sat down, undid my canvas bag, took out my Polaroid and Simon's manual camera and flashgun, and, fearing that it might constitute a nineteenth-century imperial insult, I shared out my handfuls of precious beads. The women took them eagerly, turning to each other and talking very fast. Trading had begun at once: the large, cheap, plain red ones, it seemed, were worth about eight of the small, multi-coloured, expensive, hand-painted variety.

Galvis, coming into his own and telling the Yanomami loudly in Spanish that he was a cook to be reckoned with, built up one of the fires from a pile of split logs and wedged the pot of risotto on top with an arrangement of short poles.

Jarivanau squatted down and beckoned Chimo to sit beside him. He patted the top of his own shaved, smashed skull and then ran his fingers through Chimo's wiry frizzle. He punched his own muscled stomach and then felt, with obvious amazement, the massy curve of Chimo's rounded paunch. Chimo took his pipe out of his mouth and, to order, with scarcely a pause, produced one of his gigantic Le Pétomane-like farts. Everyone laughed. The tension eased. The rest of the men sat down.

Juan and Culimacaré, opening our other bag, produced the fish hooks and shared them out, fifty to each man. Pablo began to measure out ten-metre lengths from our spools of fishing line, cutting each free with his machete as he went, and rolling them up and distributing them. Jarivanau and another man, small, wiry, with an equally high chest and an equally large wad of tobacco in his mouth but with an undamaged head, tried to re-measure their gifts, not by holding one end against the chest and extending an arm with the other, but in a stretched diagonal from the big toe of a straight left leg to the forefinger of a straight right arm. The calculations, however, soon conjured up that look of blank pain and unfocused anger that only mathematics can produce, and with a sudden grin and a shrug they gave up.

Galvis announced the start of his banquet by banging the side of the cauldron with his ladle.

'Kings, Chiefs, Ministers and all you young ladies with beautiful breasts,' he sang in Spanish, 'dinner is served.'

'We thank God and the Virgin for this food,' said Chimo, crossing himself.

'The agouti,' I said, 'might shake her up a bit.'

'From now on,' said Chimo, taking me by the elbow and whispering in my ear, 'we must not annoy the Mother of God. Reymono – she must help us to stay alive.'

Galvis piled up one of our mess-tins with hot risotto and cold spaghetti, added a fistful of dry manioc, and handed it to the nearest Yanomami girl. Jarivanau stopped Galvis by holding up his hand, snatched the tin away and took it instead to his favourite wife, the healthy-looking girl with the matchstick in her lip. She, in turn, fed her son, who was perhaps five years old and wore two half-pencil-size rods in his little ears. Jarivanau then gathered up each family's wooden bowls and supervised their filling and distribution, disappearing, lastly, into the darkest corner of the hut and forcing the emaciated girl with malaria, and her equally frail child, out of their hammock and onto the mud floor, where he fed them. The Yanomami licked their bowls clean and came back for more; it was easy to forget, I thought, how desperate a business finding enough food in such a place can be.

When they had finished there was a ladleful left for each of us; and the dogs lapped up the remaining slop of spaghetti.

Jarivanau had chosen to eat with Chimo; the two of them were actually engaged in slow, laboured but excited conversation.

'Gabriel has taught him some words,' said Chimo, slapping Jarivanau's thigh, '*I think he says he will come with us.*'

'Emoniteris,' said Chimo, turning to Jarivanau and pointing upriver, 'cuántas días? How many days?'

'Muy lejos,' said Jarivanau: very far. Stretching his arm and pointing index finger well back behind his head, he brought it forward with tremendous force towards the east. '*Mori!*' he shouted, and then, repeating the gesture each time and immediately cradling his head on his hands: '*Mori! Mori!*'

Perhaps he meant, I thought, that the Emoniteri were just three dream-times, three sleeps away; but mori, I now know, is simply the Yanomami word for one – their entire mathematical notation consists of one, two, and more than two. Three ones meant more than two.

I picked up the Polaroid, fitted a bar of flash bulbs and, in the ensuing silence, took Jarivanau's portrait. The dogs yelped at the burst of light and crept behind the pile of yucca. Everyone tensed. The men stood up.

I gave the still-wet print to Jarivanau; gradually, the image appeared. The Yanomami jostled round warily and then, as his face became unmistakable, they grinned with delight. I took everybody's picture, handing them out, and slipped in shots with Simon's Minolta in between takes.

Galvis, perhaps realising that he was temporarily free of mosquitoes, dry, and surrounded by half-naked girls, burst into song. In his high tenor he sang the sad songs of the llanos, the latest Venezuelan pop songs, and then, eventually, exhausted, he turned to his audience and indicated that now they should sing their songs to us.

The girl with the matchstick marshalled all the young women into a line and began a high-pitched, nasal, dissonant chant to which the others provided a chorus. They stood quite still as they sang their eerie song, impassive, unsmiling, without moving their hands and feet, and after about five minutes they all sat down. We clapped and shouted for more, but Jarivanau, shaking his head, got up, went to his hammock, and came back bearing his yoppo pipe and a small glass phial of brown powder.

He squatted in the middle of the mud floor and two other young men joined him. Neither of them had shaved their heads; but one was disfigured by a deep, badly-healed scar which ran from his right shoulder down his right arm to his elbow. Jarivanau beckoned to me and I went and squatted in line.

'Reymono,' said Chimo, 'don't be a fool. You don't know what you're doing.'

'Don't make more stupids,' said Juan. 'It damages the brain. It hurts the head.'

'It's all right,' I said, grinning nervously.

'How do you know?' said Juan.

'I've read about it,' I said, regretting everything.

'Read about it!' said Juan, disgusted. 'Read about it!'

'You take the camera,' I said.

'I'll take you being sick,' said Juan, 'like the dogs.'

Jarivanau and the two men smiled at me.

'Kadure!' said the one with the scar, thumping his chest.

'Wakamane!' said the other.

I shook hands.

'Reymono!' I said, completing things.

Jarivanau tipped a handful of powder into his thick palm. He cupped it into the open end of the yoppo pipe and flicked the barrel to distribute it evenly. Kadure took the nozzle, inserted it in his left nostril, and shut his eyes. Jarivanau drew in an enormous draught of air, expanding his high chest, and blew long and hard down the tube. Brown dust hissed out of the nozzle, up Kadure's nose, but also, such was the force of the blast, mushroomed out at the edges and clouded his face; he dropped the tube, put both hands to the back of his head, and sat, staring at the floor, gasping; brown slime trickled out of his nostril, down his lip, and into his mouth. Jarivanau re-loaded the pipe and waited. Kadure dribbled a long stream of saliva down his chest; he bent forward, pummelled the ground with his fists, and inserted the nozzle in his other nostril. Jarivanau blew. Kadure put his hands to the back of his neck, his face contorted. 'Whooooaaa!' he said. He started to his feet, grabbed a support-post, and was horribly sick.

Jarivanau, ignoring his distress, ministered to Wakamane. At the second blast, Wakamane sat, shaking, coughing and spitting for some moments, his hands clasped at the back of his head, brown gunge glistening down his lip and chin and throat. 'Whooooaaa!' he said, collecting himself and struggling, very slowly, to his feet. He began a powerful stamping to and fro, his arms bent above his head as if carrying a small planet which, but for his support, would crash to earth. His eyes unfocused, his lungs tugging for breath in desperate spasms, he called to his hekura, his spirits, in a deep, monosyllabic chant, pausing only to spit. After ten minutes, drained and faltering, he sat down, withdrew into himself, and became quiet.

It was, I realised, with the kind of panic that shrivels the penis, my turn.

Jarivanau blew the dust into my left nostril. Someone at once seemed to hit me just above the bridge of the nose with a small log. I put my hands to the back of my head, to stop it detaching itself. Someone else eased a burning stick down my throat. My lungs filled with hot ash. There was no water, anywhere. Jarivanau offered me his re-loaded tube. Bang. My ear, nose and throat system went into shock. I sat, unable, it seemed, to breathe, my hands pressed to the back of my head, my head between my knees. And then suddenly I was gulping oxygen through a clogging goo of ejaculating sinuses;

I mouthed for air as yoppo-stained snot and mucus from nasal recessess whose existence I had never suspected poured out of my nostrils and on down my chin and chest.

The pain went. I realised that I was still alive; that it was all over; that I was taking the best breaths I could remember. (Well, you would, after such a clear out). I looked up. Kadure and Wakamane, who were squatting, to my surprise, on either side of me, put their arms briefly across my shoulders. The Yanomami seemed the most welcoming, the most peaceful people on earth. I felt physically invulnerable: a mere bash on the head from a club, I thought, could not possibly do me any damage. The hut had grown larger; there was more than enough room for us all; I could sit on the mud floor, happily, for ever. Given the opportunity, I could have seen across vast distances; as it was, every detail in front of me was extraordinarily clear – a long black bow and two reed-cane arrows, with notched points of a different wood bound on and stained black with curare, their flights cut from the wing feathers of a Black curassow, seemed luminously themselves, leaning between the angle of the roof and the floor, a work of art. It all seemed so safe and familiar: the frayed, red-dyed, split-vine hammocks; the worn rim of a wooden bowl; the hand-smoothed bands a third of the way up the central support-posts. Indeed, given enough yoppo, it occurred to me, becoming a Yano-mami would be a desirable and simple matter. Hekura, I knew, the tutelary gods who lived in the rocks and in the mountains until summoned to live in our chests, appeared, coyly at first, as small shards of light, a migraine of spirits. I searched the periphery of my field of vision. Nothing. But in it, instead, very obviously, sat the matchstick girl.

She was really there, it seemed to me; she sat, cross-legged, no more than ten feet away. She gave me the most enormous, encouraging, kind smile; it was not simultaneous, this smile, in its spread to the left and the right across her cheeks: the matchstick tilted first one way and then the other. I smiled back, giddy, overcome with slow tenderness and deep desire. We had, after all, more time than any man and woman could possibly need: it stretched away in all directions across six million square kilometres of jungle. She appeared to be perfect in every way. I admired her, slowly. I stroked, in imagination, her cropped neck. I ran my hand through the round tuft of thick, fine black hair on her head. I kissed her stubby nose, her strong chin. I wiggled her wooden ear-ring plugs. I ran my hands over her square shoulders and short, straight back. I explored her spatulate toes and the built-in platform soles of calluses on her feet. I felt her round calves and I undid the single strand of tight vine-bonding beneath each battered knee. I kissed the old scars and newish cuts. I ran my tongue, for several night-times, up the long, soft insides of her thighs, devoid, as far as I could see, of even the downiest hairs. It seemed a sensible idea, too, at the time, the Yanomami idea that sperm comes straight from the lower abdomen, has nothing to do with the testicles, and that, in order to enjoy a week or a month of uninterrupted erections, all you have to do is constantly replenish the reservoir by eating equivalent amounts of well-chewed meat between each bout of love-making.

'Matchstick girl,' I wanted, very much, to say to her, 'I know I am old and hairy, and that, unlike you, I sweat and I smell horrible and I happen to be filthy, whereas you are clean, and used to all this, and know what to do, and anyway have the most beautiful brown eyes of all the Siapateri — but just supposing we slipped outside together . . .?'

I was suddenly grabbed from behind. I tried to shake myself free, but could not. The hands pinioning my arms were large and powerful. I looked up. An enormous stomach seemed to curve away above me into the far dark of the roof.

'Get up,' said Chimo, 'it's time to go.'

The matchstick girl grinned. She had seen it all before.

Male Peccary

16

'Holy mother, Reymono,' said Chimo, when he had got me outside, 'you were about to kill the lot of us, without even trying. The Yanomami have always killed the Curipaco and the Baré and they kill each other, too; we are afraid of them; we cannot help it. And you, also — you should be afraid of them. Did you know you were staring at Jarivanau's woman for *several hours*? Did you know he is the Capitan?'

'I was only looking,' I said, grumpily, as I was bundled into the boat.

'Looking!' said Chimo, really quite angry. 'You gazed at Jarivanau's woman like a young boy who's only just got his balls! You looked at her like a boy who still lives in his mother's hut!'

'It's revolting.' said Juan, joining in, 'you look at everything like a man in a drink.'

'Ah, but Chimo,' I said, suddenly struck by a wonderful thought, 'if *these* are not the proper Yanomami, *what will the real thing be like?*'

'Holy Mother,' said Chimo.

I woke up; exploding shells of thunder cracked and ripped the air just above our heads. It was still dark. Culimacaré, wet through, was moving intently about with Chimo's big torch, poking great sagging pools of water off the tarpaulin-roof with a pole, thrusting up extra stiffening-sticks, and adding new lines of parachute cord to surrounding trees. Whenever he stepped out of the shelter he became a small glow of watery light and then disappeared entirely beneath the cascade. I licked my forefingers, cleaned the yoppo paste from my eyes, switched on my own torch and looked about. Rivulets ran past and over the groundsheet; the bergen sat in its own small pond; water ran down the posts to which I had slung my hammock, and I was now lying, protected by my improvised tube of groundsheet and anti-mosquito plastic bag, on a length of soggy cotton; leaves and twigs spattered down onto the roof and were waterfalled off the edge. I congratulated myself on my ability to pick companions made of the right stuff. Given the choice, always go for the man with the three thumbs.

'Tomorrow we must hunt for báquiro with the Yanomami,' I shouted to Culimacaré, above the noise of the storm, as he worked his way up to my end of the shelter. 'I want to see them shoot a peccary with those big arrows of theirs.'

'We've arranged it, as you wanted before,' said Culimacaré, looking suddenly nervous, standing by my hammock. 'But you don't want to come hunting with us. You want to stay in your bed.'

'What?'

'Yes you do,' said Culimacaré, jigging his hand up and down. 'Don't you worry about a thing. You just stay where you are.'

'Culimacaré, what the hell do you mean?'

'It's nothing,' he said, looking embarrassed, 'it's just that Chimo says you're not right in the head.'

In the morning the storm had passed but the sky was still grey-black with cloud; after a breakfast of arepas, Galvis's own maize-flour fried buns, and the last of our spaghetti, we left Pablo, Valentine and Galvis to guard our camp and motored across to the Yanomami settlement. The river had risen in the night, almost up to the top of the bank. The bongo was not at its mooring. Only the two old women came out to greet us.

'Jarivanau?' shouted Chimo.

The old women giggled shyly, and one raised an arm towards the forest upriver.

'Where's the bongo?' shouted Juan, pointing at the empty landing-stage.

They spread their arms in distress and held their hands out towards us.

'It looks as if they're in a mess,' said Juan. 'The bongo has gone. Jarivanau has gone hunting. You see how primitive they are? They do not tie their boat properly! And the plantation – if the water rises again – they'll lose everything: yucca, plantains, tobacco, everything.'

'We'll go and get it,' said Chimo, swinging our dugout round with the current.

'Chimo is worried,' said Juan, confidentially, as we sped downstream. 'He thinks we do not have enough tanks of gasoline for the Emoni.'

'Of course we do,' I said, 'we've got yours from the Research Station.'

'I think Chimo took some away when we stopped in Solano,' said Juan, 'and gave it to his sons-in-law. He is a big rogue. It is only natural.'

'Well then,' I said, suddenly anxious, 'if that's the case, when the time comes we will paddle; and after that we will walk. We will all paddle.'

'Maybe yes, maybe no,' said Juan. 'You cannot tell them what to do. If they like you, they help. If not, not. And again, last night, when you were full of drugs, Chimo talked a long, long time. He is worried about the real Yanomami: from us they have different customs, Redmon. The Capitan becomes a bigger, better Capitan if he makes a trick. You ask a village you do not like to be your friends, to make a fiesta with you. You promise to give them banana soup and monkeys and báquiros. You promise to dance and take drugs and trade baskets and dogs and make marriages and I do not know what; and then you send away secretly to your real friends. And your real friends – they hide themselves outside your village, in the forest, when the guests come to your fiesta. When the guest-men lie in their hammocks, without their bows and arrows, to show their feathers to you – then your real friends, they run in, covered in black paint, and they shoot, they kill with curare arrows, with poison so there is no escape, all the guest-men as they lie in their hammocks. You do not have a fair fight. Not like us. You take all the guest-women – you and your real friends jiggy-jiggy with them and then you share them for wives. There are never enough women among the Yanomami; if your first baby is a girl-baby you must put a stick across her throat and stand on it: you can not have a girl-baby until you have had a boy-baby. There is not enough food. There is not enough food and there are not enough women. The soil is very poor. Game is hard to find. The forest is a cruel place.'

'But we haven't got any women,' I said, shaken.

'Chimo says they will kill us for his gun,' said Juan, looking pale and in earnest, 'for our machetes, our shirts, our trousers, everything.'

'Lizot wouldn't agree.'

'Oh yes he does,' said Juan, bridling, 'he only does not say so because Chagnon does say so. And Lizot is a poet for the Yanomami. Sometimes, Redmon, you make me in a rage! It is only in the English language that I am not a scholar. I learn it because I have to learn it, because my country is a poor country and there are no jobs for ecologists in Colombia: you are not the only man to read Napoleon A. Chagnon and Jacques Lizot. I read his other book, too, *El Hombre de la pantorrilla prenada y otros mitos Yanomami*, *The Man with a Baby in his*' — Juan held and shook his calf muscle — 'published in Caracas in 1975. The Yanomami think they are the first people that are made and we are — how do you say it? — like the bubbles on the river.'

'Scum,' I said.

The lost bongo came into view, wedged beneath the branches of a fallen tree on the far bank. As we came alongside, Juan, presumably in a real rage now, grabbed one of our tins and jumped in, beginning to bail out the big canoe with excessive ferocity.

We re-tied the bongo to its mooring post with a decent length of our parachute cord and set off to find Jarivanau.

'Whooooooo!' sang Chimo into the jungle, at intervals, as we motored slowly up the right bank. Eventually, about three miles upstream, there came an answering shout, 'Whoooooo! Whoooooo!' at a higher pitch. We pulled in to the foliage and waited. A group of startled Scarlet macaws flew out overhead, turning their big heads to look down at us. 'Ha ha ha!' they said.

'If it's the Yanomami *and* you coming hunting with bows and arrows,' said Chimo to me, looking uncharacteristically gloomy, 'then I'll just stay in the boat. If you don't mind.'

'But I'm not even armed,' I said, hurt.

'It doesn't matter,' said Chimo. 'Yoppo makes a man mad, whether he's armed or not. It makes no difference. The spirits of the Yanomami come out of the rocks and live in you. Reymono — you don't know who they are. You're not used to them. Anything could happen. You and Jarivanau – maybe you'd better go to find those people-in-the-centre on your own.'

'It wears off,' I said, suddenly inspired, 'the spirits left me in the night. I felt them go. And besides, I'll offer you, and every man who comes with me, 500 bolivares extra if we find the Emoniteri.'

'It's not your *money*,' said Chimo, somehow brightening even as he scowled, 'there's nothing wrong with your *money*.'

With no warning noise whatever, the Yanomami materialised amongst the leaves and branches and creepers.

'Whooooooo!' yelled Jarivanau.

Juan and I squatted down behind Culimacaré in the bow and the Yanomami filed past us, smiling, obviously pleased to be getting a lift to the day's hunting ground, holding their six-foot bows and arrows upright in front of them, tobacco wads in their mouths, their arrow point quivers slung high in the centre of their backs by a string round their necks. There were eight men, besides Jarivanau, two very old, and one, who I had not noticed in the hut the night before, very young, seemingly unmarked by scars, and carrying no bow. He was almost European-looking. He held something small and shiny-brown in the palm of his hand.

'Juan,' I whispered, 'look at that young one. He looks like an Englishman. I could have gone to school with him.'

'So what?' said Juan, loudly. 'So what is special about an Englishman?'

The young man put the brown object to his lips, holding it delicately between both his hands. A thin, clear, pure series of notes, sad and distinct, rose above the purr of the motor and seemed to hang under the grey sky. It was a mesmerising sound, the quality of the ordinary dawn call of the Blue-crowned motmot, *hudu, hudu,* taken and made intelligent and sustained and yearningly sad. It seemed to me, for a moment, that he made the birds speak.

'It's a flute,' said Juan. 'It looks as if he made it himself. You find the seed of the yucca. You must have skill and be patient. You make four holes and take out the insides – you must exactly make your holes, for the sound.'

We came to a small cove. Jarivanau stood up and pointed at the bank; Chimo ran the dugout through the overhanging branches and we all filed ashore.

Two falcons, very small and black with bright rufous stomachs, were perched on the topmost twigs of the tallest tree opposite us, clearly outlined against the watery sky. They were Bat falcons, I decided, in the few moments which Jarivanau allowed me to watch them through the binoculars. He pulled my arm excitedly, almost detaching it from its socket.

'Báquiro! Báquiro! Báquiro!' he said, rubbing his stomach, his eyes shining. He mimed loosing an arrow. 'Phut! Báquiro! Báquiro!'

Chimo waved goodbye and then pretended he was very busy, tinkering with the engine.

The Yanomami set off silently and in single file, moving at an agonisingly fast pace. Their bare feet oddly turned in, pigeon-toed, they padded over the black, six-inch-long palm-spines which were strewn everywhere across the forest floor; they waded through streams without a break; they slipped under fallen boughs and looped lianas which caught me across the chest. Juan and I crashed along behind, only just managing to keep Culimacaré and the two old men, the back-markers, in sight.

After about half an hour everyone suddenly stopped. The Yanomami squatted down and stared at the ground. There was much excited chatter over some completely indiscernible marks in the leaf litter. Jarivanau sent Kadure and Wakamane off on a wide circle to our right.

Ten minutes later we paused to look at obvious tracks, hoof-marks all over a large patch of mud; Jarivanau sent two more men on a tight circle to our right; he stood still, his nose in the air, breathing in with his mouth shut, exhaling with his mouth open. The remaining Yanomami followed suit. I tried, too; and detected nothing but the usual, damp, clinging rot. The Yanomami pointed with great confidence, straight ahead: they were hunting by smell. Jarivanau sent two hunters to the left, positioned the old men in thickets behind us, and crept forward, beckoning to us to follow.

'If they come this way,' whispered Juan, 'climb a tree.'

The great buttressed trees were too big to climb; the mass of saplings, struggling upwards in the gloom, waiting for a tree to fall, waiting for their place in the light, were far too small.

'It's okay,' I said, 'I'll just hide behind you.'

And then I finally smelt the peccaries myself – a pervasive, musky, pig-sty smell. Almost simultaneously there was a drumming of hooves: a fast, compact, black confusion of shapes smashing along near the ground some twenty yards from us, bursting through the undergrowth to our right. Jarivanau arched his back, drew his enormous bow, and loosed a six-foot arrow. Culimacaré put the shotgun to his shoulder and fired. Both men ran forward; Jarivanau veering, very fast, to the right, following the herd.

When we caught up with Culimacaré he was standing over a large boar which lay dying on the leaves, wagging its snout to and fro; it was sparsely covered in long, coarse hair; its legs were surprisingly long; its soft, brown eyes were half-shut.

Culimacaré cut down a sapling and trimmed it and Jarivanau returned, looking sheepish, and clutching the rear half of his arrow. He shrugged, mimed an arrow hitting a tree, and took the pole from Culimacaré. Getting a firm grip on the mulch with his feet and standing four-square behind the peccary, he raised the pole way back and high above his head. He brought it down, with immense force, on the animal's throat: its whole body bucked, its back legs kicked convulsively. It would not be sensible, I thought, to receive such a blow on one's skull. Jarivanau pushed the pole into its windpipe and leant against it until the peccary ceased to raise bubbles in the saliva round its nostrils.

Wakamane and Kadure appeared amongst the trees beside us, much excited. They gave their bows and arrows to Jarivanau, more or less wrenched the shotgun from Culimacaré, and held out their hands for cartridges. He gave them one each, and, with Wakamane holding the gun, unnervingly, by the barrel, they disappeared into the undergrowth at a loping run. Culimacaré and I dragged the heavy peccary about fifty yards to a spot indistinguishable from anywhere else, which Jarivanau indicated was a Yanomami path, and we then set off to find the others.

Unexpectedly – because there seemed to be no possible landmarks, everywhere looked the same – we came across the two old men, still in their ambush positions. They were almost invisible, even after Jarivanau had pointed them out – one standing in a thicket, the other against the trunk of a tree, entirely encased in the wigwam-like cage of its prop roots. They came out and joined us and we all sat on a log. Jarivanau, obviously pleased to abandon us to their care, left them the two surplus bows and the broken arrow, and vanished among the saplings.

There was a shot, a long way away, and the two old Yanomami leaned forward towards the sound, their mouths open; a second or so later they turned towards us and smiled, rubbing their stomachs.

Maybe their eardrums were as wrinkled as the rest of them, like dried seeds, but, even so, they were still so much more efficient than ours that they had actually heard the fall of a peccary far off in the forest.

We made a mutual inspection of our possessions: the Jungle Formula bottle and Anthisan tube in my SAS belt-pouch bemused them – they patted the repellent onto their scrawny arms and sniffed at it with distaste. Their quivers, made from sections of bamboo with an overlapping piece of peccary skin (the sparse black hairs on the inside) as a lid, contained arrow heads: thickish slivers of bamboo, about eight inches long, stained red on one side and shaped to a point at either end, and palm-wood sticks, likewise pointed, shiny black with curare, and cut almost through in three places.

'Be careful Redmon,' said Juan, 'if you touch those with a cut on your hand you are a dead man. It's very effective for monkeys – the arrow breaks off in the body, the monkey clings to the tree, the poison relaxes the muscles – and thump, the monkey falls to the ground.'

One of the Yanomami, besides his quiver, had a very sharp, unsheathed kitchen knife slung round his neck on a string, its point hanging downwards flat against the middle of his back; the other had a long strip of cloth tied round his neck, wound into a tight little bundle in the centre. Juan gave it a tug and the old man took it off; holding one end in his toe, he unravelled it, disclosing a lump of transparent yellow resin which smelt, slightly, of incense.

'I know it,' said Culimacaré, 'it's caraña. It's from the juice of a tree. You make a fire with it or use it like a candle; and it is good, also, as medicine for the skin. You rub it on and it cures the ache in the stomach.'

There was a rustle behind us and the rest of the Yanomami appeared. Wakamane, grinning, carried a dead peccary slung across his shoulder as if it was no heavier than a sack of rice. Kadure handed over the shotgun and reclaimed his bow and arrows. Jarivanau led us to the first peccary and loaded it onto the smallest hunter. The man gripped it by the front legs, which hung down in front to his waist; its head lolled, still bleeding, on his chest and, beyond the huge bristled hump of its stomach on his shoulders, its rear hooves dangled at the back of his knees as he walked.

We made our way back past the prop-rooted trees, past the saplings encrusted with their black lagging of termites' nests, past the bromeliads with their rhubarb-like leaves growing on the jungle floor and in the forks of the biggest trees, and, after much Yanomami hooting and howling, we got an answering shout from a sleepy Chimo and filed into the dugout.

As we motored downriver I mimed a big snake (arms stretched out in a circle, for the girth) moving through the water (right arm undulating from side to side) and then raised my fingers to my eyes.

'Wai-konya!' chorused the Yanomami, nodding their heads.

'Of course they have seen it,' said Juan, 'but no one takes you to search for the culebra de agua. Everyone is afraid. Even the Yanomami are afraid. It is well known.'

We dropped the hunters off at the settlement, with the second peccary, and all the girls came out to greet us. They were wearing their beads, redistributed, colour-coded, some strung in bunches like grapes, some in necklaces, some in lines across the body; the matchstick girl had acquired more than her original share and hung them on a necklace which, at its lowest point, divided into two loops which passed across her breasts, under her arms, and joined again at the back of her neck: a big, bright red bead sat beside each nipple.

Back in camp, Pablo, Galvis and Valentine were miserable, sheltering in their hammocks under their nets. Extraordinary numbers of mosquitoes and blackfly darkened the air under the trees.

'We must leave this place,' said Pablo.

'We'll go when Jarivanau comes,' I said.

'We should go now,' said Galvis. 'We should go home.'

We stoked up the fire to boil water to pour over the peccary. Old Valentine was much troubled by a burrowing worm in his back.

'Keep me a piece of the fat, Galvis,' he said, 'I want to tie it over the hole. Maybe he'll come out.'

Valentine took his shirt off and we all inspected the site: there was an angry red swelling on his right shoulder-blade with a gentle ooze of pus in the centre. Blackfly crowded onto his back and he replaced his shirt, cursing.

'It's a good idea,' said Juan, 'sometimes they crawl into the fat.'

'Why can't you just squeeze it out?'

'It is facing head-down in there,' said Juan, 'and it has hooks round its mouth. It breathes through its anus. It comes from a fly, Dermatobia hominis. I read a paper on it. The fly sticks its eggs on a mosquito

The walk to the Yanomami.

Our first sight of the shabono.

The photograph before we entered the shabono. From the left: Culimacaré, Reymono, Chimo, Pablo, Jarivanau.

(*opposite*) A Yanomami mother.

Yanomami girls sitting round my pack.

Yanomami men.

(*opposite*) Yavateiba in his spider-monkey tail headband.

Jarivanau gets his blast of yoppo.

Up the right nostril: I get my blast from Jarivanau.

(*opposite*) The palm-frond dance.

The sneaked picture: Maquichemi, Yavateiba and their son.

or a tick – and, when that bites you, the eggs hatch and the larvae come out and they go into your skin where the mosquito or the tick sucked your blood; and they grow bigger and bigger for two or three months. It's very painful. Then one night the worm crawls out of the boil. It falls off and pupates and soon it is a fly again.'

'God knows why it chose you', said Chimo, 'there's nothing to eat on you.'

'The báquiro will help me,' said Valentine, picking up his machete and going to the dugout. Chimo followed with the pot of boiling water. They cleared one of the thick plank seats and draped the peccary across it. Chimo poured on dollops of steaming water, turning the skin white, and Valentine scraped off the hairs.

'Look at that,' said Chimo, pointing at the peccary's surprisingly large, grey-blue testicles, 'a real father. Just like me. If I was an animal, that's how I'd be – a báquiro.'

'I'd thought you'd be a fat old jaguar,' said Galvis.

'Not enough women,' said Chimo, considering the idea, 'no, I wouldn't like it – wandering through the forest all alone. It would be horrible. The biggest macho báquiro now – he fucks whoever he pleases, whenever he pleases. And besides, the báquiro has real courage. If a jaguar comes, he knows what to do: he walks up to that jaguar, and all the young men and the women they run away in a ring with the babies in the middle.'

'And what happens to the big macho báquiro?' I said.

'He dies like a man,' said Chimo.

Having finished removing the bristles, Valentine cut off its testicles, and slit the peccary open from its neck to its anus. He took out the heart and the liver and laid them glistening in the bottom of the dugout. He tossed the intestines into the river; they floated, bulbous, close in to the bank, quietly at first, and then, bobbing up and down, they drifted downstream in a patch of increasingly agitated water as the piranha pulled at them.

'Is this the big kind of peccary?' asked Juan.

'Yes,' said Chimo, gathering up the testicles, the heart and the liver and handing them to Galvis to cook, 'but I have hunted the small one, too, the chacaro. He has a white band round his neck and lives all over the place; the báquiro has a few white hairs under his mouth' (Chimo chucked the dead chin) 'and lives deep in the forest and

181

nowhere else. The báquiro, too, smells more like me. He has a strong smell. The chacaro, on the other hand, smells less like me. He smells more like a woman. He smells more like Galvis.'

'Then this is Tayassu pecari,' said Juan to me, 'the White-lipped peccary. And very little is known about it – because not many of the workers in research wish to live in the jungle.'

'*Wouldn't it be wonderful*,' I said, 'to have it with apple sauce and gravy and crackling and roast potatoes?' And then I thought of Simon, and decided to cut short this imaginative investigation of impossible pleasures at once.

'They boil it all – you'll see,' said Juan. 'It is the best way. Nothing is lost. The fat stays in the soup and not in the air. Roasting, Redmon, is for rich people.'

Night came, the frogs began to peep and croak and grunt and whistle and the cicadas began to vibrate the drumskins in their stomachs. We sat on logs round the fire drinking black coffee and waiting for Galvis to pronounce his soup – of pork cubes, head, liver, heart and balls – ready to eat.

'Redmon wants to see an anaconda,' said Juan.

'I know he does,' said Chimo, pushing more sticks under the pot, 'but I don't.'

'We'll ask Jarivanau,' said Juan, 'the Yanomami call it a wai-konya.'

'In Curipaco it's called umawairi,' said Culimacaré.

'In Geral,' said Valentine, 'it's the sucuriyu.'

'So Pablo – what is it in Baré?' I said.

'In Baré,' said Pablo, 'it's called the pinga-of-Chimo-going-for-a-swim.'

'Believe me,' said Chimo, 'they can swallow tapirs!'

At that moment the bushes by the bank moved. There was a rustling noise. Chimo knocked over his mug of coffee, jumped to his feet, and snatched his gun from its place by the stores. Culimacaré grabbed his machete, which was cleaved into the tree trunk above his head, and started forward.

'Whooo!' said Jarivanau, stepping into the firelight.

'Whooo!' said Wakamane.

'Whooo!' said Kadure, tying the big bongo up to our dugout.

'Holy Mother,' said Chimo, 'I thought it was a snake.'

*

Jarivanau carried his bow and arrows in one hand and a plastic bag in the other. He was wearing his quiver. He had something slung over his shoulder. He had his hammock slung over his shoulder.

Suddenly overcome with gratitude, I jumped up myself and clapped him on the back. Jarivanau looked surprised. He took the wad of tobacco out from between his lower lip and bottom front teeth, and offered it to me: it was tightly compressed lengthways, brown, soggy with mucus, and, altogether, looked exactly like the undelivered turds from the large intestine of the dead peccary. Thinking it might be a necessary part of some Yanomami contract that Chagnon had forgotten to mention, I put it in my mouth. It was warm, slimy and tasted bitter. Jarivanau leant his bow and arrow against a tree, mimed holding a yoppo pipe to my nostrils, and laughed. He then slapped me on the back, in return, I supposed, for my greeting, but with such force that I staggered forward and the turd ejected itself. Jarivanau bent down, picked it up, replaced it in his mouth, put his arm round my shoulder and threw his hammock down on top of the stores.

He was coming with us.

Anaconda

17

We nodded and smiled at the Yanomami, and the Yanomami, sitting with us on logs in a ring round the fire, nodded and smiled at us.

'We'll leave tomorrow,' I said.

'We'll be the first people to reach the end of the Emoni river', said Chimo, looking Buddha-like in the firelight, 'just like I always said. You can trust Chimo. But first we must feed the Yanomami. They're not allowed to have what they kill — not until all their wives and children have eaten. And one báquiro is not enough for all those people. So they've cheated and come here.'

Galvis piled our spare mess-tins with cubes of meat and pieces of heart and liver and Jarivanau, Wakamane and Kadure, adding fistfuls of manioc, ate with speed and concentration, in silence. By the time we had finished they were on their fourth helpings, their stomachs distended. After their fifth, Jarivanau grinned and laid his tin aside. Wakamane and Kadure climbed into their bongo and, without looking round, set off into the darkness.

The temperature fell, the frogs and cicadas stopped their noise. A wind bent the trees above us and we heard the dull hiss of an approaching storm. Culimacaré picked up Jarivanau's hammock and made as if to tie it in the space between his and Pablo's, beneath the communal tarpaulin, but Jarivanau, shaking his head, took a machete, cut down, trimmed and sharpened two saplings and drove them into the ground, about five feet apart, leaning away from each other, and right beside the fire. Culimacaré fetched our small surplus polythene sheet from the dugout and, with parachute cord, rigged it between the posts like a tent top.

Jarivanau piled sticks on the fire, slung his hammock and placed his bag of possessions beneath it. I dug out my last Oxford pipe and my last tin of Balkan Sobranie from the bottom of my bergen and presented them to him. He took the gifts without a word, wrenched open the tin, stuffed the pipe with tobacco, lit it expertly with a burning twig, and got into his hammock. It looked as uncomfortable as any hammock could be: he was bunched up, almost in a semi-circle, the lengths of vine (there were no cross-pieces) cutting lines into the flesh of his back.

The rain arrived. It blasted down through the trees like pig-shot, and we retreated beneath the big tarpaulin. Jarivanau, naked but for Gabriel's trousers, his pipe alight and upside-down in his mouth, his thumb over the bowl, his bow and arrows leaning against his hammock post, lay back in obvious delight, his stomach full, and his thoughts apparently wholly comprised of admiration for his new plastic roof.

It was still raining when we tied the dugouts together and left at dawn.

Jarivanau crept beneath the big tarpaulin at our backs, next to the sack of rice; his head formed an unmoving hump in the canvas, his knees supported a small lake which overflowed in two cataracts over the top of his thighs and splashed down onto the duckboards. Only his right foot stuck out — it was short but remarkably high, the skin sloping sharply down from the bottom front of his ankle to the top back of his toes, a boot of muscle. It was thickly callused at the base, with no discernible instep, cross-hatched with the scars of small cuts, and pock-marked with the purplish roundels of healed ulcers. The skin around each toenail was slightly inflamed and the nails themselves were buckled into ridges and half-eaten away by chiggers. Staring at such a record of jungle strolls I fervently hoped that my own last pair of boots would hold together.

At midday the rain eased slightly, and shortly afterwards we turned into the Emoni. Chimo, his pipe in his mouth but his tobacco too wet to burn, was so dispirited that he forgot to stand up and anoint the new river. The country was low and flooded, the tall manaca palms had disappeared.

Worryingly late in the evening we found a small island of bank, made camp in the rain, changed into dry clothes, finished the peccary soup and went to sleep.

In the morning the mist was thick and cold, but rising; and after we had travelled for several hours, it began to clear. We were emerging, too, from the flooded mouth of the river; the banks became continuous, the trees grew tall again and, for the first time since Neblina, between swathes of mist and the slow swirl of black cloud, we could make out the low shapes of forest-covered hills.

A watery sun appeared. Jarivanau came out of hiding and lay on top of the tarpaulin, our clothes began to steam a little, and a flock of Black-headed parrots sang *toot-toot-toot* from the trees beside us.

I took the lens flaps off my binoculars, pulled Schauensee out of its canvas bag, and began to feel that life still had a lot to offer.

'Juan, I just have a feeling – I think this is going to be the most beautiful river we have ever been up.'

Juan scrutinised me, like a scientist.

'The real Yanomami wait at the end of it,' said Juan, and then: 'Are you *very* happy?' he asked.

'Yes, yes I suppose I am,' I said.

'Then you have a fever,' said Juan decisively, squeezing water out of his beard and turning away.

Cuvier's toucans yapped unseen in the trees all around us and occasionally flew across the river with desperate, fast wing-beats. Flocks of Great egrets, hunched on their perches halfway up the taller trees, ruffled and preened their feathers after the rain and, as we approached, took to the air on their wide, rounded wings; trailing their long black legs, they flew in loose, stately, linear flocks of ten to twenty birds in front of the dugout for a hundred yards or so, and then, rising above the trees, white against the remnant of dark clouds, they would double back to safety. Giant herons, awkward and unsure in comparison, always alone, would flap from one low perch to a higher one upstream, and then labour, with a deep squawk, up over the forest canopy and out of sight.

The river was obviously undisturbed, unvisited; the pairs of Green ibis hardly bothered to fly from us; the big blue-and-white Ringed kingfishers buzzed our boats, at half-speed, to take a closer look. The birds were as tame as the very few species we had seen on the swampy channels of the overgrown Baria, but here in the open and the sunlight, on a white-water river with firm banks and tall palms and great leguminous trees and purple-flowering vines, they were absurdly various and plentiful.

For the first time we could compare all four green kingfishers, their backs an iridescent, dark, oily green which somehow caught the light even as they hid in the deep shadow of the overhanging foliage. The biggest, the Amazon kingfisher, would grip a twig higher up than the others and furthest from the bank, *cack-cack-cack*-ing as we drew level and he streaked downstream. The Green-and-rufous (which I only saw once), the next size down, skulked further back behind the leaves. The Green kingfisher, smaller still, was bolder but perched lower, and both birds, when flushed, made a noise like our stonechat, a gritty *tick-tick*. And lastly, the Pygmy kingfisher, which was difficult to spot, turned out to be quite common if you peered low into the darkest recesses near the bank for several travelling hours. It would flit away, never coming into the open, and *peep-peep*-ing to itself as it went. Apart from their size the kingfishers varied only in the different proportions of white and rufous and green on their throats and chests, an obvious case of one species evolving into four, a simple adaptation to different niches, to hunt different sizes of fish. It was all very satisfying, a flicker of easily comprehensible, natural logic in the impossibly complicated thrust and tangle of trees and bushes and lianas, of epiphytic orchids and bromeliads and ferns, an overarching presence of thousands upon thousands of different species most of whose names even Juan found it impossible to guess.

Rounding a bend on the narrowing river, the engine throttled back, we put a Cattle-egret-sized yellow heron to flight from its fishing-place, and, with mounting excitement, I failed to find it in Schauensee. Perhaps it was just too rare to earn a place? The unrecorded Emoni yellow snake-eating heron, *Snakonoshicus redmondius*? But no – a sharp little note informed me that the Capped heron 'becomes buffy in breeding season': they just go yellow with desire. I turned and waved my binoculars at Chimo in an onrush of pleasure; and was rewarded with the toothless grandfather of all grins.

About fifteen bends further on I was leaning back against the rice sack, admiring a flight of eight pairs of Blue-and-yellow macaws, their long, pointed tails streaming, their bare-skinned faces turned down to look at us, their dirty-old-crone laughter, their terminal, General Paralysis of the Insane, syphilitic shrieks filling the air, when Chimo suddenly swung the dugouts right round and headed back downstream, pointing at the opposite bank. Galvis, sitting opposite me in the other boat, looked up in alarm from his interminable study of the ancient copy of the *Reader's Digest*.

Something was arranged in sagging loops along a fallen tree-trunk at the water's edge, half-obscured by the lower leaves of upstanding lateral shoots. It was big and brown and coiled and glistening in the sun; it was an anaconda.

Chimo shut off the engine and we drifted down towards it in the current. It had rough star-shaped black rings set on a yellow background down the middle of its bulky flanks; overall it was a light brown, its head, resting in the middle of its circling body, a duller brown and surprisingly small — mostly mouth. I leaned closer over the side of the canoe, to get a decent portrait with my inadequate, fixed wide-angle lens and, from three feet away, found myself looking into its tiny, brown, impassive, piggy eyes. Galvis, unable to bear the tension any longer, yelped. The head reared an inch or two and flicked backwards; the coils seemed to lash only once; and the snake, with unnerving speed, disappeared into the watery undergrowth.

'It's a baby,' said Juan, as Chimo re-started the engine and turned the dugouts round again, 'it's the smallest I've ever seen. It's about nine feet.'

'They may be three feet long when they're born,' I said, annoyed, 'but then they're only an inch thick. So it wasn't *that* young.'

'When they go old,' said Juan, 'they go blue.'

'He came to see us,' said Chimo, 'because we talked about him. It is not good to talk too much.'

About an hour later Chimo pointed to a small snake's head, upright in the water, crossing the river from right to left.

'Bejuquilla,' he announced, grinning, swinging the two pole-linked dugouts towards it.

The snake, finding its way momentarily barred by the side of the dugout, simply lifted itself up and came aboard, exactly where Chimo had intended. Its narrow little head had been misleading; a full six foot of thin, green-backed, yellow-flanked, white-bellied, red-tongued snake looped down in front of Galvis.

Galvis, his imagination presumably still scaly with anacondas, began to yell as if he meant it, a long cry that began low and rose rapidly in pitch; he stood up on his plank seat and threw his copy of the *Reader's Digest* overboard.

The snake, unappeased, reared towards his crutch. Galvis, with equal decisiveness, jumped. Arms flung forward and long legs trailing, like a gibbon, he flew easily across the gap between the boats, over the front edge of our covered cargo, and into the arms of Culimacaré in the bow. Chimo, howling with laughter, zig-zagged the canoes. The snake drew itself up, spanned the gap between the dugouts and came for me as I took its long green blur of a portrait. It undulated a couple of half-cartwheels under my elbow, thrashed onto the top of the tarpaulin, and – across my spare pair of trousers, which I had spread to dry – it made for Jarivanau. Jarivanau backed towards Chimo, grabbed the trousers and flicked the snake into the water. His new pipe, which he had laid in pride of place in front of him, went with it.

Pablo gave a whoop, threw his right gumboot into the air and caught it; Culimacaré spluttered in Curipaco, jigging his arm up and down; even Valentine looked happy.

'It's a Green vine snake,' said Juan, 'it's only poisonous a little.'

Galvis climbed sheepishly back to his plank.

'Never mind,' he said, 'I have two more books. I have the story of the life of Marie Antoinette and the story of the life of Mahatma Gandhi.'

'That bejuquilla was after your arse,' said Chimo, wiping his old eyes.

In the late afternoon we made camp beside a small creek. Chimo and Pablo fished for piranhas, Culimacaré took the gun and set off into the forest to try and shoot a curassow, and I went for a swim fully clothed. The creek, half-dammed back by the river, smelt of rotting leaves and slack pools and undulating weeds – it smelt, suddenly, of childhood, of the patch of stream beneath the great willow at the bottom of the Vicarage garden, of my ten-year-old imaginings, of bubbles from sunken empty orange-squash bottles baited with bread and full of silver-bellied minnows, of sticklebacks and Miller's thumbs and water beetles, of the breathing of the crayfish and the stick-encrusted larva of the caddisfly, of the fishy hatching of a million eggs. And, that night, safe in my hammock, full of curassow soup and piranha soup, I dreamt that I was back with my 16-bore (blue cartridges) hiding behind a scraggy hedge on the high ground of Ferguson's farm, waiting for woodpigeons that never appeared, waiting for the largest flock of *Columba palumbus palumbus* ever recorded by the British Trust for Ornithology which might well be on its way towards me in numbers that would darken the sky, and which, at the last moment, would be forced by contrary winds to fly very slowly, one at a time, on a straight and steady course over my head. I looked out at a hare crouched in the stubble field in front of me; at the great sweep of downland behind; at the beech clumps and the Neolithic earthworks on the high points of the horizon; at the white chalk track which wound up and grew small on its way to the dewpond on Tan Hill; and at the group of hunters in wolfskins who grew large as they loped down it towards me, clacking their long bows and arrows above their heads.

Harpy Eagle

18

Dawn erupted with an all-enveloping roar, a great bronchitic intake of breath in the trees above us; the ends of branches shook in the canopy; I could just make out the odd patch of red fur against the light. Before I could stop him, Culimacaré grabbed Chimo's gun and fired up to the left. A bundle disentangled itself from the high leaves and fell loosely to the ground. The roaring ceased; the trees emptied away from us.

'Juan, tell them not to do that again,' I said, annoyed.

'Redmon, we need food. But you are right. When you shoot a monkey and it falls to the ground with a wound and you go to hit it with a stick – it covers its head with its hands.'

'It's better to starve.'

'It is never better to starve,' said Juan.

The Howler lay on a clump of roots, shot in the chest, dead. He was about the size of a cocker spaniel, his thick fur buff-coloured along his back and a deep red-brown along his sides and stomach. His face was small and black, his ears blackish, his eyes brown and open, and his genitals skin-white. His hands and fingers were long and black (with nails like ours) and the inside last six-inches of his tail was lined with black skin like his hands. Culimacaré picked him up under his armpits, as you would a child, and placed him in our dugout.

We finished the piranha soup, disconnected the canoes, and set off up the narrowing river with both engines throttled down to save petrol. There were small, untropical-looking white clouds in the narrow band of azure sky above us and, but for the height of the trees and the looped curtain of lianas tumbling down and trailing in the water beside us, the whirr of cicadas and the constant, mournful, double wolf-whistle of the Screaming piha, we might have been travelling up a waterway in an English wood. As we rounded a bend, there were fifty English Peregrine falcons criss-crossing the air beneath the underbelly of a cloud. Except that there were forty-nine too many of them, and their wing-beats were all wrong; their flight was graceful, delicate, buoyant; they aroused no Peregrine-like suspicion that they had just fired themselves from cross-bows.

'Gavilán plomizo,' said Chimo, lifting his pipe in salute to them.

Schauensee translated for me: they were Plumbeous kites; and, once I had found them in the sixty-six black-and-white illustrations of birds of prey in flight, I could make out the three white bands across their dark tails. There were three Swallow-tailed kites soaring with them, and through the binoculars I could see that the whole flock was feeding on a swarm of large, heavy-bodied insects – probably flying ants, in which case, I thought, considered in the long term, they had not been feeding hard enough.

The banks grew taller and the river faster flowing; forest-covered hills surrounded us, seeming to block the way ahead and, once we had passed, to shut off all retreat. In our own immediate world, beneath an overhang of large-leaved, fleshy plants on the right bank, we disturbed a bird so distinctive that I recognised it at once: a sungrebe – small, long-bodied, olive-brown, skulking – it fluttered a little distance in front of us and then splashed back into the water, its head jerking, the black and white stripes on its neck flicking back and forth as it swam. We drew level and it repeated the process until we reached the invisible edge of its little kingdom, when it flew back past the boat to safety, its legs dangling: 'Builds nest of sticks in bushes above the water,' said Schauensee, 'transports its chicks in cavities on its side; swims and flies perfectly carrying its young until they fledge.'

Further upstream, three howlers ran on all fours for cover along the wide branches of a vast ceiba tree as we approached; and an hour or two later we slid by a hundred feet beneath a pair of Spider monkeys in some kind of legume tree, who just paused in their aerial walk and looked at us, black eyes in black faces, their bodies black-furred and slender, holding on with their hands and feet, their long tails S-shaped above their backs. Jarivanau stood up, mimed loosing an arrow, and gave a high-pitched Yanomami cry. The monkeys jumped twenty feet down into a smaller tree and swung away by their arms, ape-like.

It was obviously one of those rare, rich days when everyone had come out to look at us. I lay back on the tarpaulin. Large anxieties seemed to brachiate off into the forest like Spider monkeys, small ones skulked out of my stomach like sungrebes, and, despite myself, I fell asleep.

Juan woke me with a yell. I opened my eyes — and focused them straight into the green-brown pupils of the mightiest eagle in the world. The black and white rounded wings, a good six feet across, seemed to hang above the boat for ever; the grey hood and enormous hooked black bill were turned down towards us; the wrist-thick legs and the massive talons, a startling bright yellow, were held straight back towards the long barred tail.

'Jesus!' I said.

'Harpy eagle,' said Juan.

A bird that lives by ripping monkeys and sloths out of trees, it plainly intended to amuse itself by plucking Juan and me out of the dugout, one in each foot. But then, thinking better of it, with one leisurely beat of the great wings it rose over the canopy and out of sight.

'How's that?' said Chimo, immensely proud, half-raising his fist in the air and shaking it back and forth in self-congratulation. 'Only Chimo could show you such a bird.'

We cut steps up the high muddy bank and made camp. Chimo and Pablo spread palm fronds on the ground and began to prepare the Howler monkey, scalding it with boiling water and scraping off the fur. Its skin turned white, like a baby's.

That night, when Pablo had jointed the body and Galvis boiled it, Chimo handed me a suspiciously full mess tin. As I spooned out the soup the monkey's skull came into view, thinly covered in its red meat, the eyes still in their sockets.

'We gave it to you specially,' said Chimo with great seriousness, sitting on a log beside me, taking another fistful of manioc from the tin and adding it to his own bowl. 'It's an honour in our country. If you eat the eyes we will have good luck.'

The skull bared its broken teeth at me. I picked it up, put my lips to the rim of each socket in turn, and sucked. The eyes came away from their soft stalks and slid down my throat.

Chimo put his bowl down, folded his hands on his paunch, and roared with laughter.

'You savage!' he shouted. 'You horrible naked savage! Don't you think it looks like a man? Eh? How *could* you do a disgusting thing like that?'

In the morning, while Jarivanau and Culimacaré went hunting and Juan and the others dug for carbon a little way off in the forest, I retrieved the rest of the howler skull from the communal pot. The lower jaw was wide and deep at its rear angle, and a bony box which I found bobbing in the soup exactly fitted in the space beneath it. It was a parchment-thick hanging sac, the resonating chamber which amplifies the deep and breathy roar that marks out the howler group's territory. The back teeth were evenly worn down, almost to the gums, by a lifetime's eating of leaves and buds, flowers and fruit and nuts. I picked out the brains with a small stick and the tweezers from my Swiss Army knife, peeled away the scraps of flesh and rubbed salt into my trophy to preserve it.

A small bird, robin-like, came to watch from a bush on my right. It regarded me, unafraid, cocking its head first one way and then the other, its tail stumpy as a wren's, its breast white with black spots and its back brown with white spots. I drew Schauensee out of the front pocket of my bergen and found the likeliest plate – it was a Dot-backed antbird, whose habits, Phelps and Schauensee thought, were 'probably similar to Spot-backed antbird', which, in turn, 'probably follows army ants'. So we had reached a place where the habits of some of the most common-seeming birds (birds that came and sat beside you and introduced themselves) were unknown, their nests undescribed, their eggs unseen.

Jarivanau and Culimacaré came back from hunting with a curassow apiece, and the antbird flitted off through the undergrowth. I went to our canoe, wrapped the howler skull in a torn shirt and placed it in the top of a kit-bag. Juan joined me, clutching his new carbon samples in two small sealable plastic wallets. He stowed them in his

waterproof box; and then he turned to me suddenly, a barely con-
trolled ferocity in his quick movements, a half-mocking smile on his
face.

'You will never reach to the real Yanomami.'

'What do you mean?'

'Redmon, there are many things you do not know. Until now I
am keeping them from you. Galvis has made trouble. The Indians
they want to turn back.'

'Nonsense.'

'They told me when we dug for carbon. Galvis says there is not
much manioc. And only one tank of gasoline. They say they need
one tank for the Siapa. No man could paddle through those clouds
of blackfly.'

'I've got plenty of insect repellent. We'll share out some more.
There's nothing to worry about.'

'There is everything to worry about,' said Juan. 'You must take a
decision.'

A humming-bird buzzed between us and hovered for a moment.
It was a Long-tailed hermit, a tiny blur of mad intensity between its
bronze green head and its long white tail which hung straight down,
motionless for a small part of a second.

'Not now,' I said. 'Not yet. Today we go upriver.'

Late that morning we passed beneath a great brown granite hill,
massy above the trees, its upper slopes bare and rounded.

'Toucan mountain,' announced Chimo.

The river grew still narrower and faster-flowing, the banks higher.
We disturbed otters who scrambled up to safety in the forest, water
droplets scattering from their fur; we swung round bends between
small, sandy cliffs in which kingfishers had tunnelled their nests; we
annoyed a pair of Red-throated caracaras, black, buzzard-sized birds
with white bellies, red-skinned throats and faces, and with bills like
chickens, who just stayed perched at the top of their tree and swore
at us with extraordinary volume and vehemence.

'Ca-ca-ca-ca-cacao,' they screamed, with no self-control whatever,
until a bend in the river shut them away behind us.

And then we saw something shocking, out of place. A bridge
spanned the river ahead.

'Whoooo! Whoooo!' sang Jarivanau, delighted, stretching himself.

Everyone else looked uneasily at the close banks, at the dark spaces under the leaves.

'It's okay,' said Chimo, 'it's old.'

Two long poles had been thrust into the river bed at an angle just out from the left bank and lashed where they intersected; more poles, tied together, laid in the fork of the upright, and further suspended by lianas commandeered as cables and pulled out over the water from the surrounding trees, formed a fragile walkway to similar crossed uprights on the opposite bank. But it did look reassuringly abandoned; the whole structure had been half-pushed over by the current.

'Juan,' I said, 'you must brush your teeth especially well tonight.'

'How so?'

'Because then they'll look *their very best* in a necklace.'

'If I take a sample,' said Juan, jerkily brushing a large green Leaf insect off his arm, 'I find that one in ten of your jokes is a funny, and that unit only in five per cent of content.'

Chimo motored slowly, looking ahead with excessive attention, silent. I half expected to see Conrad's 'sticks, little sticks' from *Heart of Darkness* 'flying about ... whizzing before my nose, dropping below me, striking behind me'. Maybe Galvis would suddenly 'look at me over his shoulder in an extraordinary, profound, familiar manner' and fall across his penny life of Gandhi while 'what appeared to be a long cane', stuck to his back, would clatter round and knock against our remaining petrol drum.

But the sunlight sparked white along the ridge of our little bow wave in the usual way; it fell undisturbed among the tops of the giant trees on the tierra ferme banks, picking out the moss and lichens and bromeliads high on an exposed stretch of branch; it lit the bright red of a limp cluster of new young leaves; it dropped into steep caverns of vegetation and disappeared.

And, as I watched through my binoculars, it caught the red beak of a Black nunbird, dark, contemplative, chubby, perched at the top of a lone palm tree. It was the first member of the puffbird family (large-headed, thick-necked, kingfisher-like birds) that I had seen, and I recognised it simply because its representative also sat on a very special plate in Schauensee and Phelps, one of only two illustrations (the other of humming-birds) which were painted by Phelps's wife

Kathleen. Around a male Cock-of-the-rock she had also arranged a Blue-crowned motmot; an Amazonian umbrella bird (large, black, its head thatched with blue and its lower throat sporting a matching wattle, and which, according to Snow, moos like a calf and growls like a distant chain saw); a Red-ruffed fruitcrow (which 'emits a deep, booming hollow sound resembling the bellowing of a bull'); a capuchinbird (which 'bellows like an ox'); a Guianan red-cotinga (a finch-size mix of silky crimson, dusky maroon and rosy carmine with a penchant for figs); and an oilbird flat on its stomach at the base of the page (a whiskered, nightjar-like brown bird which screams, snarls, snores, echo-locates by clicks in its roosting caves, and feeds at night on fruit that is plucked in flight and swallowed whole).

Lost in comforting admiration of plate 25, I was wondering how many years I would have to live in the jungle before I saw the Amazonian umbrellabird, and what a good idea a fixed umbrella would be, and whether Toucan mountain or the highlands ahead would prove to be the previously unrecorded home of the most exotic of them all, the White bellbird, when Juan shouted, 'Macaw!'

A shiny, bright little bird, chaffinch-sized, with a crimson head, white belly and black wings flew low over the water and up into a dead branch projecting from the shore. It was a Red-capped cardinal.

Juan laughed. Chimo sat unmoved. I put Schauensee away. There was a snag ahead. A great tree lay across the river about two feet above the surface, supported on its branches.

Culimacaré stood up in the bow, grasping the axe, but Chimo shook his head and brought the dugout into the bank. There was an ominous sound of crashing water, of rapids ahead. The tree showed dull red where branches had been ripped away in its fall. It was obviously a species of hardwood, half-a-day's cutting if the Indians worked in relays. Leafcutter ants processed along its top all the way to the other side of the stream. We dug muddy steps up the bank, cleared a patch of ground and began to make camp. Chimo laid his gun in the curiara, eased the little boat beneath the tree and paddled off upriver.

Jarivanau, relaxed with us now, pleased with the machete I had given him and dressed in a pair of Culimacaré's bright green shorts, rubbed his taut stomach and gestured at a big palm, a ceje. The fruit hung in grape-like bunches, high up under the crown of fronds, dark against the light; and the trunk of the tree was ringed, all the way up, with long black spines. The problem looked insoluble. Culimacaré had never offered to climb a ceje. It was plainly a barbed-wire, broken-glass, festering-ulcer-per-spike palm.

Forgetting whose country it was, I shook my head at Jarivanau. Jarivanau grinned and shook his own, beaten-up head at me. He ran a hand over his stubby scalp and looked about at the surrounding saplings; he then cut down four, trimmed them, and laid the poles in two X-shapes with their top Vs against the base of the palm, their ends projecting on the far side. He tugged down a coil of mamure vine from a neighbouring tree, cut it into lengths, and bound his poles loosely at their divergent points beyond the trunk, tightly where they crossed each other hard against the palm on the side nearest him. He then raised the top frame to chest height, lodged it at an incline towards him, grabbed hold, hooked his muscled toes around the bottom frame's sides and, slowly but rhythmically, edged his way into the air, three feet out from the thorns, his machete in his teeth. We clapped.

Jarivanau steeplejacked upwards, his back brown and scarred like the bark of the tree behind him, his muscles alternately bunching and flattening beneath their lichen of blood spots. The frail platform, bending horribly, rose into the crown; Jarivanau reached forward and, with tremendous swipes, severed the stem. The heavy clusters thudded to the ground. Jarivanau descended, his teeth re-clamped on the blade of his precious machete. Culimacaré and Pablo picked the hard, purple-red, plum-sized fruits from their stalks and Valentine pounded them in the big pot, like manaca. Juan and Galvis set about building a fire. Jarivanau and I sat down on the top of a big surface root and began to pluck the curassows; he pulled out each black, white-tipped tail feather, smoothed it between his fingers and gently poked it tip-first into a patch of mud beside him: spare fletches for his arrows. I mimed someone walking and pointed in the vague direction of the highlands.

'Cuántas días?' I asked. 'How many days to the Yanomami?'

Jarivanau put down the half-naked bird, swivelled round on the root, brought his arm back behind his head and then shot it straight out five times towards the west, repeating the gesture he had used that night in his communal hut. Its very emphasis suggested an insane effort. Five days' walking for a Yanomami, I thought; maybe eight days' for us.

From the landing-stage there came the kind of wet snort a bull gives when inspecting a cow on heat; a bucket-sized gob; a fart from a siege mortar. Chimo had returned. He clambered up to the camp carrying a small cayman by the front legs and dumped it in front of Galvis.

'Reymono,' he said, wiping his mouth quickly with the back of his hand, 'we will never get past the rapids. If we *walk* into the Chori lands, anything could happen. We are not welcome here. It is not our country. We must turn back.'

So this was it – the moment I had feared more than any other, a moment for which I thought I had prepared myself. In my imagination I was always calm, forceful, measured, persuasive. But it was not like that; it caught me from behind, silently; I needed a piss; I was tired; it was all over. I began to shake.

Chimo took his helmet off and hung it on the hammock-post beside him. He rubbed both hands over his face, as if clearing sleep from his eyes.

'I'm going on with Jarivanau,' I said, feeling ridiculous even as the words formed themselves. 'So who's coming with me?'

I stood up. Nobody moved; Galvis looked away and poked at his fire with a stick. Juan was right; they really did mean to desert. On a leaf by my right boot a large red ant was waving its antennae about; I felt suddenly disconnected from everything, cut off from myself. I tried to smile, but failed; it was as though I had ceased to inhabit my own face. Through the gap we had cleared in the bushes I could see the desolate brown river eddying past. A Screaming piha called.

Chimo looked up; he put his helmet back on his head and he began to sing softly. He was absurd in his army shorts, his yellow gum boots. 'I'm by far the biggest girl in town,' he sang, 'but, just for you, I'll take my knickers down.' And he came and stood beside me.

Sungrebe

19

Shamed, Culimacaré and Pablo picked up their machetes and joined us.

'Then that's settled,' said Chimo, 'my old friend Valentine can have a rest at last; and the girl Galvis can cook for himself and guard the boats. But we'll mark the trail well, Galvis, so that when the Yanomami have killed us they will walk here – and kill you, too; you won't hear a thing – and believe me, those arrows can lift a man right off the ground and stick him on a tree.'

Valentine, looking much older than he had that morning, silent, unsmiling, his movements querulous, set about building a smoking rack for the cayman. Galvis, on the other hand, temporarily released from his great fear of the Yanomami, re-found his usual talkative and cheerful self, opened his personal medicine box (which, I now saw, consisted entirely of different-coloured soaps and shampoos), hummed one of his pop songs, and shuffle-danced himself down to the river for a wash.

Juan and I began to cut up the cayman, and Jarivanau, Chimo, Pablo and Culimacaré wandered off into the forest.

'I am worried,' said Juan *sotto voce*, his face close to mine. 'Redmon, I am worried that I am not strong enough. It will be like the peccary hunt, but it will go on for days and days. We will have to keep up with Jarivanau. I will not be able to walk so far and so fast.'

'Nonsense,' I said, secretly hoping that he might be diabetic; or possess only one lung; or suffer from congenital crutch decay — anything to slow down the pace. And as if in answer to my wish, he stood up, undid his belt with extreme awkwardness, and dropped his trousers.

'Look!' said Juan. 'It hurts me a lot. It even hurts at night.'

Two red patches, slightly scaly at the edges, spread widening up his inner thighs and disappeared under his pants. The fungus had got him.

'Why didn't you tell me? Why didn't you ask for some cream?'

'I thought you made a fuss about nothing. I thought you were ridiculous.'

'I am ridiculous,' I said triumphantly, feeling like a veteran, going to my pack, taking a spare tube of Canesten from a side-pocket and handing it to him with a flourish, 'but you've only lived in research stations; when you're in the jungle all the time every man's crutch should be a Venus bug-trap.'

Juan dabbed the white goo onto his raw skin. 'And last night I caught two brown ticks feeding on my balls: they must have come from the howler. It's how you get yellow fever.'

'Not here,' I said firmly, assuming more knowledge which I didn't possess. 'There's no yellow fever here.'

Jarivanau and the others returned bearing long bundles of green palm fronds. They squatted on the ground and, watching Culimacaré who was obviously the expert, they began to plait the leaves together. In ten minutes they had made Curipaco bergens, sixty-pound-capacity palm-leaf backpacks. Chimo then selected the right tree, a medium-sized sapling, made a machete-cut at the top of his reach and tugged off long strips of bark, about six-inches wide, which he wove into the rims and sides of the baskets to make head-bands and shoulder straps.

'Catumarés,' said Chimo, pleased with himself, testing one by trying to stretch its fretwork of leaves and stems. 'Now we can walk till our pingas drop off.'

As the tree frogs quacked and piped and trilled above and around us we parcelled out the stores — all the remaining plastic bags of beads, fish hooks, fishing line, mirrors and combs; medicines; a machete each; and half our remaining supply of all the food we had left — salt, sugar, coffee, cornflour and lentils. On top of my share of the common cargo I packed the Polaroid and our last one hundred exposures; Simon's Minolta and all the film we possessed; my spare pair of spectacles and my gym shoes, my last reserve footwear. I decided against D'Abrera's *Butterflies of South America* and my copies of Chagnon and Lizot, but for Schauensee. There would barely be room, at the top of the bergen, for the outsize, wet, heavy, Colombian hammock: for the first time I regretted leaving the compact, light, canvas SAS version in San Carlos. I wrapped my precious notebooks in two plastic bags and stowed them uneasily in Galvis's medicine box.

'300 extra bolivares,' I announced, 'to everyone who comes with me – if we find the Yanomami.' And, after supper, as we washed our mess-tins free of cayman grease in the river, '300 bolivares extra to you, too, and to old Valentine,' I whispered in Galvis's lemon-shampoo-scented ear, 'if you guard my notebooks.'

'What use is that to me,' said Galvis, 'if you don't come back?'

Chimo, stoking up the fire, whistling, talking to himself, woke us well before dawn; we packed our hammocks and mosquito nets, and Pablo and Culimacaré bound one of our smaller canvas shelter-tops apiece on top of their loads. Jarivanau simply wound his split-vine sleeping-net into a ball and stuffed it into his catumaré, beneath half the smoked tail of the cayman, wrapped in leaves.

I went down to the dugout, my torchlight diffusing into the heavy mist, to fetch a potent talisman which James Fenton had given me in Oxford. With great care, I took it out of its plastic wallet in the number one kit-bag. The prize of one of his contemplative journeys round the city's antique shops, it was the Fenton award for great bravery in Borneo in the face of no discernible danger whatever. I admired it afresh before slipping it into my pocket. One side was embossed with a profiled head of a respectable gentleman in glasses like mine: '50 JAHR PAUL LEWY HEISS ICH. 26.XII. 1926,' ran the inscription: 'MY NAME IS PAUL LEWY AND I'VE LIVED FOR FIFTY YEARS;' and, on the other side, equally boldly, were cast his buttocks: 'WAS AUCH WAR TÄGLICH SCHEISS ICH,' they announced: 'AND, WHAT'S MORE, I'VE HAD A SHIT EVERY DAY.'

*

Exactly at first light persons unknown began cutting wood with two circular saws. It was unnerving, insistent: a frantic reverberation of screaming and whining and rasping.

'Viudita carrablanca!' shouted Chimo, hoisting his catumaré onto his shoulders.

'It is the White-faced saki,' said Juan. 'He is very rare and we have luck to hear him. He is small and black and his wife is brown – and for a long time they were thought to be two different species. He lives with his wife and the children in the middle layer of the trees and they eat fruit and seeds. He is little known. This is the first time I hear him.'

There were two more bursts of sound, then silence.

I swung the corpse-like weight of my bergen onto my back, shook hands with Galvis, and waved to Valentine who was standing apart, leaning on a tree by the steps to the boats. The old man came up to me and took both my hands in his. He seemed smaller, as if he had withered slightly in the night. He studied me with his profoundly sad, watery, inefficient eyes.

'Thank you,' he said, 'for the pipe you gave me.'

I formed up behind our new leader, Jarivanau. Barefoot, he had his face forced down to his shoulders by the weight of his palm-leaf pack pulling on the strap across the top front third of his head; the scars on the other two-thirds were red with pressure and excitement; he grasped his new machete with one hand and held the shotgun tight round the barrel with the other; he grinned uncontrollably, horribly eager to start.

Juan stood behind me, tense; Culimacaŕe and Pablo waited behind him and Chimo, still whistling, wandered up from the rear. Jarivanau bounded off like a peccary.

Four foot six inches tall, brutally fit, he slipped under lianas that caught me round the waist. He swung his catumaré to his side and stooped beneath the branches of fallen tree trunks which forced me to take off my bergen and crawl through on all fours, dragging it after me. His bare boot-feet propelled him through the small creeks and up their soft, dark, rotted banks without a change in his half-loping rhythm, while I slid in and floundered out. But, most impressive of all, I could see, through the sweat and mist on my glasses, that he was constantly alert: despite the weight hanging from his head which made the tendons in his neck stand out like chicken legs, he kept scanning the underside of the canopy for palms in fruit, for bees' nests, for the unwary guan, for the movement of leaves that might betray a Howler or a Spider monkey.

After an hour or so of such a pace my sole preoccupation became judging the moment, in the short stretches between the sluggish streams and deep, full gulleys, when it might be possible to unbutton the flap on one of my SAS water-bottle holsters, pull out the aluminium bottle without losing sight of Jarivanau's ever-receding back, unscrew the black rubber top, take a desperate swig and replace it.

Mindless with fatigue, I had just completed such a manoeuvre and even re-filled a bottle from a ditch we were crossing, when Jarivanau, jumping over a tree trunk, suddenly spun round and pointed at the rotted bark. I moved closer and stooped down to peer at the place he indicated: I could see nothing unusual, just ridges of dark brown lichen and straggles of fungus. Jarivanau yelled, waving me back. Juan, catching up from behind, grabbed my arm.

'Mapanaré!' he shouted.

Culimacaré caught up with us and took hold of my shirt.

And then I just made out a short length of brown, brushed velvet, dropped along a slight hollow in the wood. It was, I realised dimly, a snake; its head was triangular, the sides of its body shaded into black.

Jarivanau darted forward, hit it with his machete, impaled it behind the head and tossed it into the undergrowth. Its belly flashed yellow as it turned in the air.

'Mapanaré! Barba amarillo!' shouted Juan, still excited, letting go of my arm. 'You nearly died! You nearly make your last stupid! Why do you want to kiss a snake?'

'I didn't see it,' I said, weakly. 'I had no idea.'

And anyway, I thought, it was difficult to believe that anything so fundamentally peaceful, so well camouflaged, could actually rouse itself and kill you.

Culimacaré, looking anxious and protective, jigged his arm up and down, still holding my shirt, and then let me go.

'You call it the fer-de-lance,' said Juan, 'and it is very common here. A lot of people die when they clear the ground for their conucos. Every female has sixty or eighty young, all born alive, and with all their poisonous equipment ready from the day one.'

I stepped over the tree trunk. The now-machete-scarred surface was on a level with my upper thighs. The fer-de-lance was about eighteen inches long. My own equipment retracted, sharply.

Culimacaré pushed past me without a word and fell into step behind Jarivanau, marking the trail as he went, cutting a plant stem or a twig with his machete every twenty yards or so. The pace eased, the country grew even flatter, and there was time to look about; the soils were obviously poor, big trees were rare and dwarf species common — miniature palms, no more than ten feet tall, and small trees with tufts of enormous leaves sprouting from their tops grew among the saplings. Yet even in the lowered, more broken canopy formed by the middle-sized trees, bromeliads clustered in every fork of the branches, their leaves half-furled together at their bases, funnelling upwards and outwards, and the water trapped in them, I knew, would be a seethe of mosquito larvae: a marsh still stretched endlessly away in all directions above our heads.

Several hours later we came to our first deep river, about thirty yards across. Jarivanau took off his catumaré, laid down his gun and, after careful inspection of its bark and crown, he selected a tree which looked like any other. I slipped off my bergen and, as my legs gave way, sat on it. There would be at least half an hour's rest, I thought: I could undo a water-bottle as slowly as I liked; I could clean my glasses; maybe there would even be time to suck on a smoked cayman chew bar.

Jarivanau hit his tree at chest height with a flurry of machete blows; grinning all the while, he stood for a minute in a shell-burst of white wood fragments. The tree creaked forward, split above the cut and toppled across the river, let down slowly by a tangle of stretched lianas; it was obviously the softest tree in the forest, there would be no rest for anyone.

Pablo emerged from the trail, looking fresh; and a few moments later Chimo appeared, carrying his paunch in front and his pack behind and whistling as if he took such a walk every day of his life.

Jarivanau set off along his Yanomami bridge, his feet like gecko's suction pads, lopping off branches and vines as he went, clearing a passage. Culimacaré cut us each a sapling and then, fully laden, using the pole like a tight-rope walker, he crossed to the far bank in one untroubled saunter. The others followed suit. In fact it looked so easy, and I was so tired, that I forgot the advice of the SAS Major in Hereford: 'Whatever you do, lad, never cross a river with a bergen on your back.'

My ruptured boots gave me no purchase on the slimy bark. The pole took on a life of its own, parrying the blows of invisible assailants to left and right; the river tilted up to look at me one side, lay flat, and then repeated the process with an increase in tempo. I felt like a pilot in a dragonfly, and then I fell, it seemed, from the highest point, with the maximum force. The world went black and gurgled; something closed on my leg and something else bore down on my shoulders, holding me under. This time it really is an anaconda, I thought, trying to raise my head – I have fallen into one of Colonel Fawcett's sixty-foot-long anacondas. And then there was a push on my chest; I was gulping air; and, through the water streaming down from my hat, still held in place by the chin strap, I looked into Culimacaré's slightly hooded, dark brown eyes. He was treading water, roaring with laughter, displaying his gums, and easing my arms out of the bergen which he anchored on a broken branch of the tree. As I struggled to free my foot, he submerged beside me, and forced it out of the snag.

When I climbed out on the far bank, Jarivanau, Pablo and Chimo were howling with laughter, too.

'Reymono!' spluttered Chimo, clapping me on the back. 'You'll *never* make a monkey.'

But Juan was unsmiling, anxious.

'I do not understand,' he said, folding his arms tight across his chest. 'What will you do? What will you do if they kill Jarivanau? What will you do if *we have to run from the Yanomami?'*

For the next three rivers (or perhaps they were loops of the same one) I gave my bergen to Culimacaré to carry in front of him over Jarivanau's felled trees, and swam across. The all-in soakings made little difference; everything was already as wet as it could be.

As the afternoon sweated on, Jarivanau seemed less eager to push ahead; we all walked in sight of each other. The ground became firmer, the intersecting gulleys less frequent, the trees much bigger. And then, from a near-hypnotic state, a trance induced by the slop-slop of my broken boots on the wet leaves, the rhythmic shifting of weight in my pack, I awoke, sharply, to full consciousness.

Jarivanau and Culimacaré had stopped in front of me. We had

come out into an open space. The crowns of the giant trees met overhead, the understorey was intact around the perimeter, but the area before us had been cleared. Some thirty little leaf-shelters were spaced out on it, looking as if they had grown where they stood. Their triangular roofs of saplings and palm-leaves were supported by a single six-foot pole at the front and two four-foot poles linked with a cross-piece at the back; some of them still had split-vine hammocks inside, slung to the uprights front and rear. The leaves were brown and withered, the hammocks decayed, the trodden earth bare of recent footprints. Yet we all fell silent: a lot of people had been here; this was not our place and we should not be in it.

Jarivanau took off his catumaré and walked purposefully across the clearing. I followed at once – perhaps he was looking for some ritual sign, some formal message always left in Yanomami camps? He flitted from tree to tree at the far edge of the clearing, looking embarrassed, secretive, gesturing at me to stay away. He became more emphatic, shooing at me with both hands. I became even more intrigued; I was about to make some small but crucial anthropological discovery. Finally, exasperated, he retreated between two plank buttresses, turned his back on me, dropped the green shorts that Culimacaré had given him, and took a shit. Jarivanau had diarrhoea.

'We must camp soon,' said Chimo gloomily, leading the way. 'And well off the path. We must be close to the Choris. They may be only one day's walk away – and we must light no fires, Reymono. I would rather risk a jaguar in the night than a visit by these people.'

Half an hour further, on a small headland formed by a tight bend in a stream, Chimo stopped and unloaded. It was an exceptional place: huge trees, clearish water, and, beneath the overhang of bank, there was even a narrow stretch of muddy sand. I cleaned my glasses, washed my face, filled my water bottles, and tried not to think about the unmapped territory around us.

Pablo and Culimacaré put up the two tarpaulins over a rectangle of cut saplings and we slung our hammocks. Chimo fussed about, his great buttocks in the air, pursuing shiny, black, inch-long veintecuatros across the jungle floor and flattening them with his machete, a task altogether too serious to permit of whistling.

'Thanks to the Holy Mother,' he said, finding their nest at last, a small clear hole by the roots of the giant tree. He went to his catumaré, took out a plastic bottle of kerosene, poured half of it down the opening and dropped in a match. There was a brief spurt of blue flame.

'That's a waste of cooking fuel,' said Juan.

'They can knock a man unconscious,' said Chimo, aggrieved.

We chewed strips of smoked cayman, said very little, changed into dry clothes and collapsed into our hammocks. Darkness fell.

Fireflies, with two green lights apiece, cruised back and forth beneath the trees; the ground around us glowed with phosphorescent fungi and lichens – a pale yellow light, brighter than I had ever seen before.

'Quack! Quack! Quack!' said something, like a duck being squeezed.

'It's a duck,' I said.

'It's an agouti,' grunted Chimo. 'We must be camped near his burrow. He's annoyed with us.'

Then, very loud, came the hooting of an owl.

'It's an owl,' I said.

'Zambullidor de sol,' said Chimo.

'So *that*'s what a sungrebe sounds like, I thought, getting excited, pleased with myself.

Something else joined in, a long burbling call.

'It's a Green ibis,' I said.

'It's Jesus Christ,' said Chimo, heaving himself over in his hammock so that we shook all down the line. 'Go to sleep.'

A reverberating cackle, followed by a long, loud groan, very close, woke me in the dark. Chimo was already up, rootling about in his catumaré.

'What's that?' I said.

'Pájaro vaco,' said Chimo. 'It's *all* the Pájaro vaco. But why ask me? Don't they tell you everything in those books of yours? Eh?'

Even Chimo, I realised, was getting tense. My stomach turned slightly at the thought.

I switched on my torch and took out Schauensee, always the best therapy: Pájaro vaco, he said, was the Rufescent tiger-heron, big, black and brown, with chestnut head and shoulders: 'Usually solitary, not shy. Active at night. Remains motionless when alarmed. Feeds on fishes, insects.' There was no word as to his speech-patterns; no advice as to whether or not he was given to imitating ducks and owls and girls on broomsticks.

We broke camp, chewed some more cayman, and set off the moment we could see the undergrowth.

Around midday I noticed a party of small birds flitting about us on twigs and on the ground; and a pace or two later we were walking over a mass of medium-sized black ants, a chaotic, hyperactive crowd of insects running in all directions and even streaming, for two or three yards, up the stems of ferns, the trunks of trees – they were, I assumed, one of Henry Walter Bates's species of army ants (he found ten kinds, eight of them new to science); but Jarivanau was too far ahead for me to shout and stop him; in five minutes we had passed across the column; and I just paused briefly to brush a few particularly brave individuals off my trousers.

Jarivanau paused, too. We had come to a path. There was no doubt about it this time: we had come to a well-trodden, four-foot-wide path which intersected our route at right angles. We waited for Chimo, who laboured up, stopped, took his pipe out of one pocket and his plastic tobacco pouch out of another, filled his pipe, replaced his pouch, firmed down the full bowl with his thumb, stuck the pipe in his gums, lit up, and smiled.

'How's that?' he said, as if he had found the way himself.

He gave me a leathery wink.

'Now we can all die together,' he said. 'Just to please Reymono. Just to see what it's like.'

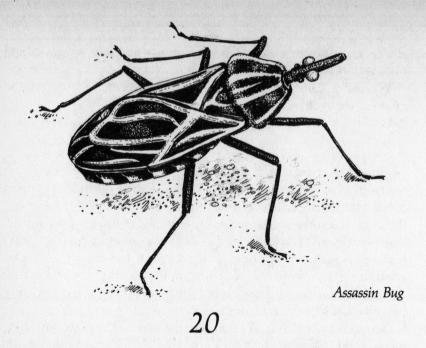

Assassin Bug

20

The path led to a plantation, a large, long-established conuco of plantains. The sunlight bore down on us, stark and hard and open.

We clambered over the well-scuffed horizontal trunks of old, half-burnt trees, down to a small stream, and up into a belt of uncleared forest. There we stopped to piss as if by agreement, our bladders water-pistolled by fear.

On the other side of the hill we halted again. A young plantation sloped down in front of us; a wooded mountain filled the horizon behind. In the hollow stood a massive, enclosed, oval construction of palm-leaf thatch, yellowed with age, its back to us; the skeletal tops of poles, facing inwards, stuck into the air along its upper edges. Eight Cattle egrets sat hunched in a tree to our left.

'Redmon,' said Juan, setting down his pack and unwrapping his camera, his movements suddenly as exaggerated, as jerky as when we first met, 'will you please take my picture with Chimo and the others? For my wife?'

It was a bizarre idea. I thought I knew what he was thinking: one day, maybe, some anthropologist or missionary will come here and find a rusty, unopened camera — and then the small mystery of our disappearance will be explained.

Despite myself, I handed him my Nikonos, too, and we photo-graphed each other: lined up against the forest edge with Pablo and

Culimacaré in their Neblina boots; Chimo with his machete in his hand and his pipe in his mouth; and Jarivanau, clutching the shotgun to his chest.

As I handed Juan his camera back, Jarivanau, unable to bear the delay of his homecoming a moment longer, took off down the path. I chased him in earnest, the bergen bumping up and down on my back, my camera and binoculars swinging across my chest.

Half-way there he paused, put the gun to his shoulder and raised the barrel towards the sun.

'No! No!' I yelled. 'Don't do that! Not here!'

The explosion, unmuffled by trees, seemed extraordinarily loud; it reverberated round the hills. The egrets shattered into the air. And then, from inside the shabono, a long, undulating, sustained scream rose into the sky.

Jarivanau beckoned to me and ran, crouching low towards the curving wall. He threw down a small panel of thatch, stooped through, and disappeared. I followed, forced by the bulk of the bergen to crawl through on all fours.

I looked up from the dry ground – straight at the shafts of a pair of six-foot-long arrows. They were fitted, I noticed, with notched, syringe-sharp, curare-blackened monkey-tips. The two young men stood, their great bows fully drawn, their backs arched, their faces expressionless. Their penises were held flat up against their stomachs by the foreskin, hooked under the waistband of bark string. They had small, neat tufts of black pubic hair.

'Real Yanomami! Chagnon's Yanomami!' I thought in a rush of pleasure and relief and adrenalin. 'Doing exactly what they're meant to do!' And then, 'Jesus Christ,' I thought, 'they're going to kill me.'

'Whooo-hooo-hooo!' whooped Jarivanau, pulling off my hat.

The young men lowered their bows and smiled. Jarivanau jammed my hat back on my head and helped me, shaky, to my feet. More men were running towards us across the huge oval expanse, waving their arms in the air.

'Whooo-hooo-hooo!' they shouted.

An old man put his emaciated arms around Jarivanau and then stood beside him, rubbing a hand fondly back and forth across his quarter-inch crew-cut and damaged skull.

Juan and Culimacaré, Pablo and Chimo appeared behind me. We stood in a group, staring stupidly at the press of people about us. The women wore red or ochre loincloths, and pudding-basin haircuts, like the men. Almost all of them had a baby or a toddler at the hip, its buttocks firmly supported by a red sash from the mother's opposite shoulder. Sticks pierced their nasal septums and projected horizontally to the edge of either cheek; three shorter sticks, spokes of a semi-circle, stuck out from holes just beneath the centre and corners of their lower lips. Larger wooden plugs were lodged through their ear-lobes and some were further embroidered with small bunches of leaves. Casual kissing, I thought, was obviously not an option; it would be like diving into a thorn bush.

I raised my arms in the air, waved them about, yelled like the men – and was immediately mobbed, touched, it seemed, by a hundred hands. An old woman elbowed everyone aside and stood in front of me. She had spindly legs, a big belly, enormous hanging triangles of breast, and bunches of withered leaves in her ears which she had obviously forgotten to change for a week or two. I looked into her kind, weak, grandmotherly eyes. She bent down slowly – and fetched me two resounding slaps across the knees. I was too surprised to move and she hesitated – before clouting me across the thighs. It was like being bashed with carpet beaters. 'I'm going to lose the lot,' I thought, as she paused again, and I held both hands in front of my trouser zip. At this point, I was vaguely aware, the Yanomami doubled up with laughter, *en masse*. She hit me across the sides of my stomach, my arms, my shoulders, and then, not quite so hard, she slapped my face. My glasses, until then safely anchored by the top of the ear pieces under my sweatband, propelled themselves off my noise and landed on the ground between us. I bent down and picked them up, half-expecting her to shuffle round and kick me up the bum. Instead she grabbed my beard in both hands and pulled it, hard.

The Yanomami in my restored field of vision were laughing, jumping up and down, showing full sets of protein-fed teeth, miming extreme horror and holding both hands over their balls. Chimo was choking and gobbing and generally betraying me.

The old woman smiled, took out a slimy wad of tobacco from between her bottom lip and gums, readjusted it to her satisfaction with a squeeze or two here and there, acknowledged the laughter of the crowd with a coy little wave, and wandered off without a backward glance.

In the shade cast by a part of the great roof I took off my pack and sat on it, rubbing my cheeks. Old women, I remembered ruefully, were very rare and very privileged. If a group was lucky enough to have one, according to Chagnon, they treated her well: old women were the only ambassadors who were allowed to collect your dead warriors from an enemy; they were the only messengers whom you could send to a hostile shabono without their being gang-raped on the way and then cut in half when they arrived.

'That was very interesting,' said Juan, taking his own pack off and sitting beside me. 'That was a greeting ceremony.'

I forbore to reply.

Children came and sat in the dust around us; one bright-eyed girl, perhaps eight years old, with a very long stick through her nose (not quite centrally balanced in the hole in her septum, so that it tilted at a rakish angle) bolder than the others, picked the burrs off my trousers and socks, poked her fingers through the holes in my boots, ran her hands over my stinking shirt, stroked the hairs on my scratched and bitten arms, and was plainly fascinated by my beard. Her own skin was pale brown, very clean, and entirely free from blackfly bites.

The two warriors who had greeted us with their drawn bows squatted down on either side of me. They were unarmed, and had changed into small red loincloths. They spoke with extraordinary emphasis and vehemence, jabbing their thick forefingers within an inch of my eyes to mark important turns in the argument. They punched my bergen and indicated that I should get off it, stand up. Their aggression, their taut faces close to mine, made them seem huge men, not to be gainsaid, and it was a surprise to find that when we all got to our feet they were even smaller than Jarivanau and reached no higher than my chest.

Chimo, Pablo and Culimacaré were surrounded by an equally insistent group of older men. Jarivanau stood apart, still talking to the delighted old man I took to be his father.

'They want our packs,' said Chimo, looking uncharacteristically anxious. 'You must give out some presents, Reymono – *but not everything at once, or we're lost.*'

I unwrapped the Polaroid, found the bag of film, walked over to Jarivanau, claimed his protection by putting my arm across his shoulders and led him out to the hot, bright centre of the open arena. The huge lean-to roof enclosed us at a distance on all sides; in one of the sectioned dwellings behind us, the gaps between the regularly-spaced main support-posts, a middle-aged man was lying in his hammock with two small children perched on his stomach, his bow and arrows propped within reach against the low back wall, watching us, impassive. I was sure we were his first visitors from the outer world and yet, I realised, unnerved, such was his sureness in himself, so capacious the depths of his disdain, that he had not even bothered to swing his legs out and take a closer look.

I stepped back from Jarivanau, knelt down, took out a film from the waterproof bag, loaded the camera, and looked up again to take his picture. Jarivanau had changed: he was shaking all over as if he had malaria. He stared at me, but as if he could not see me, keeping his eyes blankly fixed on mine, not glancing away for a moment. Perhaps he could not bear to be photographed? Perhaps he thought I was about to capture his soul? Yet he had never objected before — in fact I knew he kept with him several of the Polaroids taken that night in his hut on the Siapa. And then I dimly remembered a passage in Chagnon and began to shake a little on my own account. I was now, unwittingly, obeying the dictates of Yanomami decorum which I had so signally failed to observe in the shock of our arrival (and perhaps that lapse of manners was why the old woman had given me her own aberrant greeting — there was nothing about *that* in Chagnon): the visitor must stand motionless in the centre of the clearing for two or three minutes with his weapons held vertically in front of his face; if someone has a score to settle (and a reputation to make) he must shoot the intruder there and then or not at all. So if this really was Jarivanau's first visit after the feud that split the village, he had every reason to shake, and so did I. I stared hard, in my turn, at the developing print in my hand, aware of the unbroken skin between my shoulder blades.

Jarivanau stood erect a moment longer, then bent forward and snatched his picture; we walked, fast, back to the crowd still gathered by the entrance. The photograph was passed from hand to hand, an object which Chagnon's people called noreshi, the same word they used for the most vulnerable part of the soul.

I beckoned everyone forward into the sunlight. The dignified man who, I decided, must be the chief, got out of his hammock and stood in front of the crowd, indicating that I should take his picture first and then place it at once in his hand. His portrait turned out perfectly and he gave me a lordly smile; excitement grew; I took everyone's picture in groups: only one film had become hopelessly blotched and speckled by its long journey in the heat and humidity; forty adults got a picture each and I still had twenty left for emergencies. The women giggled and pushed each other and compared their magical squares of card. They were beginning to be pleased to see us.

Seizing the moment, we unpacked the combs and mirrors and distributed them. They were the shoddiest of mission-trade goods, and the faces of the Yanomami registered their disappointment; the nasty little mirrors even had a picture of Jesus on the back, sporting a halo. The men looked seriously disgruntled, so I unpacked the remaining bags of beads and they seemed even more various and colourful and precious in this far place than they had on the Siapa. I walked up to the chief and put the *pièce de resistance*, a small box of tiny, carved and painted wooden cockerels, in his callused palm. He fingered them idly, pleased but bemused. I put eight big red beads in the cupped hand of the old woman, and she pulled my beard with the other. I gave all the other women eight beads of different kinds apiece; as they held out their hands I noticed that many of them were damaged, their fingers scarred, crushed or broken. Everyone appeared to be in the last stages of pregnancy.

'They've got worms,' said Juan. 'They suffer terribly from worms.'

The women withdrew, chattering happily among themselves, planning something. The men, however, waited. There was nothing for it – I dug out all but a few packets of hooks and almost all our line.

'I warned you', said Chimo, measuring it into lengths. 'Now what are we going to do? We have no food and no presents.'

'We've got lentils.'

Chimo spat.

The men bore their fishing tackle back to their hammocks; and I sat on my depleted pack, unmolested for the first time, able to look about me. Juan was wandering about the shabono, eager, conscientious on my behalf, photographing everybody at home, intrusive, annoying, getting much closer to people (you needed to with the wide-angle lens on the Nikonos, the only one I possessed) than I would have dared to do myself. Chimo, Pablo and Culimacaré sat in a row against the thatched back wall behind me, silent, as if shell-shocked.

Jarivanau had left his father's side and now lay in a hammock two sections down, cuddling an adolescent boy. They stroked each other, whispering like lovers. Ah, I thought, my head too crammed with Lizot and Chagnon to imagine for one moment that they might simply be enjoying themselves, then that is Jarivanau's young brother-in-law, the only man with whom he is allowed to be tender – with all other men of his peer group (including his brothers by blood) he must demonstrate that he is waiteri, fierce: other men are potential rivals for women and so it is impossible even to ask them directly for help of any kind, let alone to trust them as friends.

The space between the main support-posts in which we sat happened to be empty: the roof sloped down behind us over an unoccupied sleeping area and there was no rough storage platform of lashed poles above it; the roof sloped upwards in front of us, way above our heads, out over the communal covered walkway to an outer upright, about forty feet high. A fringe of long-stemmed leaves hung down from the high edge of the thatch, an adaptation, I knew, peculiar to the Yanomami in the highlands, where temperatures can drop sharply and trapped smoke from the household fires helps to keep their naked bodies warm at night.

A mother lay in her wide, split-vine hammock to our right, studying her Polaroid portrait. A baby sucked at her left breast and a young boy snuggled at her other side, his legs on her stomach and his head close up against her feet; her heels stuck down between the strands of vine. Another, empty hammock was slung directly above her from the same posts, and on the ground beside her were the remains of a fire – four logs were arranged in a cross with ashes in the centre: she could stoke it at night by leaning out of bed. A pet Grey-winged trumpeter, bantam-sized, delicate, with long legs set well back and a short yellow bill, pecked about its edge. An open-work basket hung from a sloping pole in the thatch and two tightly-woven round baskets hung by their bark carrying-straps from a projecting rafter of the platform. Two bamboo quivers, a dangling bundle of deer or peccary bones, three arrows, and a bunch of plantains strung up by a length of liana completed the household goods.

To our left, the old woman sat in a hammock, ignoring us, intent on the supervision of basket-dyeing, maintaining standards. She was bossing a young woman, perhaps her daughter, who sat on the ground at her feet, ladling water from a gourd onto a bright red pile of crushed onoto seeds on a palette of plantain leaf. The young woman then rubbed the mixture with her hands into a big storage basket, her nipples and the lower half of her breasts brushing rhythmically against its sides as she worked and themselves turning scarlet. A second basket was upended to dry by the back wall and a third awaited completion. Each Yanomami village specialises in overproducing one of the few items they need (and can all make) in order to trade with their neighbours – if you are not trading with the next-door shabono, sooner or later you will be at war with them. So perhaps, I thought, this was a scarlet-basket-manufacturing group, its entire production master-minded by the visitor-spanking grand-mother.

The men, including Jarivanau, had gathered in front of the chief's section. The whole front of his storage platform was closely hung with ripening plantains – a sure sign of social power: the men with the biggest families, the most numerous wives, can cultivate the biggest gardens and are expected, in turn, to provide the bulk of the plantain soup when neighbouring villages are entertained to a feast. Two other dwellings, I noticed, boasted plantain displays that were almost as large – Yanomami headship is rarely unchallenged; alliances are complex; villages above a certain size tend to fight amongst themselves and break up; life is not relaxing.

But I could see a King vulture wheeling on a thermal thousands of feet above us, majestic as an eagle, unconcerned; perhaps his widening, lifting spiral came from the shabono itself, an oval of reflecting heat in the otherwise unbroken jungle. Maybe Chagnon just happened to have picked a particularly violent set of societies, disturbed, too near mission stations, over-aggressive, confused. After all, no one here apart from Jarivanau had shaved his head to show off his duelling scars. So thinking, still looking up at the ever-smaller King vulture, I felt the lightest of tickles on my neck. I put my right hand up to brush off the mosquito – and withdrew it, fast. I had caught something in my fingers. It was a bug, almost an inch long, kicking its long thin legs about. It was an Assassin bug, black and red with yellow lines down its wing cases. It was Rodnius prolixus, the carrier of Chagas' disease, with a stout injecting apparatus where its nose should have been. I eased my notebook out of my left-hand trouser-pocket and clapped it inside, pressing it shut. I stood up, felt faint, and sat down again.

Juan came back from his tour.

'They have almost nothing,' he said. 'Three old axes, two machetes, a few metal pots, and eight pairs of swimming pants. That is all – for eighty people.'

'Swimming pants?'

'Chagnon says everything gets traded inland from shabono to shabono, for hundreds and hundreds of kilometres. Maybe they came from his place, from Mavaca.'

'*Look at this*,' I said, opening the notebook at the flattened-bug page and pushing it in front of his face as he sat down. 'I just caught it on my neck. In fact – *look at my neck*, will you? Is it punctured? Is it?'

'No,' said Juan, inspecting the spot. 'It's filthy. You need a wash.'

'What,' I said, my voice rising an octave, '*is this bug*?'

'Rodnius prolixus,' said Juan, airily. 'It is a member of the family Reduviidae. It carries Chagas' disease. But not here. It is very common all over the forest. But it is not infected here.'

'How do you know?'

'Well,' said Juan, with a rare grin, 'you swear to me that the monkeys do not carry yellow fever. I swear to you that Rodnius prolixus does not carry Chagas' disease. Then we both feel better.'

I looked up at the thatch behind us, wondering how many more were rustling into the dropping position, dying for a suck.

'Reymono!' came a shout from the other side of the shabono.

Jarivanau was standing next to the chief, who was waving a yoppo pipe.

I crossed the shabono, ridiculously pleased to be invited, feeling as though I had just won a school prize. The chief had painted his forehead and the bridge of his nose with onoto dye and drawn a wavy red line from the base of his neck to the top of his crutch; he had strapped two bunches of parrot feathers to his upper arms, where they stuck out like the leaves of an impossible plant, an incandescent green; the left-hand cluster was further adorned with three scarlet tail-feathers from a Red-and-green macaw. He had changed, too, into something rarer and equally resplendent: a pair of blue swimming trunks. Eight men of about the same age sat in a line beside him, the shabono elders. The man on his immediate left wore a red loincloth, and a lesser, tattier bunch of parrot feathers – topped with only two macaw plumes – and only on his left arm; the rest wore white cotton armbands or just dangling strips of white or red cloth. They welcomed me with quick, friendly smiles. They looked excessively healthy, flat-stomached, fit; no men, it seemed, suffered from worms or broken hands.

Jarivanau, on the end of the line, scruffy in Gabriel's trousers, patted the ground beside him and I sat down. On my left a pet macaw perched on an upturned basket, chattering to itself, and looking even less respectable than Jarivanau because its tail feathers had been plucked out. Around the shabono the women, much exicted, were gathering up their children and making for the exit. Jarivanau's father wandered over and climbed into the middle hammock of a tier of three slung in the chief's section behind us. A man who appeared to be blind, perhaps from onchocerciasis, sat on a log near the back wall.

The chief took out a small bottle (the only one I had seen – perhaps an old coffee jar) from a basket at his feet, tapped out a palmful of light brown dust, cupped it into the end of the pipe and flicked the barrel along its length with his index finger. The man with the two macaw plumes then took the pipe, squatted in front of the chief, raised the barrel to the chief's left nostril, took a deep breath, inflated his cheeks, and blew long and hard. The chief gasped, shut his eyes, pushed the pipe away with his right hand, coughed, spluttered, threw back his head, held it with both hands, slapped his thighs and groaned; tears ran down his cheeks and brown slime dribbled out of his nose. The man with two plumes re-filled the pipe; the chief collected himself, opened his eyes, presented his right nostril and took another terrible blast. The process was then repeated, twice in each nostril. The chief sat still, stunned, agonised; he bowed his head and gobbed up slow cupfuls of phlegm onto the ground between his feet.

I at once recovered from the pleasure of my privileged position. I remembered the pain and began to sweat. Chimo waved from the other side of the shabono. Juan walked over to take a picture. The pipe was gradually passed down the line – each man in turn administering a charge to his neighbour but never, I was relieved to see, more than one blast per nostril.

The chief got to his feet, swayed, spat, leant against a post with his head down for a moment, and then stamped slowly fowards, his right arm bent, palm upwards. He began a very loud, deep chant. He stared with glazed eyes at the mountain top, at the middle sky. He raised his right arm in time with his harsh, emphatic song and clenched his fist; with both arms spread he urged the hekura towards his chest; he reached the end of his short line of advance and spun round, striking his hands together; he walked rigidly back upon the same path, his eyes fixed on the spirits of the forest. With exaggerated, immensely forceful movements, his voice rising to a shout, he paraded back and forth in front of us until, exhausted, he reached his home, his own hammock-post, and, as if after a long journey, flung himself down into a sitting position and fell silent.

The man with the two macaw plumes then began his chant; and the yoppo pipe reached Jarivanau. He slapped it on his thigh like a swagger-stick, tweeked my hat, winked, grinned all over his big rough face and stuffed in the powder. The pain was much worse than I remembered it, the yoppo probably stronger; after the second blast I struggled to my knees, holding my head with both hands, suffocating in a tank of acrid dust, dying. Through the heat, the red haze of no breath, no air, Jarivanau's face loomed up even larger, concerned; he put his arm around me and squeezed like an anaconda. As if in response, my sinuses opened, and in one delicious rush of liquid I added to the line of mucus and puke on the ground in front of us.

Jarivanau slapped me on the back, winked again, and beckoned his father out of the hammock to come and give him his own dose. I knelt with my hands tight against my hips, retching, dizzy, trembling inside my arms and legs as if from scorpion stings. Gradually the ground stopped moving and I sat back; the trembling passed and I stretched my legs. A Magpie tanager, black and white and familiar, flew over the shabono, trailing its long tail. The man who was currently dancing stopped, roared out his song and followed its passage with a taut, outstretched arm, as if he had personally summoned it from the trees of another world.

I blew the thick dust off my glasses and I wiped the snot off my lips and the sick off my chin with my shirt sleeve. I again felt I could hear with abnormal acuteness and see with extraordinary clarity. I thought I could pick out the different foliages of all the trees of the overhanging mountain, which itself seemed to be the most numinous, the greenest, the kindest mountain on earth. The sky appeared fixed, immobile, the interior blue of half a great eggshell placed over our heads, a Yanomami sky.

I thought of Lizot's idea, that for the Yanomami the central arena of the shabono represents the celestial vault, and that the low rear of the roof is a replica of the low part of the sky where it meets the flat disc of the earth. Leaving their bodies, the shamans travel into the superior world – to rescue a stolen soul or to capture the noreshi of an enemy child – by using the high posts as heavenly ladders. Chagnon's diagrams of the Yanomami cosmos seemed eminently sensible, too: immediately above us was hedu kä misi, the layer of sky, onto which the sun, stars and planets are stuck and move from east to west along their own paths, and invisible to us on its upper surface was a mirror-image of the jungle, peopled by the souls of dead Yanomami who lived exactly as they do on earth. Above that was another layer, a clear world, duku kä misi, a layer of origins where almost everything began but which is now abandoned.

Sitting in the shabono, staring at the mountain, I felt I had indeed been honoured, temporarily admitted to the centre of hei kä misi, this layer, the ellipse of earth, where the first people were created and where the first, correct form of the Yanomami language is spoken. This layer is filled, in its entire extent, with jungles and gardens, with jaguars, ocelots, monkeys, peccaries, tapir, anacondas and Harpy eagles, with rivers and hills. On its far edges live weaker, degenerate people of no account, foreigners like myself, men and women who can no longer even speak properly.

This layer, the earth, derives from a piece of hedu, the sky layer, which broke off one day and fell to its present position. And in fact the whole system is geologically unstable: when another piece of the sky-layer came loose it smashed right through the flat earth, carrying a group of Yanomami, the Amạhire-teri, with it – and on down to land on the bottom layer of all, heitä bebi. This bottom layer, however, is barren; the Amạhire-teri have nothing but their shabono and their garden, no forest to hunt in, no game to eat. So they have been forced to change, horribly; they indulge in the foulest practice that a Yanomami can imagine. They have become cannibals and eat raw human flesh just like the jaguar does: they send their spirits up to grab the souls of children on the earth layer, carry them down to their shabono, and eat them.

In the bright sunlit calm of the mountainside canopy where even now the Mouse opossums and Tree porcupines and kinkajous were taking their siesta, and which seemed to spread over me in waves of heat shimmer, in the sudden tranquillity, like a gentle hand on the back of the neck, the four layers of the Yanomami cosmos seemed no more and no less probable than the five layers of heaven, paradise, earth, limbo and hell. But their ideas of creation were much more entertaining. Women are derived not from Adam's hard little rib, but from Kanaboroma's big fleshy calf. The Amạhire-teri lived on earth at the same time as the no badabö, the original human beings, part men, part spirit, part animal. Moon was then a terrible scourge, Great-horned-owling it down to earth to eat the souls of children. Finally the ancestor Periboriwä, a champion archer, managed to hit Moon when he was right overhead. The arrow was nearly spent; it was only a surface wound in the stomach; but Moon bled profusely as he flew. The first spurt of blood fell near the mountain called Maiyo and the droplets changed into men as they hit the earth. Where the blood was thickest the new men were so fierce and their wars so maniacal that they almost exterminated themselves; where the blood was thinner or mingled with water vapour on its way down the warriors were more restrained and a few more survived. But because they were born of blood, all Yanomami are fierce.

One day Kanaboroma, a man of Moon blood, became pregnant in both calves: men who were more docile than the men of blood emerged from the right leg, and women, for the first time, appeared on earth from the left.

An alternative or complementary version adds that the men of Moon blood went out collecting vines one day, pulling them down from the trees. On one of the vines, the chief noticed, a newly opened, inviting wabu fruit had stuck (a fruit from a tree whose bark is used to prepare curare and which must itself be submerged in water for several days before its poison is leached out and it is safe to eat). The chief tossed it on the ground. Behind his back it changed into a woman – and she at once developed an exceptionally large and long and hairy vagina. As the men took the vines on their shoulders and began to drag them home the brand new woman stepped on the trailing ends, pulling the men off balance and popping behind a tree every time they looked round in alarm. Finally she could bear it no longer and trod down hard: the men turned round, stared at her, saw her vagina, and burst their penis strings with lust. They all copulated with her in turn (still standard practice when enemy women are captured by a raiding party) and brought her back to the shabono (where all the men left at home had a go, also still the custom). Eventually she had multiplets of daughters – and there were enough women for everyone to copulate with whenever they wanted (this is no longer the case).

And then of all the hundreds of Yanomami stories, myths and beliefs documented or sketched in Lizot and Chagnon, which had long since made their way into my own dreams, I thought of Titiri, once the black Nocturnal currassow-spirit and now the white-haired demon of the night, whose death by an archer created darkness and dreaming, who lurks against the back wall of the shabono where the layer of sky rests on the disc of earth, and whose penis, says Lizot, 'is inordinately long and thick. He couples with women and sodomises men, without their knowledge, while they are asleep, tears their flesh with his member, and captures their souls after he has ejaculated.'

There was a burst of sound in my right ear.

'Leapopuei! Leapopuei!' shouted the chief, shading his eyes with one hand and pointing at the mountain with the other. He had obviously recovered from his trance. The brown slime on his upper lip had caked dry.

All the other men were pointing at the mountain, too, laughing at me and then shading their eyes, miming an idiot in a trance, their mouths open, their eyes rolled up.

'Leapopuei-teri!' said the chief, pointing a finger at his own chest. 'Leapopuei-teri!'

My joints were stiff, my neck ached, my buttocks were numb; I must have been staring at Leapopuei for a very long time.

Juan still sat beside me.

'I took your picture,' he said. 'You were sick.'

A Grey-winged trumpeter with three chicks in tow fussed past us, pecking about like a hen and offering whatever it was she found, too small for me to see, to each of her brood in turn. Her wing feathers were certainly grey, but wispy at their edges, with odd hair-like filaments which ruffled in the slightest breeze; and the short velvety feathers on her throat shone metallic purple or blue or green, bright as the backs of scarabs, according to the angle of her neck against the sunlight.

'Whooooooo!' yelled the chief, sending her scuttling to safety, her chicks at her heels.

'Eeeeeee-yiee!' came an answering cry from outside the shabono.

'The women!' said Juan.

Two very small boys came through the entrance in a flying stumble, as if shoved from behind by their mothers. They picked themselves up and ran towards us along the edge of the shelter, each carrying a stick in his right hand; they were painted black from head to ankle. An equally small boy, onoto red, pitched through, fell over, and ran in the other direction around the oval, towards Chimo.

'Eeeeeeeee!' wailed the chorus without.

The two boys stained with charcoal from the cooking pots (the warpaint camouflage used by their fathers on raiding parties) paused in front of us; they wore only headbands of black Spider-monkey tail decorated with white vulture down. The youngest looked at his audience, became mesmerised with stage fright and, seeking comfort, with his free hand he pulled his willy and his nose alternately; the ends of both turned light brown on black. The men laughed, issuing a barrage of instructions in guttural, glottal-stopping banter. The boy put his hand on his head, catatonic with embarrassment. The elder boy shrugged his shoulders with manly disdain, and launched into the dance: a series of stamping back-steps; a short leaning-forward prancing; a walk holding his stick horizontally above his head; a repeat of the whole display; and then a dash on round the shabono to the next group of admirers. His young partner recovered from the horrors of it all and ran after him.

Chimo, Pablo and Culimacaré were cheering and clapping the boy in red, who then ran in our direction, swerving to avoid the boys in black, and repeated much the same steps in front of us. All the other children filed into the arena, two by two, peeling off to run left and right, singing an unending, simple chant. They were painted with small circles all over or with curved, straight or wavy lines back and front, in red or purple or black. The boys carried sticks and the girls held lengths of palm-frond whose long spear-shaped leaves had been cut off along one side and shredded into thin hanging strips along the other, light green tresses of plant which they swirled about their bodies as they danced.

The high ululating chorus from outside the shabono suddenly ceased. The women made their entrance in succession, one left, one right; they were painted like their daughters but they carried larger fronds in their left hands – and they wore white flowers in their ears, puffs of white cotton on their armbands and tiaras of vulture down on their heads. In their right hands three of them held up objects that were obviously particularly prized: a mirror (larger than the ones which we had given to them) and two much-sharpened, half-worn-away machetes.

Each of the women in turn danced and chanted before us with unsmiling concentration, swirling their fronds, never glancing at us, and waving their machetes or shaking their fists above their heads, perhaps in imitation of the swaggering, weapon-brandishing dances of visiting warriors at a feast.

Maybe the cells in my cerebellum were still gurgling in yoppo slime, their synapses firing backwards through tubefuls of dust particles, or maybe I had simply been travelling in the jungle far too long, but I just sat and stared at the young women, too absorbed even to clap. The sunlight threw long caressing flickers of light over them through the moving fronds, their unclothed skin was extraordinarily smooth. The woman with the mirror, who was last in line, danced with more passion than the rest: she had drawn squiggly lines down her cheeks and two more ran down the centre of her forehead, between her eyebrows, to either side of her nose beneath the long white stick in her septum, and then bent outwards to the corners of her bottom lip where two fresh sticks projected. She had covered her body with large, irregularly spaced round blotches like the spots on the coat of a jaguar; those on her breasts were as big as the aureoles round her erect nipples; they stretched vertically into ovals as she raised her arms above her head and her breasts tautened and flattened, and then became circular again as her breasts fell forward and rounded in the shuffling dance. I thought of the reply which Chagnon's Yanomami gave him when he suggested to them a rival anthropologist's theory – that their constant warfare was not really about the capture of women at all but in order to win the maximum possible extent of hunting territory because they were protein-starved, meat-hungry: 'Certainly we like meat,' they said, 'but we like women a whole lot more.'

All the dancers formed up, the children at the rear, and processed once round the shabono; they then laid their fronds and sticks, the mirror and the machete on the ground and gathered in the centre of the arena. Following a lead woman, the children yelling with excitement, they jumped wildly on the spot with their arms alternately raised and lowered for a minute or two until, tired out, the party broke up and they drifted back to their separate dwellings.

I got up stiffly, still slightly dizzy, and walked across the open space to our allotted section.

'We're hungry,' said Chimo. 'You stay here and guard everything. We'll go outside and prepare the soup. If we do it here they'll want the lot.'

The grandmother was splayed out in her hammock next door, fast asleep, with two equally unconscious babies at the erstwhile sucking position on the end of either breast and another, nipple-less but just as contented with its own thumb, eyes shut, on her stomach. All three rose and fell gently as she snored, safely cradled beneath her wrinkled arms. She had taken her tobacco wad out of her mouth and stuck it on the rim of a red basket on the ground by her head. She obviously knew all there was to know about babysitting.

Very probably, I thought, as I sat on my pack and watched her, there was a secret Yanomami baby-knockout drug, a powdered bark of morphine-equivalent which you mashed up with honey and full, fat, soft palm-maggot extract and then administered down the drip-tip of a leaf. There was certainly, I knew, a powdered love-potion which every young warrior carried wrapped in a leaf at the bottom of his quiver: you crept up behind your beloved and clapped it across her nose (careful not to bang the septum-stick). One deep sniff and she was moist all over. In fact it acts so quickly that you must first lure her to your chosen bush (and make sure that the ground beneath it is prepared well in advance). But watch out — because girls too have chemical weapons. If you are a bad hunter, or a coward, or just plain ugly, she may get you first with an equally powerful powder that shrivels the penis: one sniff and it goes back where it came from. And again, but then this is an incomparably better idea, she has a lithium-like powdered mega-tranquilliser which if, and only if, she knows that you are a champion hunter, brave, and irresistibly hand-some, she will throw over you when she thinks your club-duel has gone too far, when your skull has fragmented about your ears. One sniff and you can disengage with dignity, scoop your brain back into its case, and retire to your hammock for a terminal sleep.

A circle of children gathered round me and a little boy clambered onto my knee, smudging the red-painted squiggles on his side against my sweaty shirt. I took out my notebook, which intrigued them, and ran through my entire artistic repertoire: goose flying, cat sitting, rabbit sitting, mouse rampant. The little boy wiped his nose with scorn. So I looked through the binoculars and then handed them to him. He put them up to his eyes, paused, got the idea, looked over the top, put his eyes back to the rubber eye-cups, trained the tubes at a woman on the other side of the shabono who was presumably his mother, and shrieked with delight. She was sitting on the edge of her hammock suckling a baby. He whipped the binoculars down, peered at her, and then whipped them back up again as if expecting her to disappear in the interval. I turned them round and let him look through the other end. Too late, I realised, she had shrunk to hekura size and was already journeying to another world. He got off my knee, his lower lip trembling. Looking at the ground, he handed back the binoculars, his eyes filling with tears, and then he ran screaming back across the arena to wrap himself around his mother's legs.

The older children laughed. Everyone wanted a go. They pointed them in turn around the shabono and, tiring of that, withdrew to look out through a small hole I had not noticed before in the thatch of the back wall. Every shelter, I saw, had such a hole. It was for spotting raiding parties, I decided.

Chimo returned with the others and set down our cooking pot full of lentil soup. The children immediately replaced the binoculars on my bergen and squatted round us again. Everybody began to hurry in our direction.

'There's another plantation at the back,' said Juan, 'and a stream where they wash and fetch their water.'

'This piss is for us,' said Chimo, stirring the pot with a stick. 'There is not enough to give away. They have their own food.'

A crowd assembled in front of the pot. The grandmother woke up, and three of the women who had been in the dance reclaimed their babies. The chief, carrying a large gourd bowl in one hand, pushed his way forward and strode up to Chimo. He had washed the yoppo mucus off his face and no longer wore his parrot-and-macaw feather armbands. He was quieter in his movements than all the other men, more assured; he simply held out his bowl an inch or two in front of Chimo's stomach.

Chimo, without so much as a gob or even a mutter, as if he had never intended otherwise, bent down, picked up a mess-tin and ladled the bowl full to the brim. The chief stood back a couple of paces, blew on the surface of the liquid, took two long draughts, and beckoned to his family: a young boy in a red loincloth stepped forward and then the little boy in black, the one who had forgotten his dance steps, edged closer, too, trying to hide behind his brother's legs. A young girl with the full array of sticks in her face and holding a boy toddler by the hand moved up behind them, and the woman who had brandished the mirror and an older wife who had not taken part in the dance brought up the rear. The chief went down the line in that order, holding the bowl to their lips. He then calmly dipped it back in the pot and began to feed himself, properly.

Chimo broke out of his horrified trance and filled our own bowls faster than I had ever seen him move and without a single one of his formulaic witticisms. We ate in silence, watched by the crowd. No one returned my smile and it stuck on my face in a rictus of embarrassment. Chimo looked at the ground; Juan looked at me; Pablo turned away, his shoulders hunched forward and his head lowered with stress; Culimacaré ate behind us, by himself as usual, standing against the back wall, where, I noticed with fresh unease, he had half hidden his gun behind a pile of logs. Only Jarivanau had done the right thing, giving his bowl to his father. A gust of the evening breeze puffed up dust at his feet and the old man swung himself in its direction, muttering some vehement spell at the spirit of wind, perhaps telling him to go away before he blew the leaves off the roof.

We had offended the Yanomami deeply, behaving like barbarians. Because there are really only two imperatives in social life: to be waiteri, fierce in avenging every insult, and to be generous, ready to share every possession except your wife — but especially to give away your food. On your personal day of judgment, when the central part of your soul, your will, your bahii, has shinned up the hammock vines and a support-post and reached the upper layer, the spirit of thunder will direct you to your own people's shabono of shades if you have been generous, to the place of fire if you have not. We were clearly destined for the flames.

The shabono elders who had taken yoppo with me pressed up to Chimo in a body and jabbed their fingers in his chest. They began to shout, their foreheads ridged and furrowed with anger, their nostrils flared, the tendons standing out on their necks. Chimo shrugged, backed away, and then, on an impulse, surrendered his own now-empty bowl and so his only chance of that second helping without which, I knew, he considered his life to be no more than a writhing ball of intestinal worms. He found a log in the shelter next door and sat on it with disgust.

The grandmother sat, equally forlorn, on the edge of her hammock on our other side. I walked over to another spare log by her feet and sat down; I gave her my quarter-full mess-tin, the remains of the warm sludge of soup, and she took it with a small, weary smile. Since waking, she had made herself up again — she had evidently rubbed both her palms round a cooking pot and then patted the sides of her face, but it had failed to raise her spirits. The black smudge on her left cheek set off a terrible raised scar beneath it at the corner of her lip, an outward-facing tear in the flesh from the hole in which she had once worn a stick. Maybe a husband had yanked on it one day — perhaps because she had not prepared his own soup quickly enough. And as her face half-disappeared beneath my upturned mess-tin I wondered how many fights she had seen; how often she had waited for wars to end; how many of her husbands and sons she had seen placed on a funeral pyre in the centre of the shabono, their bones and teeth then collected from the ashes, mortar-and-pestled and drunk in plantain soup, a symbolic preservation of their body and blood, a holy communion that would keep something of them here on earth.

All our own soup had gone and most of the adults had dispersed back to their dwellings. Two mothers remained sitting near us delousing a toddler apiece, and four small boys sat in a tight row beside them delousing each other: they searched carefully through the mop of hair in front of them, picked off the grey lice, cracked them between their teeth, and giggled at us. After a short interval the boy at the back would move to the front.

I left the grandmother, who was still lost in her own thoughts, dabbing her finger in the mess-tin and licking it, and wandered off for a pee. I chose the exit towards the mountain. It was obviously the most used; a wide door of poles and dry brushwood had been leant back on two posts. The path led into a plantation and down through a patch of mud to a stream. Stepping stones had been laid across it but there was no sign of the usual flat slab in the shallows worn smooth by women pounding and rubbing clothes with a stone; the Yanomami, I supposed, had nothing but loincloths (and blue swimming trunks) to wash. I peed on the downstream bank at the edge of a patch of yellow and brown butterflies, who immediately crowded onto the freshly steaming ground, flicking their wings open and shut as they fed.

When I got back to the shabono preparations were being made for the night. A pet Red-billed toucan had escaped onto the roof, bouncing from one projecting rafter-sapling to the next, pausing on each new perch to cock its head and enormous bill twenty degrees to the left and then twenty degrees to the right, fixing one round black eye at a time on its owner below, a boy of about five years old, who was howling uncontrollably. His mother came to the rescue bearing a long pole and other women joined in, likewise armed. Little boys yelled directions. Someone knocked the bird over and it fluttered down to squat half-unconscious at Juan's feet. Juan picked it up and I clipped its wings with the scissors on my Swiss Army knife, feeling helpful. Its bill was surprisingly light to hold, dark red in the centre, yellow along the top and blue on the underside at the base — its throat and chest were white, its rump yellow, the rest black, and the whole ragged and dirty with handling. Its owner, still snuffling, popped it in a floppy basket and tied the tope with vine loops.

Jarivanau's father and the chief pulled the big door across the entrance towards the river. All round the shabono, women were taking kindling and logs from the piles against the back walls of their dwellings, arranging them on the hearths beside their hammocks, and then lighting sticks at the half-blind man's fire which had smouldered all day. Jarivanau indicated that we should spend the night in the empty section adjacent to the big door and flanked by his father's dwelling on the other side — exactly, I thought, where any sensible raider would burst in and start shooting.

We unfurled our stinking hammocks and slung them to the posts of our new home. A baby agouti streaked past against the back wall, pursued by two little boys screaming with excitement. As it dodged and feinted, five sections on, travelling faster than a whippet, the chief's youngest son, the boy in black (now washed brown again) caught it with a rugby tackle and held it aloft, shouting in triumph, all his miseries forgotten. The pursuers fetched a basket and bore it back to their hearths.

'Reymono,' said Chimo, sitting down heavily on his hammock and rubbing his face with both hands, 'we must go tomorrow. You've given away all the presents. We have no food but lentils. They'll kill us. They'll kill us for our shirts. Everyone knows. It's simple. They club you to death in the night.'

'Eeeeeeee-aiyeeee!' screamed the chief's young wife across the shabono.

Chaos ensued. Women seemed to run in all directions. Jarivanau's father jumped out of his hammock. Culimacaré grabbed his gun.

A piece of thatch, a concealed entrance midway between us and the chief's hearth, fell flat, pushed from outside with tremendous violence. 'This is it,' I thought. 'This is a raid.'

A young man, carrying his bow and two arrows vertically in front of his face, stepped through the gap, closely followed by twelve others. Wearing red loincloths, superbly fit, their heads bent forward slightly against the headbands of enormous loads on their backs, they marched across the arena to their various dwellings, expressionless, looking straight ahead. Three of them had terrier-like dogs at their heels. Each man shed his load outside his home, leant his bow and arrows against the back wall, and climbed into his hammock. They lay there, silently. When the glance of the hunter in the section beyond Jarivanau's happened to fall on us he shut his eyes, tight. He looked away emphatically, as if merely seeing us had fouled his world.

Chastened, we sat on our hammocks, saying nothing. His wife rolled a wad of tobacco from leaves in a basket, moistened it in a gourd of water and handed it to him. He took it without a word. She broke six plantains off a bunch hanging from the platform and poked them into the edge of the fire.

The chief and three elders got out of their own hammocks and began systematically to cut open the vine-bound bundles with a machete, laying out the game. In a week of hunting, maybe more, thirteen men had brought back three Spider monkeys, four armadillos, a small pile of curassows and four peccaries. The Spider monkeys and armadillos were intact, but the peccaries had been cut up and smoked during the evenings of the hunt. The chief and his assistants began dividing up the meat, distributing it to every family in the shabono.

After about half an hour the young men bounded out of their hammocks and crowded round us. They pointed at their mouths. They wanted food. They pulled Chimo to his feet, felt his paunch and then rubbed their own flat, muscular stomachs. There was no doubt about it. They were fit. We were over-privileged. Chimo had got that extra meat from somewhere.

I showed them our empty cooking-pot and then got the remaining hooks and line out of my bergen: there were only enough for three hooks and four metres of line each. They took the meagre gifts back to their homes and then returned to inspect us closely. They were much more demanding, more immediately bold and psychologically overpowering than the older men. With half-shouted jokes or insults, I could not tell which, they tried on Chimo's helmet and Pablo's gumboots; they felt the canvas of my bergen, puzzled by its texture; they passed round the gun, clicking their tongues in admiration and putting it up to their shoulders – but when Culimacaré began to jig his right hand up and down in spasms of anxiety they handed it back at once. They fingered my biceps and shook their heads in sympathy. One of them, slightly older than the others, serious and intelligent-looking, nudged his companion and pointed at the triple-granny knots with which I had tied my hammock to the posts. Amid much hilarity, he mimed me falling to the ground in the night, and then re-tied the hammock with Yanomami knots of such compressed power that I half-expected the rope to break. One of the hunter's dogs snorted and snuffled at my trousers, wagging his tail, stuffing his muzzle into the cotton; used only to bare legs, he was hyper-ventilating through an unaccustomed library of smells. His owner picked him up, stroked him tenderly, kissed him full on his wet nose and set him down again.

Night fell and the men went back to their own hearths. The air filled with the smell of woodsmoke from the small fires all round the shabono, and then, more immediately, with the smell of singed fur and burnt meat from the fire next door, where a Spider monkey, cursorily gutted, was being roasted whole. By the light of a flame which temporarily shot up from the fire around the monkey's tail I watched the young mother leave her cooking, reach down a plantain leaf from a pile on the platform, spread it on the ground, disengage her toddler from its sling and hold it, legs dangling, over the leaf. The baby, well trained, produced a milky shit on cue. The mother folded the leaf carefully and pushed it out through the hole at the back of the shelter. So that was the purpose of those little windows — when the thatch and brushwood doors were shut, when jaguars or raiders might be waiting outside, you used the lavatory half way up the wall.

Large frogs began to call from the river, a deep, slow *co-aaaaark, co-aaaaark, co-aaaaark*, and from the same direction, but with much greater volume, came waves of sound I had not heard before: a steam train labouring out of a roofed-over station, followed by a brief burst from a smooth-running two-stroke motor.

'Chimo, what's that?'

'How should I know?' said Chimo testily, heaving himself over in his hammock and so trampolining me in mine via our shared head-post. 'It's the mother of all toads. And the last we'll ever hear. We should not be staying with these people.'

From inside our own hut, over by the back wall, there came the lesser sound of someone being sick. Jarivanau was throwing up without apparent effort. He had obviously had more than a bowl of lentil soup. Perhaps he had cadged something from his brother-in-law. The puke hit the ground in a steady jet and then ceased. He had managed to lean well out and miss his father in the hammock beneath. The old man's wheezing breaths continued in their rhythm.

A shouting chant broke out on the far side of the shabono and edged louder and closer in the darkness.

'Holy Mother,' muttered Chimo, turning over in his hammock and bouncing me about again, 'here they come.'

'Redmon,' said Juan accusingly, 'it is a war dance.'

It was certainly a violent song, an insistent two-note repetition like a pair of drums being struck alternately *donya donya donya donya* followed by an equally emphatic glottal stop and then the quick phrase *oi ai coi ya* (or so it sounded), the whole endlessly repeated with gathering force.

As the noise drew level and we heard the stamping of feet accompanying the song, Chimo, presumably wanting to know if the singers were carrying clubs, momentarily flicked on his torch. Four young men were briefly caught in the beam, dancing backwards and forwards in front of our section of the lean-to and carrying nothing more dangerous than two ripe plaintains apiece. I took an involuntary long breath which seemed to travel from my chest to my feet and told me how afraid I had been: this was not the build-up to a clubbing, but the ritual hunting dance that Lizot describes: all night long the young men walk and dance and sing around the shabono in a test of stamina, and as everyone else falls asleep in their hammocks the singers pause in their song to chew pieces of plantain, spit a mouthful into their hands, and lob the white, warm, sticky, sperm-like goo onto the genitals or buttocks or faces of the unconscious girls, waking them up. It is a time of jokes and obscenities; and indeed, now that I no longer expected to die there and then, I could hear occasional shrieks and laughter all round the shabono as the singers passed.

An electric storm played over Leapopuei and soon the rain pitter-pattered steadily on the thatch above us. Men made sporadic, shouted speeches into the darkness on one side of the shabono and were answered from the other. The chanting itself increased in volume as more young men joined the dance, the interminable *donya donya donya donya* becoming even louder as they passed us, receding almost to a hoarse whisper as they lapped the far side of the perimeter, and then swelling once more as they returned.

Chimo stopped his mountainous heaving and began to snore. I closed my eyes, still gritty with trapped yoppo dust, and fell asleep.

I awoke to the sound of Jarivanau and his father dragging open the big door to the stream. It was a cold, grey dawn, the shabono full of mist. People slipped out through the gap, the women carrying gourds to fetch the morning's water. This was the time of day for secret, pre-arranged meetings in the forest beyond the plantation. It was also prime time for raiders, who might have travelled for days from an enemy shabono and camped undetected nearby, to capture women. All the mothers, I noticed, took their children with them, not wishing to be separated, just in case.

Chimo had already made a fire to boil up our lentil soup and Jarivanau had roasted us a plantain each. No one bothered us until the mist began to lift, when the hunters crowded round. The man who had re-tied my hammock rope grabbed my arm. He held a Polaroid in his other hand, a picture of the most beautiful woman in the shabono, who was obviously his wife. He released me, pointed at the picture, and then at himself.

'Yavateiba!' he said.

'Reymono,' I said, shaking his hand.

I took out the Polaroid camera and the last of the film. The hunters ran to their dwellings and fetched their bows, or, in one case, the community axe in the right hand and a Grey-winged trumpeter held against his chest with the left. A particularly aggressive young man, wearing a monkey-tail headband speckled with King vulture down and with a ball of monkey fur hanging down his back from a string round his neck, demanded that I take his picture first. He posed with his bow drawn, his untipped arrow pointing at the sky. The rest followed suit. I took all their portraits with the Polaroid and Juan photographed them with the Nikonos. Everyone was happy.

Jarivanau ostentatiously took down his hammock and packed his catumaré in the front of our shelter. He tied our cooking pot to his load with a length of vine and placed a bunch of plantains on top. He grinned at me and nodded towards the door by which he had entered on the far side of the shabono.

If Jarivanau thinks we should go, I thought, then we had better go.

'We must leave at once,' said Chimo, rolling up his hammock, 'and walk fast. They come after you in two groups, way out on either side, silent as the ghosts. They wait in front. You see nothing. Even the arrow makes no noise.'

I could see that he really believed it. There was no twinkle in his hooded eyes. It was just another fact to him. And it was difficult to imagine Chimo walking fast. You really are a very brave old Indian, I thought. And how extraordinarily lucky I had been, in the long term, that great Chimo, Chief of Salano, the famous navigator, had bragged to all and sundry in Solano, San Carlos and Culimacaré about the Maturaca – and then failed to find it. Nothing but his endangered reputation would have driven him to take me to these people.

Culimacaré helped me undo the Yanomami knots and Juan and I packed our hammocks and nets. Yavateiba, suddenly and unnaturally friendly, joined us. Oddly he carried two bows and two arrows and had slung his quiver on his back. It's just another hunting ritual, I thought, half-seriously. He's propitiating the spirits of his prey before the ambush.

Jarivanau's brother-in-law, also carrying a bow and two arrows and with a quiver on his back, wandered over and put his arm around Jarivanau's shoulders. He was very young, his flesh new and unmarked, his body unhardened. He had Jarivanau's and Yavateiba's high chest but had not yet developed their massive, half-breast-like pectorals, or their packs of muscle across the shoulders. He and Jarivanau stood and smiled at each other, saying their farewell, as I imagined.

We strapped on our loads and walked towards the far entrance, accompanied by Yavateiba and the boy. I waved goodbye to the few people still left in the shabono. Only the grandmother waved back.

The chief got out of his hammock as we passed, swung himself up onto his platform and untied a bunch of yellow, ripened plaintains from his hanging store. He stopped us with a lordly gesture, holding up his hand, jumped down, and presented the plantains to Yavateiba who passed them to the boy. The chief turned his back on us and returned to his hammock.

Yavateiba walked over to his own hearth and picked up a round basket with a headstrap. His wife stood beside the smouldering fire, parrot feathers in her ears, sticks through her nose and lip, a toddler held against her hip by its sash – and her head bowed forward against the weight of an identical basket on her back.

I whooped like a Yanomami. They were coming with us.

In reply the woman walked over to my side, lifted up her head as if her load was of no consequence, looked up at me, smiled, opened her mouth and flicked her tongue between her teeth.

Jaguar

21

Jarivanau and Yavateiba disappeared through the entrance. I turned round for a last look at the shabono. Two little boys, one of them the chief's son, were shooting at something, perhaps a lizard or a cicada, with miniature bows and arrows in the centre of the arena. Jarivanau's father had returned to his shelter and leant with his arm against a post, watching us go.

I followed Yavateibi's wife as she picked her way carefully up through the plantation, her feet turned slightly inwards as she walked. Beside her main basket, dyed onoto-red with two rows of black circles painted round the sides, there hung another, much smaller, openwork carrier. Through the vine-loop fasteners at its top, a Grey-winged trumpeter peeked its head out at me. The family were travelling with everything that they possessed.

Once in the jungle, Yavateiba dropped back to be with his wife. He was much kinder to her, now that he was alone with us, than he had ever been in the shabono. It was obviously only in front of his peers that he had to be fierce and assertive all day; as we hardly counted as men at all, and as Jarivanau and the boy were several hundred paces in front of us, he could be as relaxed as he liked. He helped her through the gulleys and across the streams; he encouraged her constantly; and on our frequent stops so that she could feed their toddler or let it run about, he took brazil nuts out of his basket, cracked them between his teeth and popped the kernels in her mouth.

'Maquichemi!' he said proudly, stroking her head.

She gave us a shy smile.

The cruel difference in their loads, I thought, must be simply because he needs to be able to draw his bow at any moment. And in fact that was the only unnerving habit he had – he checked, every time we paused, that he had not accidentally knocked his arrows out of true or snagged their curassow flights as we walked: he compulsively smoothed their feathers and held their shafts in front of his right eye up against the light. And he remained excessively watchful as we walked, his weapons in his hand, scanning the spaces between the trees to either side of us and listening, every now and then, his mouth open – but whether for peccaries or enemy Yanomami I could not tell.

It was unsettling, too, as we followed them hour upon hour, to think how differently Yavateiba knew this forest. Not just in the sense that he would have been able to describe the habits of twenty species of bee by the time he was six but also that he would be wary, at night, not only of the jaguar but also of the no uhudi, that fraction of the soul which is released by the funeral fire and which wanders forever through the jungle with eyes like glowing embers and a penchant for attacking sleeping men with sticks and clubs.

To side-step sudden sickness and death he must guard the main part of his own soul, the möamo in or near his liver, against the targeted spells of enemy shamans; and at all times he must take care not to shoot his noreshi-soul counterpart, the animal alter ego of his lineage. Yavateiba would share a Spider monkey or a Harpy eagle or a Collared forest falcon with his father and his brothers and his little son. Now that he was travelling his noreshi animal would also be travelling. Should he or Jarivanau or the boy be unlucky enough to kill it in the hunt he would die instantly. Maquichemi's noreshi animal would be ambling through the jungle, too, but at the female level, close to the earth – an armadillo or an agouti or a snake.

So as he walked Yavateiba was not the essence of freedom which he appeared to be, but intimately held by the unseen tendrils of his spirit forest at every step. And further, if he was hunting seriously, he would have to observe the rules of sympathetic magic: were he to shit before looking for armadillos he would find only empty burrows; were he to fart, all curassows would fly away and disperse amongst the leaves like his own wind.

However, on this dank day, walking slowly, we saw almost nothing except a snake which I at first took to be the venomous coral. It was about three feet long, winding gently away from us beside our path, its ringed lengths of pink-on-black as unexpected as a runnel of flame against the drab brown and green of the jungle floor. Yavateiba and Maquichemi walked past it without a second glance, their bare feet within easy striking distance of its little black head. They know it is slow, I thought, they know its fangs are short and that it has to hang on and chew before it can inject enough poison to kill you. And then I noticed that it lacked the tell-tale yellow bands between the black and the red – it was not a true coral at all, but a harmless mimic.

We reached our camp in the late afternoon; it seemed to me that after our stay with the Yanomami everything should have changed – but there were our old shelter posts ready to take the tarpaulin, the charred veinte-cuatro nest at the base of the great tree, the stream with its same little curve of beach.

Chimo and Pablo chopped up a rotten log with their machetes and made a fire with the last of the kerosene. Jarivanau and Yavateiba cut four saplings, drove them into the ground at an angle a few paces away from the flames and slung their tiny split-vine hammocks. Maquichemi took her son to the stream for a wash. Juan and Culimacaré dug a shallow trench for carbon samples in the wet, sandy soil. The Trumpeter, released from his basket, dashed over to help, convinced that they were doing something sensible, like digging for grubs.

The boy hung round me as I unpacked my hammock, so I spread the entire contents of my bergen out on a plastic liner. He leant his bow and arrows against a tree and squatted down for an inspection. Somewhere along the way he had simply dumped his load of plantains in the bushes, presumably because they were too heavy for him. Not all Yanomami are potential chiefs.

The binoculars intrigued him as much as they had the children in the shabono, and then, with a deep frown of concentration, he fingered my mould-covered shirts and socks and y-fronts, the assorted plastic bags full of vitamin pills and water-purifying tablets, the bandages and dressings and sealed syringes, the morphine syrettes and two spare pairs of glasses and one pair of gym shoes, the last tubes of Betadine and Savlon, Canesten and Jungle Formula. Naked but for the short flap of loincloth covering his genitals, his buttocks bare, he was shivering, his skin goose-pimpled. It was a mystery of Yanomami life – why had they not invented nightshirts, at least, of monkey skins? How did they survive in their hard, open lattices of hammocks when we slept fully clothed in several extra shirts and a sweater and, in my case, further rolled up in a groundsheet?

Bizarrely, he decided that he wanted a pair of glasses (he liked the way the red case clicked shut), my gym shoes, three empty plastic bags and the least-rotted pair of y-fronts, picking them out of the collection of riches and laying them at his feet. We settled for the plastic bags and the y-fronts. He riffled through the plates in Schauensee, clicking his tongue in admiration, but eventually the excitement of his new possessions was too much for him and he withdrew to make a catumaré of his own in which to place them.

Pablo and Culimacaré tied our tarpaulin onto the frame of saplings and rigged up a shelter over the Yanomami with Chimo's outsize cape. Chimo himself, stirring miserably, boiled up our lentil soup. Yavateiba and Maquichemi, sitting on the roots of the great tree, ate brazil nuts and played with their offspring.

Yavateiba pretended to tie his son's penis up to an imaginary waistband, making a warrior of him; he then bent forward and flicked his tiny stomach repeatedly until the little boy, provoked, suddenly struck his father on the head as hard as he could and fell over with the effort. Yavateiba whooped with approval. His son, lying on the leaves, howled and kicked his legs with rage. Maquichemi squatted down and poked his stomach too; he sat up and slapped her on the knee. Yavateiba whooped again, broke a stick off a shrub and forced it into the little boy's hand. Still enraged, the toddler beat his mother across the legs. All the Yanomami cheered.

Maquichemi gathered up her son and sat in her hammock, holding him tight until the sobbing ceased; Yavateiba climbed in facing her, hooked his legs around her waist and lifted his son onto his chest. Peace was restored.

It was such an unusual picture of happy Yanomami family life that I sneaked up from the side with the Nikonos, set the distance ring, over-exposed two stops against a small patch of filtered sunlight which was speckling the bushes behind them, and released the shutter.

Yavateiba turned his head, quick as a fer-de-lance; he thrust his son onto Maquichemi; he leapt out of his hammock and came at me. He raised his arm as if to strike, thought better of it, hissed, and spat at my feet. Chimo, heroic as ever, shoved a mess-tin of soup into his hand.

I went to my hammock as ashamed as a defeated Yanomami and lay in it. Yavateiba had been delighted to have his picture taken in the shabono with his bow drawn and his arrows tipped with those diamond-shaped points for killing peccaries, tapirs and men; so perhaps my offence lay in stealing the image of a warrior in a shameful attitude of weakness, a moment of unmanly tenderness with his family; or perhaps I had endangered the fragile noreshi of his child.

Chimo, shaking his head, brought me a bowl of soup and then fed everyone else in relays. Nobody spoke until Yavateiba got out of his own hammock, took nine plantains out of Maquichemi's basket and pushed them between the burning logs. He pointed at each of us and then at the fire. The plantains were a peace offering. Chimo talk and Yanomami banter began again.

That night, above the rasping of cicadas, there rose a simple, caressing, repeated three-note song. Maquichemi was singing a lullaby to her son. It put me to sleep at once.

In the morning I sent Jarivanau on ahead with the gun, and the rest of us followed slowly, at Maquichemi's pace. She trod surely and deliberately in her husband's footprints through the leaves and mud, avoiding the long black thorns shed from the palm trunks and strewn in patches almost everywhere across the jungle floor. Carrying her son, the trumpeter and her basket of plantains she walked easily over Jarivanau's slimy tree-trunk bridges, laughing at me as I waded or swam across beneath her.

On one of the stops to feed the baby I finally decided to discard my boots: the soles had rotted away from the toe caps and flapped backwards as I walked. I took out the laces and tossed the boots into the undergrowth – whence the boy retrieved them and clumped about in front of us, grinning, walking with exaggerated clumsiness, tripping up, banging into trees, falling into imaginary gulleys and rivers, like me. We clapped. Even Yavateiba laughed. I put on my thin gym shoes and felt half-naked about the feet, wholly naked about my fer-de-lance-inviting ankles.

Around midday we heard a blurred, distant shot, and when we caught up with him Jarivanau had already plucked the wing feathers from a male Lesser razor-billed curassow, the one with the chestnut rump. He was sitting beside a hole like the entrance to a fox's earth. Yavateiba stuck his head in the entrance and sniffed. Jarivanau held his fingers up to his temples like two long ears and mimed a long snout. It was an armadillo burrow.

Yavateiba cupped his hand to his ear and listened. Maybe the Yanomami would now show me the orthodox armadillo-asphyxiation technique. I wanted them to break open an old termite nest, place the dense contents at the burrow entrance, light the pile and fan the slow, thick smoke down the hole – as it emerges from other entrances they are found and blocked and everyone crawls about on hands and knees, putting their ears to the ground and listening for armour-plated digging noises. The Yanomami then dig down themselves with sharpened stakes and drag out the half-stupefied armadillo. But Yavateiba thumped the ground at the top of the entrance, listened again, and shook his head. Nothing. There was no one at home.

Several hours after nightfall, close together, silent with exhaustion, following Chimo and his torch which followed the outlines of the Yanomami, we reached the camp by the Emoni river.

As we approached there came a high-pitched cry full of uncertainty, of rising horror.

'Who's that?' yelled Galvis. 'Who's that?' And then, after a pause, 'We'll shoot!'

'It's cannibals,' growled Chimo. 'We've come to eat your liver; and then, maybe, the cheeks of your buttocks.'

'Chimo!' shouted Galvis, his voice dropping from a sonic bat-squeak to his normal register. 'It's Chimo!'

A great fire was blazing, with a neatly stacked pile of logs to one side of it and Galvis on the other, wild, legs apart, grasping a paddle, ready to bat incoming arrows. He flung it down and hugged Jarivanau to his chest in a great spasm of relief and friendship which was nearly his last – because the loaded gun, which Jarivanau always clutched by the barrel, jerked up and came to rest with its muzzle to his throat. Jarivanau just stood there, looking sideways at Yavateiba, racked with embarrassment. Galvis disengaged and in a frenzy of welcoming, embraced everyone, including Maquichemi.

'Mucha alegría!' he repeated over and over again, as if in a trance. 'Mucha alegría! Such happiness!'

He smelt clean, soapy, good to eat.

As we slid our packs off I decided that I was fond of him after all – far from deserting us as I had half-expected him to do, far from slipping away downstream to safety in one of our dugouts, he had withstood the torments of his large imagination and transformed the camp. He and Valentine had built a new shelter for the stores and baggage we had left behind; they had cut new steps down to the boats, paved them with split logs and added flanking handrails of saplings; they had cleared all the bushes and young trees for twenty yards around the perimeter of the camp, a touching precaution against surprise attack; they had constructed a palatial new smoking-rack – and on it lay row upon row of blackened piranhas. They had even, as I later learnt, dug two pits for carbon samples for the hated Juan.

All that devoted labour had obviously been too much for Valentine: the old man was asleep, stretched out in his hammock, a crumpled shirt and both arms wrapped around his head. Chimo, motioning to us to be quiet, went down on all fours, pulled up the bottom edge of the mosquito net and crawled beneath the hammock. He lifted Valentine's skeletal body on his back. He made a deep, grunting-coughing noise, like a jaguar.

Valentine kicked out with both legs and scrabbled awake. He tried to sit up, but Chimo, round and fat and jammed under the hammock, bumped him flat again.

'Ouooof ouooof', said Chimo, 'urrrgh urrrgh urrrgh.'

'Fuck off! Fuck off!' shouted Valentine with surprising force and very fast. 'Fuck off! Fuck off you motherfucking fucker!'

Chimo roared.

'In the name of the Mother of God,' sang Valentine. 'Fuck off. Get away from me! Fuck off!'

Chimo began another *ouooof*, spluttered, gave up, and helpless with laughter, collapsed onto his stomach. Valentine dropped to the bottom of the hammock.

'So who doesn't,' yelled Chimo from the prone position, his huge buttocks wobbling as the laughter shook him, 'so who doesn't believe in shouting bad words at a jaguar? Eh?'

'I should have known,' said Valentine, recovering, outraged, trying to extricate himself from the folds of hammock and tangle of old clothes. 'It smelt too strong for cat.'

'So who's not a Christian?' howled Chimo, bumping Valentine about again. 'Who never prays to the Virgin? Eh?'

'I was asleep, you fat old fool,' said Valentine.

'Old yourself!' howled Chimo, crawling out a few yards and then lying down with laughter.

'Valenteenie! Valenteenie! You'll have to do better than that! You can't just say fuck off at a jaguar! You have to think of *really bad words.*'

Valentine struggled out of his hammock, put on his gumboots, rubbed his eyes and stood smiling at us and Yavateiba and Maquichemi, looking as bemused as a little boy.

'Valenteenie! Valenteenie!' chanted Galvis, doing one of his auto-dances, shuffling in a circle, his arms above his head, his fingers clicking, 'Valenteenie! Valenteenie! *We're going home!*'

Pablo and Culimacaré stood by the smoking rack, pulling the heads and tails off piranhas, peeling the flesh from the sharp little bones and stuffing it into their mouths. They were much hungrier than I had realised – two disconnected fish-heads lay at Culimacaré's feet, staring up with one cooked eye apiece: not only had he started tearing at his food without a word, he was doing so in full view, too desperate to care whether we saw his deformity or not; as his true thumb on the right hand opposed his index finger in shredding the flanks of a third piranha, his extra thumb, mounted on the base joint, picked back and forth at the air.

Everybody began to eat, standing around the dully smoking fire. But one piranha was enough for me: my stomach seemed to have contracted from rugger-ball to cricket-ball size and judging by the length of slack which I had had to pull in on my water-bottle belt I thought I must have lost two or three stone. Surreptitiously I checked Chimo's belt: his paunch curved outwards over the same worn notch like an oncoming wave. The master was undiminished.

Galvis, singing one of his llanos songs, went to the medicine box, which rested in pride of place in the middle of the new shelter, and produced one golden-foil sachet of coffee and one plastic jar of sugar.

'I kept it for this moment,' he said.

He knelt down, placed the treasure on the ground (and from the way we stared at those containers they might well have enclosed frankincense or myrrh), tossed his head back, closed his eyes and muttered to himself.

'I promised the Virgin,' he said, looking up, 'I promised her that if she protected us and let us go away from here we would drink to her in coffee and sugar.'

'Get on with it,' said Chimo, sticking his lips and gums like the sucker of a giant lamprey onto the side of another piranha.

'I told her,' said Galvis, standing up and hanging the cooking pot from a slanted stake by the fire, 'that if she would only let me return to San Carlos and see my children again I'd say ten rosaries a day. I'd go to mass every Sunday.'

'You'll be drunk,' said Chimo, spitting out a clump of bones, 'you'll be lying in the grass. And anyway, don't count on it Galvis – that wife of yours has got more sense; she'll be in Puerto Ayacucho with a guardia by now.'

'Stop it,' said Valentine, 'he's had enough. He's been away too long. Leave him alone.'

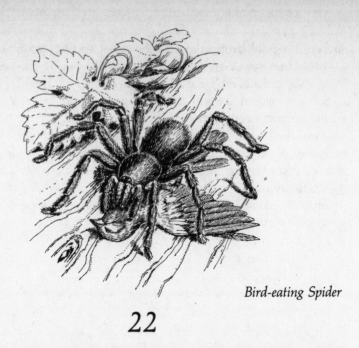

Bird-eating Spider

22

In the morning we ate more piranhas, dismantled the camp, doused and grubbed out the fires, loaded the much reduced baggage into the boats and bound them together. We would drift and paddle downstream. The one tank of petrol was to be kept for our dash through the blackfly swarms of the Siapa.

Jarivanau perched as before on the tarpaulin behind Juan and me and Yavateiba sat on an old manioc tin opposite us. Straight-backed, dignified, he held his bow and arrows vertically in front of him and studied the lower vegetation on either bank ahead as it moved gently, tousled and tugged by the current. Maquichemi lay on the tarpaulin behind him with her legs curled up and her baby sprawled across her stomach. There were very few moments in the baby's life, it occurred to me, when his naked body was not held against equally warm and naked skin; even when he shat, Maquichemi merely leant over the low gunwale with him in one arm and washed the shit off his legs and her stomach with the other.

Galvis, perhaps in preparation for another attempt on the mayoralty of San Carlos, read his pocket life of Gandhi. The boy squatted happily in the bow of our dugout with Culimacaré: he had temporarily transferred his adoration from the less exotic Jarivanau and watched his new hero's every move; Culimacaré, obviously flattered by the intensity of such unaccustomed, owl-monkey-eyed admiration, let

246

the boy take the paddle on straight stretches and use the pole when we swung too close to projecting trunks. They pointed at different palm-fruit clusters together, swapping names in Yanomami and Curipaco.

I took the last exposure of my last film, a picture of Maquichemi and her child, and packed the worn, scratched, gritty but still functional Nikonos deep inside my bergen. To my surprise, I felt relieved rather than disabled; it was pleasing to know that if a six-foot electric eel blew a fuse and flipped aboard on top of Galvis I could actually watch it bite him rather than fuss about with the rangefinder. I lay back against my bergen. A Great black hawk slipped quietly out of a tall tree to our left and flapped slowly across the river, looking much bigger than it really was, a broad-winged patch of night against the white, building clouds.

Around noon we drifted past one of the rare Emoni sandbanks, backed by ferns and small palms and curving out into the slack water on the inside of a bend.

'Jaguar tracks!' shouted Chimo, standing up in the stern. '*He was here last night!*'

There was a flurry and crashing in the ferns at the rear of the sandbank, a frantic, low-pitched grunting, a large turning flank of brown fur. I sat bolt upright – just in time to see two baby capybaras gallop after their mother and disappear into the vegetation.

'Jaguar tracks!' scoffed Valentine.

'He was after them last night,' said Chimo, sitting down again. 'Everyone likes capybara.'

A little further on, Yavateiba and Jarivanau turned round, shouted in Yanomami at Chimo and waved the boats imperiously in to another small sandy beach. Jarivanau mimed eating nuts and rubbed his stomach. Maquichemi and Yavateiba picked up their now empty baskets and stepped ashore. We left Valentine and Galvis to guard the boats and followed the Yanomami up the bank.

'See you in a week,' said Chimo to Galvis. 'Watch out for that jaguar.'

After about half an hour we came out into a clearing, its edges thick with undergrowth.

'Yanomami,' said Jarivanau with a proprietorial grin, gesturing at the open space.

'This is very interesting,' said Juan, examining one of the tangled bushes. 'The old shabono must have stood here. This is a secondary succession. Invasive species are re-colonising this habitat.'

We climbed up a path on the far side, past a huge clump of arrow-cane, and the invasive species blocked our way at every turn. Yavateiba handed his bow and arrows to the boy and he and Jarivanau and Culimacaré took the machetes and cut a tunnel through the profusion of thorn bushes and lianas. The trunk of a plantain came into view. Jarivanau cleared the ground beneath it and climbed up; we reached a group of peach-palms and halted. Yavateiba hacked away the undergrowth and discovered a pair of climbing frames still wedged tight round a palm stem; the rotted poles came away in his hands. We could see the small, yellow and purplish-red tumbling clusters of fruit hanging forty feet above our heads, beneath the crowns of the trees, protected, all the way up the straight thin trunks, by rings of black spines. Yavateiba cut a long sapling, gave it to the boy, took back his bow and arrows, and, with a nod of the head, ordered him up a silver-birch-like tree to our left. The boy hugged the smooth bark with his arms and legs and arched and flattened himself upwards like a caterpillar. Forty feet up, he edged along a branch until he was just within range of a cluster and thrashed it with the end of the pole. Fruit scattered down around us and we scrabbled for them in the undergrowth, dropping them into Maquichemi's basket.

Jarivanau joined us, pleased with himself, and launched into an impassioned argument with Yavateiba. He shrugged his shoulders, spat, and, turning away, suddenly attacked the trunk of a fresh peach-palm with his machete. The tree fell neatly into a gap. Jarivanau lumberjacked another.

'Whooooo!' he sang, curling his machete above his head like a sabre.

Yavateiba stood quietly for a moment, his right hand tensed round his bow. He was clearly shocked, and so was I. We could easily have made new climbing frames. Jarivanau, powerful, irrepressible, scarred by a lifetime of combat, was clearly a gangster — but then perhaps that was why he had the bravado to come with us in the first place.

We lugged the massively heavy clusters of palm-fruits to Jarivanau's pile of plantain bunches and divided up the loads. Culimacaré made me a loose carrying net of vines with a loop to go over the top of the head. I filled it with a clump of plantains and put it on. The weight began to compress the vertebrae in my neck to a puddle of bone marrow between my shoulders, so I heaved it off and held it in front of me, waddling along. Maquichemi, carrying her child in its sling and bent low by her basket of peach palm, laughed and chattered behind me and her child giggled back. I thought I knew what the joke was. 'Tiddlywink,' she was saying (or something like it), 'have you ever seen a man look so stupid?'

As we dumped the fruit by the boats so that Chimo and Pablo could stow the new cargo where they thought best, I slipped on a patch of mud and put my hand against a small tree to steady myself. Now this tree was probably, unbeknown to me, a species belonging to the genus Myrmidone, one of the many genera of trees and bushes described by Spruce which have sac-bearing leaves infested by ants:

> of Myrmidone I gathered four species, including the original *M. macrosperma* of Martius. They are low-growing, sparingly-branched shrubs of 3 to 8 feet; the leaves of each pair are very unequal in size, the smaller one sometimes even obsolete, the larger saccate, as in the Tocaca Anaphyscae, but the sac always rugose as well as unisulcate; flowers solitary, rather large, terminal or axillary, rose (turning red); hairs of stem, leaves, etc., spreading, more copious than in Tocaca, and red or crimson, corresponding curiously with the colour of the minute ants – of that viciously-stinging tribe called 'Formiguinhas de fogo' (little Fire-Ants) – which inhabit the sacs, and also make covered ways of inter-communication along the outside of the stem and branches ...

But I did not stop to check on the rugosity. I alternately tore at the swarm of formiguinhas de fogo clamped into my skin and plunged my hand in the river. They really were fire-ants. It felt exactly as if I had reached into a flame. No wonder the ant and tree symbiosis, a trade of free homes for free protection, was so widespread. No thinking monkey would stop to make a cup of tea near a Myrmidone, let alone climb in for supper on its leaves.

Early in the afternoon we paddled into Toucan hill bend and made camp. Unlike the grand canyon of the great Neblina massif, it looked the kind of hillock that any fool could climb on all fours – and as we now had enough plantains and peach-palm nuts to feed a forestful of coati-mundis I decided that we would stay where we were for a day or two. Pablo took the gun and the curiara and set off downstream;

Yavateiba took his bow and arrows and quiver and disappeared into the forest.

My right hand was now so swollen that I could not use it, and Juan slung my hammock for me. No sooner had I sat on its edge, rubbing more Anthisan into my puffy knuckles, than the trumpeter, released from his cage, rushed up to me and stood still at my feet, peep-peeping to have his head scratched. Flattered, I stroked him with my one serviceable index finger; the black feathers on top of his skull were short and nobbly to the touch. He stopped peeping, lifted one leg, and went into a trance. From the edge of his eyes nearest the beak the nicitating membranes, the third lids, moved slowly across his eyeballs until both lenses were entirely filmed over.

It was odd to think that almost nothing was known about the courtship and social behaviour in the wild of even this widely domesticated bird, kept as a snake-killer and alarm-caller. I stopped stroking and he withdrew his membranes, shook himself, fluffed out his wispy back-feathers and began a desultory scratching and pecking among the fallen leaves. However, now that he had made friends with me I kept half an eye on his movements, mindful of Spruce's experience:

> When at Panuré, on the river Uaupés, we had a tame agamí [trumpeter] which so attached itself to me that it would follow me about like a dog, and never failed to kill any snake that came in our way. One day I was alone with the agamí in a caatinga about four miles from the village, where I lingered about a good while in a spot comparatively clear of underwood, but abounding in certain minute plants (Burmanniaceae) which I was much interested to gather. Whilst I hunted for plants the agamí hunted for snakes, and had already caught three or four, which it brought and laid before me as it caught them. I suppose I had not noticed and praised its prowess as I usually did, for at length – apparently determined to attract my attention – it laid a newly-caught snake on my naked feet, when I was standing erect, absorbed in the examination of a little Burmannia with my lens. The snake was scarcely injured, and immediately twined up my leg. To snatch it off and jerk it away into the bush was the work of a moment; but ever afterwards I took care to leave the agamí at home when I started for the forest.

Chimo and the boy made a fire and boiled up the peach-palm fruit, and as night fell Pablo returned bearing a large cayman. Almost simultaneously Yavateiba stepped into the clearing. He carried his bow and arrows in one hand and a brace of trumpeters in the other. He bent down in front of his pet bird, made peeping noises, and, holding up the heads of his victims, pecked their beaks in the trumpeter's face. It redrew the membranes across its eyeballs.

The dead, glossy trumpeters seemed unmarked until I noticed that they were both bleeding from their anal vents. Yavateiba had shot them from behind with his thinnest arrow-tip — and it was just possible that he had deliberately hit them up the gut in order not to spoil the already small amount of meat on their bodies. To command such accuracy, I thought, must be one of the pleasures of being a Yanomami male: when he comes across a giant turtle basking in a lake, said Culimacaré, the Yanomami hunter stands on the bank and shoots an arrow into the air at just that angle which will bring it down to pierce the one weak spot in a turtle's shell, which lies, like the central suture on a baby's head, right in the centre of the carapace.

Pablo opened his cayman with the axe and laid it out along our plank seat in the dugout for disembowelling. Yavateiba and I went down to watch; when Pablo pulled out the coils of the large intestine and made as if to tumble them into the river Yavateiba jumped into the canoe and pushed him aside. He eased out the whole alimentary canal and climbed back up the bank with it slopped in his arms. Intrigued, I followed. By the fire he grasped one end of the fishy tube in his right hand and slowly pulled the whole length through the tight sphincter made by his fingers, squeezing out the grey sludge of half-made cayman shit. The boy disappeared briefly into the forest and came back with a few large leaves. Yavateiba then wrapped up the bundle of guts, secured it with a piece of vine, arranged one leaf at the side into a spout, and pushed the whole gently into the ashes at the edge of the fire.

We sat down to wait and in about five minutes Yavateiba decided it was ready; he pulled out the leaf vessel and held the spout in front of me; honoured, I opened my mouth and he tipped in half a cupful of liquid. It was warm, thick, slimy, like a mixture of cod-liver oil and the re-cycled juice from old sardine tins. Yavateiba ministered likewise to Maquichemi, Jarivanau and the boy, finished the rest himself and threw the leaves and guts into the undergrowth.

Abducting Chimo's torch, Juan looked through his interminable notes on the carbon content of the tierra firme, caatinga and riparial forests of the Rio Negro, Casiquiare, Pasimoni, Baria and Emoni rivers. Galvis plucked, gutted and jointed the trumpeters and added them to the peach-palm stew. Valentine and Culimacaré built a smoking rack for Pablo's cayman and Yavateiba purloined the cayman's head. He pushed it, too, into the fire, and when it was cooked he and Maquichemi extracted the small, backwardly curved, yellowish teeth and stowed them in one of their baskets. They then hacked open the skull with a machete and ate the brains.

It was the beginning of a feast; later that night we gorged ourselves on stringy peach-palm fruit and even stringier little bits of trumpeter meat; we ate Jarivanau's baked plantains and we chewed pieces of cayman which he skewered on sticks and placed upright in a ring round the fire. Chimo and Valentine swapped stories. There was a man in Brazil, said Valentine, who had set the stone from the head of an electric eel into his hand: whenever he punched someone, he electrocuted them. That was nothing, said Chimo, there was a hill somewhere near here that was made entirely of gold. His father had told him about it before he died. You'd know when you were close: if you shot a curassow and when you went to pick it up you found that its legs were gold, you were close all right − that bird had spent its life treading in gold dust.

'Reymono,' said Culimacaré from his hammock, 'where are aeroplanes made?'

'All over the world. They even make them in Brazil.'

'Then that is where I would like to go,' he said quietly. 'I would like to go where aeroplanes are made and learn to be a pilot. I would like to fly over the trees.'

Jarivanau, bored of all the talk which he could not understand, gave me a conspiratorial smile, walked casually over to my bergen, undid the ties and took out Schauensee as if he owned it. He carried the book back to Yavateiba, Maquichemi and the boy, and huddled them up closer to the fire. Very slowly, he turned over the plates.

I went and sat beside him. Yavateiba grew increasingly excited, talking very fast in his stressed language. A great naming of birds in Yanomami took place; they seemed to know almost every bird in Amazonas; and when Jarivanau reached Kathleen Phelps's painting of the cotingas it was obvious that Yavateiba was as entranced by it as I was: he leant forward to look more closely and called softly to himself: *hudu! hudu!* for the Blue-crowned motmot; a sequence of differently pitched bellows for the Amazonian umbrellabird, the Red-ruffed fruitcrow and the capuchinbird; a high *krioow* for the cock-of-the-rock and a quack whose supposed author escaped me.

Unwittingly, I brought the party to an end by taking the book and flicking through the black and white drawings from the back to the front. Yavateiba shook his head at pictures of the gulls and terns of Venezuela's Caribbean coast and by the time we came to the figure of Leach's storm-petrel and the Dusky-backed shearwater his faith in the book of the nabë, the foreigner, the non-Yanomami, the non-human being, had obviously evaporated. He did not believe it. Yavateiba did not believe in the sea.

As Juan and I lay in our hammocks preparing to go to sleep – in my case I had reached the stage of plumping up my pillow, or restuffing my torn shirt in a half-rotted pair of blue Y-fronts of which I had grown inordinately fond – a shadow launched itself from a small tree behind our heads and landed with an appreciable thud on the leaf litter between us. Juan, who still had Chimo's torch, leant over the side of his hammock and shone it at the ground.

In the circle of weak light there was something flattish, motionless, dinner-plate-size, furry, brown.

'Quick!' yelled Juan suddenly. 'It's a tarantula!'

But it was not the much smaller animal which tarantula signifies in English. I realised, with a rush of adrenalin, that I was looking at the largest spider in the world, the Bird-eating spider, whose habits Maria Sibilla Merian, an artist working in Dutch Guiana, was the first to describe and paint in her book *Metamorphosis Insectorum Surinamensium* (1705). Her spider has an unlikely looking hummingbird by the throat and is dragging it from its pillbox nest. Everyone ridiculed her account until at Cametá, on the Tocantins river in Brazil, Bates

chanced to verify a fact relating to the habits of a large hairy spider of the genus Mygale, in a manner worth recording. The species was M. avicularia, or one very closely allied to it; the individual was nearly two inches in length of body, but the legs expanded seven inches, and the entire body and legs were covered with coarse grey and reddish hairs. I was attracted by a movement of the monster on a tree-trunk; it was close beneath a deep crevice in the tree, across which was stretched a dense white web. The lower part of the web was broken, and two small birds, finches, were entangled in the pieces; they were about the size of the English siskin, and I judged the two to be male and female. One of them was quite dead, the other lay under the body of the spider not quite dead, and was smeared with the filthy liquor or saliva exuded by the monster. I drove away the spider and took the birds, but the second one soon died. The fact of species of Mygale sallying forth at night, mounting trees, and sucking the eggs and young of humming-birds, has been recorded long ago by Madam Merian and Palisot de Beauvois; but, in the absence of any confirmation, it has come to be discredited. . . . Some Mygales are of immense size. One day I saw the children belonging to an Indian family, who collected for me, with one of these monsters secured by a cord round its waist, by which they were leading it about the house as they would a dog.

Bates's monster was probably a female, the web an old cocoon and the crevice just a lair to which the finches had been dragged, because Bird-eating spiders do not generally build webs but run their prey down in quick dashes along branches or on the ground at night. The Yanomami are said to eat their legs roasted, but obviously not after a banquet of peach-palm fruit and cayman pieces – Jarivanau crept up behind it, very warily, and hit it once with a long pole.

'They can jump three metres from standing,' said Juan. 'They inject you with a powerful enzyme which digests the flesh – and be careful in the morning, Redmon, because all the hairs on their bodies are poisonous.'

The camp settled down again. A Marbled wood-quail began to crow like a rooster. A Black-and-white owl called his explosive, deep, dismissive, single *boo* every ten to twenty seconds from somewhere nearby. I fell asleep and dreamed, not of becoming a milkshake for spiders, as I expected, but of Kellaways. I was back, eight years old, on another family expedition to the Avon. We carried the two-seater canvas canoe through the archway, across the fields, and lowered it into the river. As usual, my father and I paddled upstream. At the fifteenth bend the unreachable railway bridge came into view through the gap in the stand of bullrushes, unimaginably far away from the landing-stage and the picnic basket behind us. Yet this time we did not turn back; my father kept paddling and, three bends later, there was the bridge ahead of us. But as we approached the pitted stone pillars and the rusty iron girders they slowly metamorphosed into a line of poles supported by sapling X-frames and handrails of liana. We passed beneath it; and suddenly I was suffused with an intense happiness.

In the morning, as soon as it was light enough to see properly, Pablo took the gun and paddled downstream in the curiara, and I borrowed Juan's scissors, wrapped my left hand in a leaf, straightened out the mangled body of the spider and cut away its long brown fangs, tough as crab-shell. I dropped them into one of Juan's plastic bags and stowed it in my bergen.

Trumpeter feathers from Galvis's plucking pile were drifting gently about over the rotting leaves, propelled by the tiny breezes that got up as a few oblique lines of sunlight filtered down to the jungle floor and spotted it with warmth. I picked up three breast feathers and laid them in my notebook. Delicate, fan-shaped, they appeared to be a uniform grey when lying flat on the page, but when held at an angle to one of the neighbouring lines of light, each feather shone at its top with a crescent of purple whose inside edge was radiant with minute bands of green and orange and gold.

There was a loud bang and ten minutes later an excited Pablo pulled into the bank.

'Now we have meat for days and days,' he shouted.

'Take it easy,' said Chimo, 'you'll upset the boat.'

A huge, wet capybara, the world's largest rodent, lay in the bow of the curiara. Chimo and Culimacaré helped Pablo lift it ashore. About four-feet long, a male, its deep, massive body was covered in grey-brown, bristly hairs, and its short legs ended in four partially webbed toes on the front feet and three on the back. Its nostrils and eyes and little rounded ears were set high on its broad, squarish head, further adaptations for its semi-aquatic life. Chimo and Pablo butchered it and gave me the two cheek-teeth from its upper jaw. Backwardly curved to unequal degrees so that one was almost semi-circular, they were yellowish white with a shallow groove down the centre of their front surfaces, worn to a sharp, angled cutting edge and, as measured by Juan's ruler, they were three and a half inches long.

Valentine stoked up the wood under the smoking-rack and moved the remains of the cayman tail to one side. Jarivanau skewered slabs of muscle and fat on sticks and sat down to monitor his roasting system, a fence of meat around the fire. Yavateiba commandeered the offal, but instead of squeezing out the intestines he lodged all the guts at the edge of the river on the upstream side of a half-submerged log, fetched one of Chimo's lines, baited the hook with bits of capybara skin and began to pull in furiously thrashing piranha, their backs dark blue, the small scales on their flanks sparks of silver.

After a slow, remarkably quiet breakfast of capybara chunks, which tasted like sirloin-on-the-bone, Pablo, Chimo and Valentine wandered off into the forest to find exactly the right kind of buttresses from which to carve four more paddles – so that we could all help propel the dugouts down the Siapa if the one tankful of petrol should prove insufficient to force us clear of the blackfly; Maquichemi took her son to play in Galvis's part of the canoe, where he had stored all the empty plastic containers that had once held oats and all the sounding tins that had once been full to the brim with crude brown sugar; Galvis himself settled down on his medicine chest to read about unarmed resistance with Mahatma Gandhi; and Yavateiba, Jarivanau, the boy, Juan and I set off to climb Toucan hill.

The ground began to rise almost at once and we emerged abruptly from high, thick forest onto bare rock in the open sunlight. The immediate angle of the slope, perhaps forty-five degrees, was far too steep for any plant to gain a purchase; only a species of blackish algae grew in its runnels. But the rough, nodular surface of the dark brown granite provided a good grip for my gym shoes. The sun beat down on our backs and, bouncing off the rock in front of us, beat back up into our faces.

Juan and I kept level with each other and Culimacaré bounded ahead of us with half-jumping strides, his stomach and chest almost parallel to the slope. The Yanomami, however, hung back: Jarivanau followed without the slightest sign of enthusiasm; Yavateiba, carrying his bow and one arrow, ambled up below us; the boy, holding Yavateiba's spare bow and second arrow, climbed about three hundred yards, and then gave up and returned to the forest. Perhaps the rock was simply too hot for their feet; or perhaps the whole exercise just seemed pointless because there was nothing to hunt; or maybe they were reluctant to come with us because Toucan hill was rising into that Yanomami otherworld where the hekura live. Perhaps the powerful rays of light were dangerous here, potential pathways for the malignant, brightly-coloured hekura of enemy shamans, hekura which, catching you in the open, far from the counter-magic and healing powers of the familiar shamans in your home shabono, might touch you with the tell-tale sign which every Yanomami fears, your personal guarantee of sickness and death – two small, crossed curves at the back of the throat.

We spread out as we climbed, and in about half an hour we reached a ledge which curved round the shoulder of the hill. I sat down on a large stone and wiped the sweat from my glasses with my shirt-tail. When I put them back on I was astonished by the height we had reached in such a short time. At the lip of the platform the rock disappeared into space: heat or no, we would have to descend backwards on all fours.

In front of us the jungle stretched endlessly away across five horizons, across a receding, diminishing series of broken lines composed of rounded hills and flat-topped tepuis, the majestic boundaries of five different river systems. To our left a pair of King vultures were soaring, only a little higher than we were and much closer than I had ever seen them before, their bellies and wing linings the purest white, the black flight feathers of their broad, flat, six-and-a-half-foot wingspan fully spread, and through the binoculars I could clearly see the odd, bulbous, orange wattles above their bills. Two Greater yellow-headed vultures, velvet-black, were quartering the air immediately over the trees beneath us, probably hunting by smell for carrion. Standing up, I could make out, directly below us, a few thin, curved gaps in the forest, which was all that marked the course of the Emoni river.

Near at hand, the ledge was loosely covered with bromeliads, gorse-like bushes, some kind of orchid, and small-leaved shrubs about fifteen feet high. And from the closest of these, I suddenly noticed, two yellow-ringed, bright red eyes were watching me. Above a rough clump of sticks in a fork of the bush an anxious bird with a heavy yellow beak like a hawk, a brown head, a chestnut back and an enormously long, white-splotched brown tail was trying to flatten itself from view. A Squirrel cuckoo was sitting on its nest.

Seeing me in a trance, staring into the bush, Juan and Jarivanau walked over to investigate from their resting places further down the ledge to my right. Jarivanau put his arm round me as he had done when I had first taken yoppo (but because I was standing up he actually gripped me round the chest) and blew a soft, breathy 'whoo!' up into my ear. He then signalled to Yavateiba who had just arrived on the platform. Yavateiba hurried towards us, notching the arrow into his bowstring – so I clapped my hands and the bird flew off the nest and away between the bushes.

'*Psit psit psit!*' it called.

'Whoooo!' sang Jarivanau after it.

He grinned at me and scratched his battered scalp. Yavateiba sat down with disgust on my boulder, Juan and Jarivanau joined him, and I wandered off to the left to find Culimacaré.

I had walked about fifty yards when a nightjar flicked silently from the ground in front of me, twisted over a patch of bromeliads, and disappeared. On the bare rock, in the shade of a low bush, lay one pink-brown egg, stippled, lined and spotted with black. I knew that very few of the eggs of the Amazon nighthawks and nightjars had been described and this was certainly not one of them. But that was not why the happiness from my dream again overwhelmed me, so that suddenly the world seemed freshly made and the future ceased to matter. Beneath the tropical sun on Toucan hill, ignorant, momentarily, like a Yanomami, of the laws of science, gazing at that little egg, I might have been looking at one half of an empty eggshell, a message of brown and purple blotches on a background of browny-white, a present from a mistle thrush dropped at my feet on a Vicarage lawn.

SELECT BIBLIOGRAPHY

Alamo, C. Y., *Funes, El terror del Amazonas*, Caracas, 1979.

Aldington, Richard, *The Strange Life of Charles Waterton 1782–1865*, London, 1949.

Amuchastegui, Axel, *Studies of Birds and Mammals of South America*, London, 1967.

Anduze, Pablo J., *Shailili-ko, Relato de un Naturalista que también llegó a las Fuentes del Rio Orinoco*, Caracas, 1958.

Bates, Henry Walter, *The Naturalist on the River Amazons, A Record of Adventures, Habits of Animals, Sketches of Brazilian and Indian Life, and Aspects of Nature under the Equator, during Eleven Years of Travel*, 2 vols., London, 1863.

Beebe, William, *High Jungle*, New York, 1950.

Belt, Thomas, *The Naturalist in Nicaragua. A Narrative of a Residence at the Gold Mines of Chontales; Journeys in the Savannahs and Forests; with observations on Animals and Plants in Reference to the Theory of Evolution of Living Forms*, London, 1874.

Biocca, Ettore, *Yanoáma, the story of a woman abducted by Brazilian Indians*, translated by Dennis Rhodes, London, 1969.

Blake, Emmet R., 'Birds of the Acary Mountains of Southern British Guiana', *Fieldiana*: Zoology, vol. 32, No. 7, December 19, 1950.

Brewer-Carias, Charles, 'Cuevas del Cerro Autana', *Natura*, 58, 1976, pps. 33–48.

— *La Vegetación del mundo perdido*, Caracas, 1978.

— *Roraima, La Montaña de Cristal*, Caracas, 1984.

— *Venezuela*, Caracas, 1982.

— and Julian A. Steyermark, 'Hallucinogenic Snuff Drugs of the Yanomamo Caburiwe-Teri in the Cauaburi River, Brazil', *Economic Botany*, vol. 30, No. 1, January–March 1976, pps. 57–66.

Campbell, Bruce and Elizabeth Lack (eds.), *A Dictionary of Birds*, Calton, 1985.

Carpentier, Alejo, *Los Pasos Perdidos*, Mexico D.F., 1953; *The Lost Steps*, translated by Harriet de Onís, London, 1956.

Chagnon, Napoleon A., *Yanomamö, the Fierce People*, New York, 1968; third edition, New York, 1983.

Chapman, Frank M., 'Problems of the Roraima – Duida Region as Presented by the Bird Life', *The Geographical Review*, vol. 21, 1931, pps. 363–372.

Cocco, P. Luis, *Iyëwei-teri, Quince años, entre los yanomamos*, Caracas, 1972.

Cohen J. M., *Journeys down the Amazon, being the extraordinary adventures and achievements of the early explorers*, London, 1975.

Colchester, Marcus (ed.), *The Health and Survival of the Venezuelan Yanoama*, Copenhagen, 1985.

Collier, Richard, *The River that God Forgot, the Story of the Amazon Rubber Boom*, London, 1968.

Coward, T. A., *The Birds of the British Isles and their Eggs*, 2 vols., London 1920.

— *The Birds of the British Isles, their Migration and Habits with observation on our Rarer Visitants*, London, 1926.

— and Charles Oldham, *The Birds of Cheshire*, Manchester, 1900.

D'Abrera, Bernard, *Butterflies of South America*, Victoria, Australia, 1984.

Darlington, P. J., Jr., *Zoogeography, the Geographical Distribution of Animals*, New York, 1957.

Darwin, Charles, *The Zoology of the Voyage of H.M.S. Beagle, under the Command of Captain Fitzroy, R.N., during the years 1832 to 1836. Published with the Approval of the Lords Commissioners of Her Majesty's Treasury*, London, 1838–1843.

— *Journal of Researches into the Geology and Natural History of the Various Countries Visited by H.M.S. Beagle*, London, 1839.

— *The Beagle Record, Selections from the original pictorial records and written accounts of the Voyage of H.M.S. Beagle*, edited by Richard Darwin Keynes, Cambridge, 1979.

— *On the Origin of Species by means of Natural Selection, or the Preservation of Favoured Races in the Struggle for Life*, London, 1859.

— *The Descent of Man and Selection in Relation to Sex*, 2 vols., London, 1871.

— *The Expression of the Emotions in Man and Animals*, London, 1872.

— *The Life and Letters of Charles Darwin, Including an Autobiographical Chapter*, ed., Francis Darwin, 3 vols., London, 1887.

— *More Letters of Charles Darwin, a Record of his Work in a Series of hitherto Unpublished Letters*, ed., Francis Darwin and A. C. Seward, 2 vols., London, 1903.

— *The Correspondence of Charles Darwin*, volume 1, *1821–1836*, ed., Frederick Burkhardt et al, Cambridge, 1985.

DeVries, Philip J., *The Butterflies of Costa Rica and their Natural History, Papilionidae, Pieridae, Nymphalidae*, Princeton, 1987.

Doyle, Sir Arthur Conan, *The Lost World, Being an account of the recent amazing adventures of Professor E. Challenger, Lord John Roxton, Professor Summerlee and Mr. Ed Malone of the Daily Gazette*, London 1912.

Edwards, William H., *A voyage up the River Amazon, including a Residence at Pará*, London, 1847.

Emboden, William, *Narcotic Plants, hallucinogens, stimulants, inebriants and hypnotics, their origins and uses*, London, 1972.

Ewell, Judith, *Venezuela, A Century of Change*, London, 1984.

Ewer, R. F., *The Carnivores*, Ithaca, N.Y., 1973.

Fleming, Peter, *Brazilian Adventure*, London, 1933.

Frisch, Johan Dalgas, *Aves Brasileiras*, volume 1, São Paulo, 1981.

Furneaux, Robin, *The Amazon, the Story of a Great River*, London, 1971.

Garcia, Maria Isabel Eguillor, *Yopo, Shamanes y Hekura, Aspectos Fenomenologicos del Mundo Sagrado Yanomami*, Puerto Ayacucho, 1984.

Gates, R. Ruggles, *A Botanist in the Amazon Valley, an account of the Flora and Fauna in the Land of Floods*, London, 1927.

George, Wilma, *Biologist Philosopher, a Study of the Life and Writings of Alfred Russel Wallace*, London, 1964.

Gomez, Berenice, 'La Neblina: el encuentro de un nuevo mundo perdido', N 580 *RESUMEN*, 23 de Diciembre de 1984, pps. 17–28.

Gosse, Philip, *The Squire of Walton Hall, the Life of Charles Waterton*, Edinburgh, 1940.

Grelier, Joseph, *To the Source of the Orinoco*, translated by H. A. G. Schmuckler, London, 1957.

Guenther, Konrad, *A Naturalist in Brazil, the Flora and Fauna and the People of Brazil*, translated by Bernard Miall, London, 1931.

Guppy, Nicholas, *Wai-Wai, Through the forests north of the Amazon*, London, 1958.

— *A Young Man's Journey*, London, 1973.

Hagen, Victor Wolfgang von, *South America, The Green World of the Naturalists, Five centuries of natural history of South America*, London, 1951.

Halliday, Tim and Kraig Adler (eds.), *The Encyclopaedia of Reptiles and Amphibians*, London, 1986.

Hanbury-Tenison, Robin, *A Question of Survival for the Indians of Brazil*, London, 1973.

— *Aborigines of the Amazon Rain Forest, the Yanomami*, Amsterdam, 1982.

Harney, Thomas, 'Scientists Explore "Lost Worlds" in Venezuela', *Smithsonian News Service*, January, 1985.

Haverschmidt, F., *Birds of Surinam*, Edinburgh, 1968.

Hemming, John, *Red Gold, the Conquest of the Brazilian Indians*, London, 1978.

— *The Search for El Dorado*, London, 1978.

— *Amazon Frontier, the Defeat of the Brazilian Indians*, London, 1987.

Hemming, John (ed.), *Change in the Amazon Basin Volume 1: Man's impact on forests and rivers; Change in the Amazon Basin Volume II: The frontier after a decade of Colonisation*, Manchester, 1985.

Herrara, R., 'Soil and terrain conditions in the International Amazon Project at San Carlos de Rio Negro, Venezuela: correlation with vegetation types', *Transactions of the International MAB-IUFRO Workshop on Tropical Rain Forest Ecosystem Research*, pps. 182–187, Hamburg, 1977.

Hill, John E. and James D. Smith, *Bats, a natural history*, London, 1984.

Hilty, Steven L., and William L. Brown, *A Guide to the Birds of Colombia*, Princeton, 1986.

Hingston, R. W. G., *A Naturalist in the Guiana Forest*, London, 1932.

Huber, Otto and John J. Wurdack, 'History of Botanical Exploration in Territorio Federal Amazonas, Venezuela', *Smithsonian Contributions to Botany*, Number 56, Washington, 1984.

Hugh-Jones, Christine, *From the Milk River, Spatial and temporal processes in Northwest Amazonia*, Cambridge, 1979.

Hugh-Jones, Stephen, *The Palm and the Pleiades, Initiation and Cosmology in Northwest Amazonia*, Cambridge, 1979.

Humboldt, Alexander von, *Relation Historique du Voyage aux Régions Equinoxiales du Nouveau Continent*, 3 vols., Paris, 1814–25; *Personal Narrative of Travels to the Equinoctial Regions of the New Continent, during the years 1799–1804, by Alexander de Humboldt and Aimé Bonpland*, translated by Helen Maria Williams, 7 vols., London, 1814–29; *Personal Narrative of Travels to the Equinoctial Regions of America during the years 1799–1804*, trans. and ed. Thomasina Ross, 3 vols., London, 1852–53.

Husson, A. M., 'The Mammals of Suriname', *Zoologische Mon-*

phieën van het Rijksmuseum van Natuurlijke Historic No. 2, Leiden, 1978.

Irwin, R. A. (ed.), *Letters of Charles Waterton of Walton Hall, near Wakefield, Naturalist, Taxidermist and Author of 'Wanderings in South America' and 'Essays on Natural History'*, London, 1955.

Jordan, C. F., 'The Nutrient Balance of an Amazonian Rain Forest', *Ecology*, 63, pps. 647–654, 1982.

— and C. Uhl, 'Biomass of a "tierra firme" forest of the Amazon Basin', *Oecologia Plantarum*, 13, pps. 387–400, 1978.

Jordan, Tanis and Martin, *South America: River Trips, Volume II*, Cambridge, MA, 1982.

Kline, Harvey F., *Colombia, Portrait of Unity and Diversity*, Boulder, Colorado, 1983.

Klinge, H., E. Medina, and R. Herrera, 'Studies on the ecology of Amazon caatinga forest in southern Venezuela', *Acta Cientifica Venezolano* 28, pps. 270–276, 1977.

Koch-Grünberg, Theodor, *Vom Roraima zum Orinoco: Ergebnisse einer Reise in Nordbrasilien und Venezuela in den Jahren 1911–1913*, Berlin, 1917; translated by Federica de Ritter, *Del Roraima al Orinoco*, 3 vols., Caracas, 1979.

Lewis, Norman, 'Genocide', *A View of the World, Selected Journalism*, London, 1986.

Lieuwen, Edwin, *Venezuela*, London, 1961.

Lizot, Jacques, *Diccionario Yanomami – Español*, traducción: Roberto Lizarralde, Caracas, 1975.

— *El Hombre de la Pantorrilla Preñada*, Caracas, 1975.

— *La Cercle des Feux, Faits et dits des indiens Yanomami*, Paris, 1976; *El Circulo de los Fuegos, Vida y costumbres de los indios Yanomami*, traducción: Jorge Musto, Caracas, 1978; *Tales of the Yanomami, Daily Life in the Venezuelan forest*, translated by Ernest Simon, Cambridge, 1985.

MacCreagh, G., *White Waters and Black*, New York, 1926.

Macdonald, D. W., 'Dwindling resources and the Social behaviour of Capybaras', *Journal of The Zoological Society of London*, 1981, 194, pps. 371–391.

— 'Feeding Associations between Capybaras *Hydrochoerus Hydrochaeris* and some Bird species', *Ibis* 123, 1981, pps. 364–366.

— *The Encyclopaedia of Mammals*, 2 vols., London, 1984.

Maguire, Bassett, 'Cerro de la Neblina, Amazonas, Venezuela: A Newly Discovered Sandstone Mountain', *The Geographical Review*, 45 (1), 1955, pps. 27–51.

— and Richard S. Cowan and John J. Wurdack, 'The Botany of the Guyana Highland, A report of the Kunhardt, the Phelps, and the New York Botanical Garden Venezuelan Expeditions', *Memoirs of the New York Botanical Garden*, vol. 8, No. 2, April 27, 1953, pps. 87–96.

Maxwell, Nicole, *Witch Doctor's Apprentice*, London, 1962.

Mayr, Ernst and W. H. Phelps, Jr., 'The Origin of the Bird Fauna of the South Venezuelan Highlands', *Bulletin of the American Museum of Natural History*, 136 (5), 1967, pps. 269–328.

Meggers, Betty J. and Clifford Evans, 'Archaeological Investigations at the Mouth of the Amazon', *Bureau of American Ethnology*, Bulletin No. 167, Washington, 1957.

Ministerio de Relaciones Exteriores, Republica de Venezuela, *Summary on the Boundary Question with British Guiana, now Guyana*, Caracas, 1982.

Morón, Guillermo, *A History of Venezuela*, edited and translated by John Street, London, 1964.

Oquist, Paul, *Violence, Conflict, and Politics in Colombia*, New York, 1980.

Owen, D. F., *Tropical Butterflies, The ecology and behaviour of butterflies in the tropics with special reference to African species*, Oxford, 1971.

Prance, Ghillean T., and Thomas E. Lovejoy (eds.), *Key Environments: Amazonia*, Oxford, 1985.

Rabinovitz, Alan, *Jaguar, One man's struggle to save Jaguars in the Wild*, London, 1987.

Ramos, Alcida R. and Kenneth I. Taylor, *The Yanoama in Brazil, 1979*, Copenhagen, 1979.

Raymond, Theophile, *Mariposas de Venezuela*, Caracas, 1982.

Rice, Hamilton A., 'The Rio Negro, the Casiquiare Canal, and the Upper Orinoco, September 1919–April 1920', *The Geographical Journal*, vol. LVIII, November 1921, pps. 321–344.

Richards, P. W., *The Tropical Rain Forest, an ecological study*, Cambridge, 1952.

Ridgely, Robert S., *A Guide to the Birds of Panama*, Princeton, 1981.

Rodway, James, *In the Guiana Forest, Studies of Nature in Relation to the Struggle for Life*, London, 1894.

Rouse, Irving and José M. Cruxent, *Venezuelan Archaeology*, London, 1963.

Ruschi, Augusto, *Aves do Brasil*, 2 vols., São Paulo, 1979.

Rutgers, A., *Birds of South America, 160 colour-plates from the Lithographs of John Gould*, London, 1972.

Saldarriaga, J. G., D. C. West and M. L. Tharp, *Forest Succession in the Upper Rio Negro of Colombia and Venezuela*, Unpublished thesis, Oak Ridge, 1986.

Sandford, R. L., J. Saldarriaga, K. E. Clark, C. Uhl and R. Herrera, 'Amazon Rain-Forest Fires', *Science*, vol. 227, pps. 53–55, 1985.

Schauensee, Rodolphe Meyer de, 'The Birds of the Republic of Colombia, their Distribution and Keys for their Identification (Addenda and Corrigenda)', *CALDASIA*, Boletin del Instituto de Ciencias Naturales de la Universidad Nacional de Colombia-Bogotá, Part V., No. 26, pps. 1115–1214; I – XXXIX, Julio 1, 1952.

Schauensee, Rodolphe Meyer de, *A Guide to the Birds of South America*, Edinburgh, 1971.

— and William H. Phelps, Jr., *A Guide to the Birds of Venezuela*, Princeton, 1978.

Schomburgk, O. A., *Robert Hermann Schomburgk's Travels in Guiana and on the Orinoco during the years 1835–1839, according to his reports and communications to the Geographical Society of London*, Leipzig, 1841, edited and translated by Walter E. Roth, Georgetown, British Guiana, 1931.

Schomburgk, Richard, *Richard Schomburgk's Travels in British Guiana 1840–1844*, edited and translated by Walter E. Roth, 2 vols., Georgetown, British Guiana, 1922.

Seitz, George, *Hinter dem grünen Vorhang*, Wiesbaden, 1960; *People of the Rain-Forests*, translated by Arnold J. Pomerans, London, 1963.

Shoumatoff, Alex, *The Rivers Amazon*, London, 1979.

Skutch, Alexander F., *A Birdwatcher's Adventures in Tropical America*, Austin, 1977.

— *Birds of Tropical America*, Austin, 1983.

— *Helpers at Birds' Nests, A Worldwide survey of co-operative breeding and related behaviour*, Iowa City, 1987.

— *A Naturalist amid Tropical Splendor*, Iowa City, 1987.

Smuts, Barbara B., Dorothy L. Cheney, Robert M. Seyfarth, Richard W. Wrangham and Thomas T. Struhsaker, *Primate Societies*, Chicago, 1987.

Snow, David W., *The Web of Adaptation, Bird Studies in the American Tropics*, New York, 1976.

— *The Cotingas, Bellbirds, Umbrellabirds and their allies*, London, 1982.

Spruce, Richard, *Notes of a Botanist on the Amazon and Andes, being records of travel on the Amazon and its tributaries, the Trombetas, Rio Negro, Uaupés, Casiquiari, Pacimoni, Huallaga, and Pastasa; as also to the cataracts of the Orinoco, along the Eastern side of the Andes of Peru and Ecuador, and the shores of the Pacific, during the years 1849–1864,* edited and condensed by Alfred Russel Wallace, with a Biographical Introduction, 2 vols., London, 1908.

Stark, N. and M. Spratt, 'Root biomass and nutrient storage in rain forest oxisols near San Carlos de Rio Negro', *Tropical Ecology* 18, pps. 1–9, 1977.

Steward, T. H. (ed.) 'Handbook of South American Indians', *Smithsonian Institution Bureau of American Ethnology Bulletin* 143, New York, 1949.

Steyermark, Julian A., 'Flora of the Guyana Highland: Endemicity of the Generic Flora of the Summits of the Venezuelan Tepuis', *Taxon* 28 (1, 2/3), pps. 45–54, April, 1979.

Stone, Roger D., *Dreams of Amazonia*, New York, 1985.

Tavera-Acosta, B., *Rio Negro, Reseña etnográfica, histórica y geográfica del Territorio Amazonas*, 1906; third edition, Caracas, 1954.

Tello, Jaime, *Mamiferos de Venezuela*, Caracas, 1979.

Thurn, Everard F. Im, *Among the Indians of Guiana, being sketches chiefly anthropologic from the interior of British Guiana*, London, 1883.

Ure, John, *Trespassers on the Amazon*, London, 1986.

Wallace, Alfred R., *A Narrative of Travels on the Amazon and Rio Negro, with an account of the Native Tribes, and Observations on the Climate, Geology and Natural History of the Amazon Valley*, London, 1853.

— *Darwinism, an Exposition of the Theory of Natural Selection with some of its Applications*, London, 1889.

— *Natural Selection and Tropical Nature, Essays on Descriptive and Theoretical Biology*, London, 1891. (*Natural Selection*, London, 1870; *Tropical Nature*, London, 1878).

Waterton, Charles, *Wanderings in South America, The North-West of the United States and the Antilles, in the Years 1812, 1816, 1820 and 1824, With Original Instructions for the perfect preservation of Birds, Etc. for Cabinets of Natural History*, London, 1825.

Waugh, Evelyn, *Ninety-two Days, a journey in Guiana and Brazil*, London, 1934.

— *A Handful of Dust*, London, 1934.

Whitmore, T. C., *Tropical Rain Forests of the Far East*, Oxford, 1975; second edition, Oxford, 1984.

Woodcock, George, *Henry Walter Bates, Naturalist of the Amazons*, London, 1969.

INDEX

compiled by Douglas Matthews

NOTE: Page numbers in *italic* refer to illustrations